❦ The Ladder of Jacob ❦

THE LADDER OF JACOB

ANCIENT INTERPRETATIONS OF THE BIBLICAL STORY OF JACOB AND HIS CHILDREN

James L. Kugel

PRINCETON UNIVERSITY PRESS

PRINCETON AND OXFORD

Published by Princeton University Press, 41 William Street, Princeton, New Jersey 08540

In the United Kingdom: Princeton University Press,

3 Market Place, Woodstock, Oxfordshire OX20 1SY

All Rights Reserved

ISBN-13: 978-0-691-12122-2

ISBN-10: 0-691-12122-2

Library of Congress Cataloging-in-Publication Data

Kugel, James L.

The ladder of Jacob : ancient interpretations of the biblical story of Jacob

and his children / James L. Kugel.

p. cm.

Includes bibliographical references and index.

ISBN-13: 978-0-691-12122-2 (hardcover : alk. paper)

ISBN-10: 0-691-12122-2 (hardcover: alk. paper)

1. Jacob (Biblical patriarch) 2. Bible. O.T. Genesis—Criticism, interpretation,

etc., Jewish. I. Title.

BS580.J3K84 2006

222′.11092—dc22

2005020584

British Library Cataloging-in-Publication Data is available

This book has been composed in Sabon and Trajan

Printed on acid-free paper. ∞

pup.princeton.edu

Printed in the United States of America

1 3 5 7 9 10 8 6 4 2

For R.

CONTENTS

ACKNOWLEDGMENTS

I wish to express my thanks to my editor at Princeton University Press, Fred Appel, for his help in making this book a reality. Thanks as well to Deborah Tegarden and Vicky Wilson-Schwartz for their editing skills, and to my literary agent, Ellen Geiger. A number of the chapters of the present book have been preceded by articles published in various journals, and I am grateful to those journals for permission to use parts of the articles here. It may be helpful for readers if I mention here the names of the articles and how the present treatment is different from the original.

Most of chapter 2, "The Ladder of Jacob," is altogether new, but the section dealing with the Slavonic text "The Ladder of Jacob" is based in part on an article of mine by the same name, published in the *HTR* 88 (1995): 209–27. I should note that I have translated more of the Slavonic text than appeared in that article and have proposed some new readings as well—in particular, an interpretation of that text's reference to a strange deity named *Falkonagargail*.

Chapter 3, "The Rape of Dinah, and Simeon and Levi's Revenge," and chapter 4, "Reuben's Sin with Bilhah," appear here in essentially the same form as two earlier articles, "The Story of Dinah in the *Testament of Levi*," *HTR* 85 (1992): 1–34, and "Reuben's Sin with Bilhah in the *Testament of Reuben*," in David P. Wright et al., *Pomegranates and Golden Bells: Studies in Honor of Jacob Milgrom* (Winona Lake, IN: Eisenbrauns, 1995), 525–54. I have, however, added a brief section, "The Question of Intermarriage," to the first of these articles; I have also modified both articles to fit the present format and updated the footnotes.

Much of chapter 5, "How Levi Came to Be a Priest," is new, although the first half of it incorporates some parts of an earlier article, "Levi's Elevation to the Priesthood in Second Temple Writings," *HTR* 86 (1993): 1–64.

Chapter 6, "Judah and the Trial of Tamar," is new.

Chapter 7, "A Prayer about Jacob and Israel from the Dead Sea Scrolls," is a reworking of "4Q369 'Prayer of Enosh' and Ancient Biblical Interpretation," *DSD* 5 (1998): 119–48.

ABBREVIATIONS

11QMelch, 4QDibHam, etc.	Dead Sea Scrolls sigla (thus: the Melchizedek scroll from Cave 11 at Qumran; the *Dibre Hamme'orot* scroll from Cave 4 at Qumran)
AbrN	*Abr-Nahrain*
AbrNSS	Abr-Nahrain Supplement Series
ALD	*Aramaic Levi Document*
AOT	*The Apocryphal Old Testament*, ed. H.F.D. Sparks (Oxford: Clarendon, 1984)
Apoc. Abr.	*Apocalypse of Abraham*
APOT	*The Apocrypha and Pseudepigrapha of the Old Testament*, ed. R. H. Charles (Oxford: Clarendon, 1913)
BASOR	*Bulletin of the American Schools of Oriental Research*
BIA	*Bar Ilan Annual*
CBET	Contributions to Biblical Exegesis and Theology
CBQ	*Catholic Biblical Quarterly*
CBQMS	Catholic Biblical Quarterly Monograph Series
CSCO	Corpus scriptorum christianorum orientalium, ed. I. B. Chabot et al. (Paris: Peeters, 1903–)
DJD	*Discoveries in the Judaean Desert*
DSD	*Dead Sea Discoveries*
GA	*Genesis Apocryphon* (from Qumran Cave 1)
HSS	Harvard Semitic Studies
HTR	*Harvard Theological Review*
JJS	*Journal of Jewish Studies*

JNES	*Journal of Near Eastern Studies*
Jos. Asen.	Joseph and Aseneth
JPS	Jewish Publication Society
JQR	*Jewish Quarterly Review*
JSJ	*Journal for the Study of Judaism in the Persian, Hellenistic, and Roman Periods*
JSOT	*Journal for the Study of the Old Testament*
JSOTSS	Journal for the Study of the Old Testament: Supplement Series
JSP	*Journal for the Study of the Pseudepigrapha*
JSPSS	Journal for the Study of the Pseudepigrapha: Supplement Series
JSQ	*Jewish Studies Quarterly*
Jub.	*Jubilees*
LAB	Pseudo-Philo, *Liber Antiquitatum Biblicarum*
Lad Jac.	*Ladder of Jacob*
LAOT	*Lost Apocrypha of the Old Testament.*, ed. M. R. James (London: Society for Promoting Christian Knowledge, 1920)
MT	Masoretic text
NRSV	New Revised Standard Version
OTP	*Old Testament Pseudepigrapha*, 2 vols., ed. J. Charlesworth (Garden City, NY: Doubleday, 1983–85)
PAM	Palestine Archaeological Museum
PISBR	*Publications of the Israel Society for Biblical Research*
Praep. ev.	Eusebius, *Praeparatio evangelica*
RevQ	*Revue de Qumran*
RSV	Revised Standard Version
SBLEJL	Society of Biblical Literature Early Judaism and Its Literature Series
SBLSP	*Society of Biblical Literature Seminar Papers*

SJSJ	*Supplements to the Journal for the Study of Judaism*
T. Asher	*Testament of Asher*
T. Dan	*Testament of Dan*
T. Gad	*Testament of Gad*
T. Isaac	*Testament of Isaac*
T. Iss.	*Testament of Issachar*
T. Job	*Testament of Job*
T. Jud.	*Testament of Judah*
T. Levi	*Testament of Levi*
T. Moses	*Testament of Moses*
T. Reub.	*Testament of Reuben*
T. Sim.	*Testament of Simeon*
VT	*Vetus Testamentum*

THE LADDER OF JACOB

Chapter One

JACOB AND THE BIBLE'S
ANCIENT INTERPRETERS

*O*ne question that troubled ancient readers of the Bible was that of the purpose of the book of Genesis. This first book of the Torah (Pentateuch) was in some ways the most problematic. Those that followed—Exodus, Leviticus, Numbers, Deuteronomy—all contain divinely given laws, so their purpose was clear enough: they were written in order to guide people along the proper path in life. But Genesis has no laws or commandments to speak of; it is a collection of stories about Israel's ancient ancestors, starting with Adam and Eve and leading up to the founders of the Israelite nation, Jacob and his twelve sons. Now, history may be interesting, even important, but to a certain way of thinking, history per se does not deserve a place in the Torah. Why, then, was the book of Genesis included?[1]

Various answers were given to this question in ancient times. The author of the book of *Jubilees* (early second century B.C.E.), for example, understood Genesis to be a crypto-halakhic work; that is, although it has no overt laws per se, he maintained, its stories nonetheless contain legal teachings in hidden form, alluding here and there to divine commandments and practices that had been instituted with Israel's ancestors long before the great revelation of biblical law at Mount Sinai. Philo of Alexandria (ca. 20 B.C.E to ca. 30 C.E.), somewhat analogously, saw the various people whose lives are recounted in Genesis as walking embodiments of the laws that were to be given later on at Mount

Sinai. Many writers from the time of Philo and afterward, including the founders of Christianity and rabbinic Judaism, saw the heroes and heroines of Genesis as moral exemplars, whose lives might serve as models for generations to come. This last, indeed, has been the dominant approach to the book of Genesis from late antiquity almost to the present day.

But when it comes down to cases, this last approach runs into problems, particularly with regard to Jacob and his family. Jacob himself begins life as a bit of a sharpster: he cheats his brother Esau out of his rightful inheritance as the firstborn of the family, then tricks his poor, blind father into giving him a paternal blessing intended for Esau. Next Jacob travels to his uncle Laban's house, where he ends up acquiring, apparently by somewhat questionable methods, most of Laban's flocks (a prime form of wealth in ancient Israel). Thereafter he departs, like a thief in the night, for his homeland of Canaan. Meanwhile, Jacob's wife Rachel, Laban's daughter, is shown in a hardly better light; the narrative reports that she stole her father's sacred images (*teraphim*), then hid them in her saddlebags and lied to him to prevent their discovery. Of Jacob's children, one ends up sleeping with his father's concubine and another ends up having relations with his own son's wife. When Jacob's only daughter ends up being raped, her brothers respond by invading the rapist's town and killing every man in it, subsequently plundering all the townsmen's flocks and possessions, including wives and children. Sometime after that, Jacob's sons seize their younger brother Joseph, strip off his clothes, and throw him into a pit with the intention of killing him; then they relent and merely sell him as a slave to a passing caravan. "Dysfunctional" is probably the first word an observer would use to describe such a family in modern times; but whatever word is used, one would be hard-pressed, on the face of things, to claim that these stories about Jacob and his children could ever have been intended to provide readers with a set of moral exempla by which to steer their own course in this world.

The logical next sentence in this exposition ought to be, "Enter the biblical interpreter." If I hesitate to write it, it is because I do not wish to give readers the impression that ancient biblical interpretation is principally a matter of apologetics, touching up the biblical portrayal of various figures to remove most of their faults and so make them appropriate role models for the Bible's readers. Interpreters did indeed do such things sometimes, but apologetics was hardly their main purpose. Principally, they were interested in making sense of biblical narratives, laws, prophecies, and prayers; in particular, they addressed themselves to narrative gaps and other omissions, to apparent contradictions, and sometimes to historical references or words that were no longer understood. The questions they sought to answer—particularly the most ancient of ancient interpreters—were, Why, and how, did X do what he did? How am I to go about carrying out this law today? What was this prophet talking about, and what does it matter to us? Or sometimes simply, What do these words mean?

It is true, however, that the search for answers to such questions was hardly conducted according to the rules of modern biblical interpretation. Ancient interpreters approached their task with certain presuppositions, and some have already been hinted at above. The Bible, and particularly its first five books, comprised for them a divinely given guide; therefore, everything within it had a lesson to impart. The Torah was, in this sense, a supremely *relevant* book and not just a remnant from the ancient past. At the same time, its teachings were not always obvious; indeed, ancient interpreters assumed that much of the Bible spoke *cryptically*, saying X when what it really meant was Y. The third presupposition was that the Bible was one harmonious, *perfect* document. That is, although written down over a long period of time, by different authors in different circumstances, it was

nonetheless without mistakes or inconsistencies or internal contradictions; indeed, in the extreme formulation, no word of it was
extraneous. The fourth presupposition was that the biblical text
as a whole, despite its references to human authors and its apparent distinction between words specifically attributed to God and
the rest of its words, had altogether come *from God* or at God's
command or inspiration, so that it was essentially a divine text,
the very word of God. It is these four assumptions that animate
all of ancient biblical interpretation.[2]

THE DEVELOPMENT OF EXEGETICAL MOTIFS

The present volume consists of a series of studies of ancient biblical interpretation, all of which center on the person of Jacob and
his immediate family. Its particular focus is not so much on the
what of ancient biblical interpretation (a subject I have tried to
survey in some detail elsewhere)[3] as on the *how* of its development, including, prominently, an attempt to untangle the interrelationship of various interpretive texts and traditions. In order to
pursue this subject, it may be well to define here some of the
terms frequently used in the following chapters.

Ancient biblical interpretation is an interpretation of biblical
verses, not of whole chapters or stories or larger units. Even when
interpreters had their eyes on the larger context, they always
framed the question they sought to answer in terms of a specific
verse, or more typically, one or two words prominent in that
verse. In other words, they asked, Why does Jacob set up a pillar
(מצבה) in Gen. 28:18 instead of building an altar and sacrificing
to God? What is the connection between the brief account of
Reuben's sin with Bilhah in Gen. 35:22 and the next verse, "And
Jacob had twelve sons"? What does God mean by referring to
Jacob as his "firstborn son" in Exod. 4:22? The answers given to
such questions usually went well beyond the verses mentioned

and touched on wider issues in the sequence of events in the narrative—indeed, on Jacob's overall character in Genesis and even such matters as the election of Israel, God's role in human affairs, and sin and forgiveness—but the starting point for any evocation of such larger issues was always the precise wording of a particular phrase or verse. (This phrase or verse may also be referred to as the biblical **site** of an interpretive tradition.)

So it was that ancient biblical interpretation traveled in little packets, called **exegetical motifs**. An exegetical motif is an explanation of the meaning of a biblical verse, especially a potentially problematic one, or even of a phrase or a word within that verse. In this book, exegetical motifs are given descriptive titles, enclosed in quotation marks: "Angels Descended to Admire Jacob," "Rise and Fall of Empires," "Killed One Each," "City with a Criminal Past," and so forth.[4] The explanations of biblical verses embodied in these motifs were passed on orally, from person to person and from generation to generation, as an accompaniment to the biblical text itself. Thus, if a person were to ask, "How did two men manage to conquer and kill an entire city?" the answer would probably be some version of the exegetical motif, "Swords from Heaven," a motif that interpreted Gen. 34:25 as hinting that Simeon and Levi had acquired special armaments that allowed them to accomplish this improbable feat. Similarly, the answer to "Why were all the men of Shechem killed because of the rape of Dinah?" would be framed in terms of one or another exegetical motif dealing with a specific verse, for example, "The Other Shechemites Participated," a motif built on a particular word in Gen. 34:27.

Sometimes, the same basic explanation of the meaning of a particular verse can exist in different forms; these are called **variants** of the same **basic motif**. For example, the basic motif "Staircase of History" has two variants, one involving a series of twelve successive periods of domination, the second involving four foreign

empires that were to dominate Israel. Often, two or more different motifs were created for the same verse; these are called **rival
motifs.** For example, "Staircase of History" and "Rise and Fall of
Empires" are two rival motifs both seeking to explain a certain
detail in the account of Jacob's dream in Genesis 28.

Exegetical motifs are explanations of verses—all kinds of verses,
verses found in laws, prophecies, songs, and so forth. When they
are found in biblical narrative, they often give rise to **narrative
expansions,** that is to say, little bits of narrative that are added to
the retelling of a biblical story. For example, the motif "Saw
Bilhah Bathing"—which originated as an explanation of a problematic phrase in Gen. 49:4—gave rise to a narrative expansion in
the book of *Jubilees*, which, in retelling the biblical story, specifies
that on one occasion Reuben had seen his father's concubine
bathing in a certain place and that it was this that caused him
later to sin. An exegetical motif is by nature abstract: it is an idea,
a way of explaining a verse. A narrative expansion is always specific, the particular words of a particular text in which an exegetical motif is embodied. For example, the narrative expansion of
the motif "Saw Bilhah Bathing" in the book of *Jubilees* is essentially the same as the narrative expansion of "Saw Bilhah
Bathing" in the *Testament of Reuben*—no surprise, since the author of the latter was apparently well acquainted with the former
and copied much material. But sometimes narrative expansions
will differ in one or more **elements,** significant details that distinguish one narrative expansion from another. For example, the
motif "Bilhah Was Asleep," common to these same two texts, is
embodied in two somewhat different narrative expansions: in the
Testament of Reuben it is specified that Bilhah was intoxicated
and unconscious, whereas this element is not present in *Jubilees*.

Ancient biblical interpretation did not develop overnight but
over the course of several centuries. So it was that the existence of
one exegetical motif often contributed to the creation of another.

The motif "Abraham Saw a Dire Future,"[5] aimed at explaining Gen. 15:12, probably influenced the creation of the "Rise and Fall of Empires" and "Staircase of History" motifs, although the latter two pertained to an entirely different biblical narrative. Sometimes the same motif will be applied to two different sites, that is, it may be offered as an explanation of two quite separate verses (often with less than perfect results): this is the phenomenon of **midrashic doublets.** It also happens that an exegetical motif originally designed to explain one biblical verse will come to be associated—wrongly—with another site entirely. This is called **transfer of affects.**[6]

Finally, it should be noted that ancient interpreters—the creators of what were to become interpretive traditions—were themselves usually very respectful of earlier interpreters and their traditions. Thus, if interpreters were aware of two rival motifs, each of which explained a certain verse in its own way, they often would incorporate both in their retelling of a biblical story. The same might be true even of two narrative expansions embodying the same exegetical motif but differing from each other in one or more elements; a later ancient interpreter might blend, or simply confuse, the two previous narrative expansions in his own, new retelling. So it was that the phenomenon of **overkill** was created, whereby a single retelling of a biblical text may contain two quite independent explanations of how an event occurred, or why, or even two separate accounts of the event itself. As will be seen in the following, **overkill** is one of the most characteristic features of ancient biblical interpretation.

OTHER JACOB TRADITIONS

A great many of the exegetical motifs concerning Jacob and his children are not treated in the present study. The interested reader is referred to two of my earlier books, where Jacob's relations with his father Isaac and mother Rebekah, for example, or his early struggles with his brother Esau, as well as the tale of his son Joseph, have been surveyed in some detail.[7] If, for the present book, I have chosen to focus on other incidents and stages in Jacob's life, it is because these afford a rich opportunity to look at some of the very earliest examples of ancient biblical interpreters at work, as well as to explore the interrelationship of various motifs and texts in the emergence of the Jewish and Christian exegetical traditions.

And so: after his stormy upbringing with his older brother Esau, Jacob leaves home. His destination is the land from which his mother Rebekah had come, and the relatives that she had there: her brother Laban and his two daughters, Leah and Rachel. On his way, however, Jacob stops in a place called Luz to spend the night. It is there he has a fateful dream that was to influence the course of the rest of his life.

Chapter Two

THE LADDER OF JACOB

Jacob left Beer Sheba and went off toward Haran. He happened on a certain place and decided to spend the night there, since the sun had set. He took some of the stones from the place and put them down at his head; then he lay down in the place to sleep. He had a dream; a ladder was stuck into the ground and its top reached up to heaven, and the angels of God were going up and down on it. And the Lord was standing over him and He said, "I am the Lord, the God of Abraham your father and the God of Isaac; the land upon which you are lying I am giving to you and your descendants. And your descendants will be like the dust of the earth, so that you will spread out westward and eastward, to the north and to the south; by you and your descendants will all the families of this land be blessed. And I will be with you and watch over you wherever you go, and I will bring you back to this spot; I will not leave you until I have done what I have just said." Jacob woke up from his sleep and said, "The Lord is indeed present in this place, though I did not know it!" And he took fright and said, "How fearsome is this place! This is the very house of God, and that is the gateway to heaven." Early that morning Jacob took the stone that he had put under his head and set it up as a pillar, and he poured oil on its top. And he called the place by the name Bethel, although previously the city was called Luz. Then Jacob made a vow: "If God is with me and watches over me on the journey that I am making, and gives me food to eat and clothes to wear, so that I return safely to my father's house—then the Lord shall be my God, and this stone, which I have set up as a pillar, will be a temple of God, and everything that You give to me I will tithe back to You." (Gen. 28:10–22)

*T*he story of Jacob's dream-vision at Bethel was highly significant for ancient readers of the Bible: it marked the first time that God appeared to Jacob or addressed him directly and was thus the start, in a sense, of his career as one of God's chosen servants. At the same time, a few things in this brief passage were puzzling. Why, to begin with, had Jacob dreamt of a ladder and angels at all? Could not God simply speak to him with words alone, as He had spoken earlier to Abraham (Gen. 15:17–20)? And what were the ladder and the angels intended to communicate? Finally, Jacob's reaction to the dream was puzzling. After he wakes up, "he took fright and said, 'How fearsome is this place!'" Surely the content of the dream itself seemed altogether positive and reassuring—what could have frightened Jacob?

These were the sorts of questions out of which ancient biblical interpretation developed. For it is certainly not hard to imagine young pupils in olden times asking their teacher just such things about Jacob's dream, or listeners to a sermon on this text quizzing the preacher about such matters once he was done. Bit by bit, and often in highly creative fashion, ancient interpreters managed to come up with answers—not only to the questions mentioned, but to all manner of queries touching on the whole of the Bible's stories, laws, prophecies, and songs. A good answer—one that seemed to solve the problem, or at least addressed it in some novel fashion—would be adopted willingly by teachers and preachers (now they would know what to say!) and so passed on to future generations. Sometimes, however, different explanations would vie with one another for a long time before one of them won out in public opinion; indeed, it sometimes happened that no single explanation succeeded in eliminating all the others. In fact, that is what happened in the case of Jacob's dream.

One very early answer to the questions posed above is to be found in the writings of Philo of Alexandria, a first-century Jewish scholar who lived in the Greek-speaking city of Alexandria, Egypt. Commenting on the dream narrative, Philo observed:

> Perhaps as well [Jacob] caught a glimpse of his own [future] life in this visionary ladder. . . . The affairs of men are by their very nature comparable to a ladder because of their irregular course. For a single day (as someone well put it) can carry the person set on high downward and lift someone else upward, for it is the nature of none of us to remain in the same circumstances, but rather to undergo all manner of changes. . . . So the path of human affairs goes up and down, subjected to unstable and shifting happenstance. (Philo, *On Dreams*, 1:150, 153–56)

For Philo, the ladder in the dream seems to have been intended to communicate the "ups and downs" that lay in store for Jacob (and which characterize human affairs in general). If so, one can well imagine Jacob's anxiety upon awakening: it is one thing to know in a general way that life is not always sweet for everyone, but quite another to have a vision implying that tough times may lie just ahead in one's own life. As will be seen presently, Philo's comment in its broad outline is paralleled by exegetical traditions attested elsewhere, both in the roughly contemporaneous writings of the biblical apocrypha and pseudepigrapha and in later, rabbinic texts. But these other sources hardly speak with one voice: there were, as already indicated, several competing approaches to Jacob's dream.

Changing of the Guard

One well-known approach focused on the biblical passage's assertion that the angels were "going up and down" on the ladder. In Hebrew, going *up and down* (more literally, "ascending and

descending") is the normal order of things—as it is indeed in English as well. In fact, the laws of gravity being what they are, in
quite a few languages things are said first to go up and then, afterward, down. But in the case of angels, this order raised a slight
exegetical difficulty: since angels are normally located in heaven,
one would expect them first to have gone *down* on the ladder,
and only subsequently *up*. If the biblical passage maintains the
opposite, it seemed to ancient interpreters a reasonable inference
that the particular angels in question must have already been on
the earth—on some mission or other—before the ladder appeared;
they then ascended on the ladder to heaven while some other
angels descended at the same time. It remained only to discover
what their particular mission had been.

One hypothesis was that these angels had been sent down to
earth to accompany Jacob on the trek from his father's house to
that of his uncle Laban in Aram (that is, the journey from Beer
Sheba to Haran mentioned in the first sentence of the biblical passage cited). They went with him from his parents' house as far as
Bethel. If, at that point in the journey, they ascended to heaven,
perhaps it was because they were unable to accompany him the
rest of the way:

> The angels that accompany a person within the land of Israel can-
> not accompany him outside of the land. [Therefore, the angels who
> were said to be] *ascending*—these were the ones who had accompa-
> nied him within the land of Israel; *and descending*—these were the
> ones who were to accompany him outside of the land [to Aram].
> (*Genesis Rabba* 68:12)

Seen in this light, what happened at Bethel was a kind of
"changing of the guard": the angels who ascended were immediately replaced by another cohort that descended on the same
ladder.

Angels Had Been Exiled

Another possibility was that the angels were already on earth because they had been sent down on some previous mission quite unrelated to Jacob. Looking backward from chapter 28 of Genesis, a reader could not but notice that a group of angels had been mentioned not long before, in chapter 18: there, three angels had appeared to Abraham and Sarah at Mamre, and not long afterward (chapter 19) two of the three were sent to destroy the city of Sodom and save Lot from its wreckage. Perhaps, interpreters theorized, these were the very same angels who subsequently ascended on Jacob's ladder. But why should they have waited so long before returning to heaven?

> Said R. Levi in the name of R. Samuel bar Naḥman: [they were] ministering angels [i.e., the angels that serve God in highest heaven]. But since they had revealed the *mysteria* of God, they were cast out of their [heavenly] domain for 138 years. . . . Said R. Ḥama b. R. Ḥanina: [they were cast out] because they had been arrogant and said, "For we are about to destroy this place" (Gen. 19:13). (*Genesis Rabba* 50:9)

According to this overall approach, these angels were ministering angels[1] and thus naturally belonged in the highest part of heaven. If they were still on earth at the time of Jacob's dream-vision, it must be that they were being punished for something. R. Levi cites one opinion: at the time of the destruction of Sodom, the angels had warned Lot of the impending disaster by saying, "Who else do you have here? Sons-in-law, your sons and daughters, and anyone else that you have in the city—bring them out of this place. *For, we are about to destroy this place; the outcry made against them to the Lord has become so great that the Lord has sent us to destroy it*" (Gen. 19:12–13). Apparently, the angels gave out too much information. All they had really needed to say to Lot and his family was, "Get out." By mentioning the outcry that led to God's divine verdict against Sodom, and even mentioning the fact that they themselves had been sent by God, the angels were, according to this opinion, revealing far more than was called for, things that were in the category of divine *mysteria* and thus normally kept from human beings. The explanation given by R. Ḥama b. R. Ḥanina is slightly different. The very wording of the angels' warning—"For, *we* are about to destroy this place"—seemed terribly immodest. Were not the angels merely executing God's decree that the place be destroyed? Even Lot, no saint in the rabbinic reckoning, reworded their warning in the very next verse: "The *Lord* is about to destroy the city" (Gen. 19:14). Attributing the destruction to themselves thus seemed to be an instance of overweening pride on the angels' part, one that might have brought on the punishment of being exiled from heaven.

Whichever explanation one chooses, the idea that these heavenly angels had been exiled would account for their presence on earth at the time of Jacob's dream. They then ascended on the ladder and resumed their rightful place in the supernal realm.

A Real Ladder

One subtle fact is often missed in connection with this midrash or the previous one (that is, the exegetical motif that we have called the "Changing of the Guard"). The starting assumption of both is that the actual content of Jacob's dream had nothing to do with a ladder or angels. Gen. 28:12 may say, "He had a dream," but what follows immediately is not a description of the dream at all but an account of something else that took place while Jacob was asleep and busy dreaming: suddenly, a real ladder was stretched between earth and heaven, and some real angels ascended and descended on it. The narrative then goes on to detail God's words to Jacob while he was asleep. One might adjust the previous translation of the biblical narrative to reflect this other way of reading:

> Jacob left Beer Sheba and went off toward Haran. And he happened on a certain place and decided to spend the night there, since the sun had set. He took some of the stones from the place and put them down at his head; then he lay down in the place to sleep. He had a dream. *Meanwhile*, a ladder was stuck into the ground and its top reached up to heaven, and the angels of God went up and down on it.
>
> And [in the dream] the Lord was standing over him and He said, "I am the Lord, the God of Abraham your father and the God of Isaac; the land upon which you are lying I am giving to you and your descendants. . . ." Jacob woke up from his sleep and said, "The Lord is indeed present in this place, though I did not know it!" And he took fright and said, "How fearsome is this place! This is the very house of God, and that is the gateway to heaven."

This approach to the biblical passage had much to recommend it. In removing the ladder and the angels from the dream, it eliminated in one deft stroke the most puzzling aspect of the narrative. All that was left now in the dream were God's own words to Jacob, and these were quite straightforward. In so doing, these midrashists also succeeded in making God's manner of communicating with Jacob no different from His method of communicating with Abraham in Gen. 15:17–20: in both cases, God speaks to the person in a deep sleep, but in both He uses only words and not visual symbols, saying in both cases what lies in store for the person's progeny.

Angels Descended to Admire Jacob

Such success notwithstanding, the above explanations are lacking in at least one regard. The biblical text says the angels were *ascending and descending*. Now, the exiled angels might well have ascended because their allotted punishment was over, or because of some act of divine clemency, but why should other angels then go down? One might, of course, say—in keeping with the "Changing of the Guard" motif—that Jacob still needed to be escorted the rest of the way to Laban's house. But if so, why should the exiled angels, who, after all, had accompanied Jacob part of the way and who were thus already in place, have departed so quickly without completing the job?[2]

In fact, even the "Changing of the Guard" midrash had not really handled this problem successfully. It had created an ad hoc "rule," according to which angels who accompany someone within the land of Israel are not authorized to accompany him outside of the land.[3] But by any reckoning, Bethel (or Jerusalem, with which, curiously, "this place" in the biblical story was sometimes identified)[4] does not sit on the border between the land of Israel and Aram; the new angels would thus have a lot of accompanying to do right in the land of Israel before entering their supposed province of activity. If the second group of angels could operate both inside the land of Israel and outside, why couldn't the first?

Perhaps it was because of such considerations that a slight variation on the overall approach of these explanations is found elsewhere in rabbinic writings. According to this other approach, the ladder in the story is still a real ladder and the angels are real angels; unlike the previous versions, however, their ascending and descending had nothing at all to do with *escorting* Jacob. Instead, the angels were intent on catching a glimpse of the righteous fellow, and his sleeping at Bethel provided them with an opportunity.

It was for that reason that a multitude of angels, a continuous stream of them, went down on the ladder and back up again while Jacob slept.

Indeed, the Genesis text itself offered some support for this reading. It said that "a ladder was stuck into the ground and its top reached up to heaven, and the angels of God were going up and down *on it*." The word *bô* ("on it") in Hebrew might equally well be rendered *upon him*. If so, the text would be indicating the purpose of the angels' descent was to arrive directly next to Jacob himself—presumably, to see him up close. Alternately, "upon him" might be interpreted as an elliptical phrase—as if what the text were really saying was that the angels were descending to look *upon him*,[5] to catch a glimpse of the righteous Jacob asleep on the ground.

One early passage that depends on this line of interpretation is found in the New Testament:

> Jesus answered him, "Because I said to you, I saw you under the fig tree, do you believe? You shall see greater things than these." And he said to him, "Truly, truly, I say to you, you will see heaven opened, and the angels of God ascending and descending upon the Son of man." (John 1:50–51)

Many commentators have recognized in the words "the angels of God ascending and descending" an allusion to Gen. 28:12; but it is not simply an allusion to the biblical verse but the biblical verse as interpreted in the sense described above. That is, the word *bô* is being understood as "upon him" (here, "upon the Son of man") and not "on it," that is, the ladder.[6] In keeping with this same approach,

> R. Ḥiyya the Great and R. Yannai [disagreed on this verse], the one claimed [they were] ascending and descending on the ladder

while the other said [they were] ascending and descending on Jacob
(*Genesis Rabba* 68:12).[7]

What about the order of the verbs, "ascending and descending"? Apparently—as John 1:50–51 shows—in this midrash the
order was not taken to be significant. After all, the act of admiring Jacob might imply hundreds, perhaps thousands, of angels
going down to take a look. If so, the verbs "ascending and descending" refer to continuous, simultaneous activity—some angels go up while others go down—in which case the order in
which the verbs appear makes no difference.

Given such a scenario, there was no need to explain why, once
having descended, the angels went back up again; heaven was,
after all, their home. Nevertheless, some versions of this midrash
specify that the angels not only *descended* to look at Jacob but
also *ascended* to look at him,[8] since Jacob's portrait, by an old
midrashic tradition,[9] was engraved on God's own heavenly throne:

> It is written: "Israel in whom I [God] am glorified" (Isa. 49:3).[10]
> You [Jacob] are the one whose portrait is engraved above [on the
> heavenly throne. The angels thus] ascended to see his portrait and
> descended to see him [the real Jacob] asleep. (*Genesis Rabba* 68:12)

One of the most characteristic features of rabbinic midrash is the
blending—and sometimes, the confusing—of exegetical motifs that
were originally quite separate from one another. A good example
of this phenomenon is the treatment of Gen. 28:12 in the Palestinian targums, which combine a number of elements seen thus far:

> And he dreamt that there was a ladder fixed in the earth and its top
> reached the heavens, and the two angels who had gone to Sodom
> and had then been exiled from Heaven for having revealed secrets
> of the Master of the world and had thus been wandering about

until Jacob left his father's house, whereupon they lovingly accompanied him to Bethel—now they ascended to the upper heavens and called out: Come and see the faithful Jacob, whose portrait is fixed on the Glorious Throne, since you have desired to see him. Then the other holy angels of the Lord went down to see him. (*Targum Pseudo-Jonathan* Gen. 28:12; cf. *Targum Neophyti* ad loc.)

Here we have the motif "Exiled Angels," whose one-time ascent was designed to account for the word order of "ascending and descending." Once in heaven, however, these exiled angels invite their angelic brethren to go down and admire the faithful Jacob. This element belongs not to the "Exiled Angels" motif at all but to that of "Angels Descended to Admire Jacob." (The connection to this motif is solidified by the next clause, which explicitly mentions Jacob's portrait engraved on the heavenly throne.)[11] Note, however, how this second motif has been slightly modified. Originally, there was a continuous flow of angels up and down, as attested in John 1:50–51 and *Genesis Rabba* 68:12; in the latter text, the ascending angels were going up to see Jacob's portrait etched on the heavenly throne, while the descending ones were going down to see Jacob in person. In the targumic version, however, the arriving, formerly exiled, angels call out to the other angels, who, being stationed in heaven, have apparently already seen Jacob's portrait etched on the heavenly throne. They are therefore told to go down to see the sleeping Jacob in person, "since you have desired to see him." Thus, two originally quite separate explanations of the ascending and descending angels have been successfully fused in the targumic tradition.

Rise and Fall of Empires

All the motifs seen thus far separate the ladder and the angels from the content of Jacob's dream. But to most readers of the Bible this separation must have appeared artificial; surely the ladder and the angels were part of the dream, a significant part! A number of interpreters, therefore, sought to explain these elements (as Philo did) as symbolic, indeed, as a symbolic announcement of Jacob's own future.

The following midrashic explanation of Jacob's vision exists in several forms; the most widely attested is a remark attributed to R. Samuel b. Naḥman:[12]

> *And he dreamt that a ladder was set on the ground and its top reached to the heavens and the angels of God were going up and down on it.* . . . . Said R. Samuel b. Naḥman: Is it possible that these were the ministering angels [whose job it is to serve before God in Heaven]? Were they not instead the guardian angels of the nations of the world (*sarei 'ummot ha'olam*)? He [God] showed him [Jacob] Babylon's angel climbing up seventy rungs [of the ladder] and going down again. Then He showed him Media's angel going up and down fifty-two, and then Greece's going up and down one hundred and eighty. Then Rome's went up and up, and he [Jacob] did not know how many [rungs it would ascend]. Jacob took fright at this and said: "Oh Lord, do you mean that this one has no descent?" God said to him: "Even if you see him reach the very heavens, I will still cause him to go down, as it is written, 'Though you soar aloft like the eagle, though your nest is set among the stars, from there I will bring you down, says the Lord'" [Obad. 1:4].

R. Samuel b. Naḥman's point of departure is a question already mentioned: if the angels in Jacob's dream were (as the biblical text calls them) the "angels of God"—presumably the highest class of angels, God's "ministering angels"—what were they doing going up and down a ladder stuck into the earth rather than serving God in the loftiest regions of heaven? The answer he gives is that, despite the phrase "angels *of God*" in the biblical text, these angels were not in fact God's ministering angels but the angelic "princes" of the nations mentioned in the book of Daniel (Dan. 10:13, 20, etc.), each of whom is assigned to watch over a different country or people. Their "ascending and descending" (in that order), therefore, had great significance: what Jacob saw was actually a visual representation of the rise and fall of empires, specifically, those foreign empires which would dominate his own descendants in time to come.[13] And so, our midrash specifies that the angels that Jacob saw were, in turn, the guardian angels of Babylon, Media, Greece, and Rome. The seventy rungs that the guardian angel of Babylon ascends represent the seventy years of the Babylonian captivity as specified in Jer. 25:11–12, 29:10, and later Jewish writings; the number of rungs ascended by the guardians of Media and Greece similarly correspond to traditional chronology.[14] But what of Rome? Its angel kept going up and up—no wonder Jacob is frightened! It was bad enough for Jacob to see that his descendants were to be dominated by a succession of foreign empires, but according to this dream, the Roman domination would go on for centuries and centuries and seemed, in fact, to have no end. It was then that God reassured him with a verse from the book of Obadiah, "Though you soar aloft like the eagle, though your nest is set among the stars, from there I will bring you down, says the Lord." These words, addressed by the biblical prophet to the nation of Edom, seemed particularly appropriate in context since, by a well-worn midrashic act of identification, Edom, along with its founder, Esau, were typologically identified with the Roman empire.[15] Rome's domination might thus appear endless right now, but its guardian angel, like the previous ones, would eventually have to end its climb on the ladder and go back down.

Of all the interpretations of Jacob's dream examined thus far, this last one certainly had the most to recommend it. Every element of the narrative was well accounted for: the ladder and the angels, God's (now necessary) words of reassurance to Jacob, and Jacob's fear on awakening. Indeed, by this interpretation Jacob was understood to have had a full revelation of his descendants' future, much as Abraham had at the "covenant between the pieces" in Genesis 15. (In particular, the motif "Abraham Saw a Dire Future" may have served as a model for "Rise and Fall of Empires.")[16] What is more, if one imagines this interpretation being put forward by a Jewish sage of the late third or early fourth century, at a time when Roman dominion over the Jewish people and their national homeland did indeed seem utterly unchallengeable and destined to last forever, the interpretation of Jacob's dream it espouses must appear as a inspiring message of hope in the most trying of times: even the greatest of obstacles can eventually be overcome if one only has the patience and courage to outlast it.

Ensnared on the Staircase of History

A somewhat similar, but nevertheless distinct, explanation of Jacob's dream is sometimes conjoined with this one:

> R. Berekhya and R. Ḥelbo and R. Simeon b. Yosina: R. Meir explained the verse, "Despite all this they still sinned; they did not believe despite his miracles" (Ps. 78:32). This refers to Jacob who did not believe and did not ascend [the ladder]. God said to him: "Jacob, if you had believed and gone up, you would never have had to go down again; but now, since you have not believed and have not gone up, your children will become entangled with nations and ensnared with empires, [and will go] from empire to empire, from Babylon to Media and from Media to Greece and from Greece to Rome." He said to Him: "Ruler of the universe, forever?" Said God to him, "Do not fear, my servant Jacob, and do not be dismayed, Israel" [Jer. 30:10].[17]

At first glance, this passage might appear to be rather similar to "Rise and Fall of Empires": once again we have the ladder and the four empires. But here, strikingly, it is not the four guardian angels who are to ascend the ladder; in fact, there is no mention of these guardian angels, just the four empires themselves. Instead, apparently, it is Jacob himself who is asked to ascend. Unfortunately, Jacob loses his nerve; he does not sufficiently trust in God and so does not go up (that is, he "did not believe and did not ascend"). As a result, his descendants will now become "ensnared with empires," going from one to the next, "from Babylon to Media and from Media to Greece and from Greece to Rome." That is, since Jacob did not ascend, his children will have to—but they will not have an easy time of it. Apparently, Babylon, Media, Greece, and Rome are the four rungs of this ladder: Jacob's descendants are to go (as the text says) "from empire to empire" by *climbing*, slowly making their way to the top. But since they will become "entangled" and "ensnared," impeded in their climb, the ascent will not be rapidly accomplished. If only Jacob had trusted in God, he himself would have gotten over these rungs unscathed! But since he did not believe, rough times are in store.

This overall scenario sets the reader up for the punch-line of this midrash, the biblical verse cited at the end, "Do not fear, my servant Jacob, and do not be dismayed, Israel" (Jer. 30:10). A normal reader would see the two halves of this verse as virtually synonymous: "Israel" is another name for Jacob, and "fear" and "be dismayed" are near-synonyms. But "Jacob" might also be differentiated from "Israel," the former referring to the patriarch himself and the latter to the nation descended from him. Moreover, the word normally translated as "dismayed" here, *tḥt*, can, if one wishes, be understood to derive from the root *nḥt*, meaning "go down," "descend" (and not from *ḥtt*, "dismay"). This is precisely the playful switch being proposed by this midrash. For, by substituting this other meaning, the midrashist can make God out to be simultaneously telling Jacob not to fear and "Israel" (that is, Jacob's descendants) *not to go down*, not to give up because of the difficulties of the climb in which they are engaged.[18] For this pun to work, of course, one has to imagine the personified people of Israel halfway up a ladder somewhere—that is to say, one has to have precisely the picture presented by this midrash, in which Jacob's descendants are in the midst of the rough climb that leads "from Babylon to Media and from Media to Greece and from Greece to Rome."

AN ANCIENT MIDRASH ON JACOB'S DREAM

I wish now to consider an ancient, and certainly a rather strange, treatment of Jacob's dream, the one found in a short biblical pseudepigraphon called the *Ladder of Jacob*.[19] Known only from the medieval Slavonic *Tolkovaya Paleya*, this text exists in a number of versions; in addition to retelling Jacob's dream itself, it contains a prayer[20] and angelic revelation nowhere present in the biblical narrative. The Slavonic text is clearly a translation from a now-lost Greek version; it appears likely to me that the Greek is itself a translation from an original Aramaic or Hebrew text dating from, roughly speaking, the Second Temple period.[21]

There are many mysterious elements in this text that I cannot explain; here I would like simply to examine an area of overlap between its basic understanding of Jacob's dream and some of the rabbinic explanations just surveyed. Jacob's dream-vision is presented in the opening verses:

Jacob then went to Laban, his uncle. He found a place and, laying his head on a stone, he slept there, for the sun had gone down. He had a dream. And behold, a ladder was fixed on the earth, whose top reached to heaven. And the top of the ladder was the face of a man, carved out of fire. There were twelve steps leading to the top of the ladder, and on each step to the top there were human faces, on the right and on the left, twenty-four faces, including their chests. And the face in the middle was higher than all that I saw, the one of fire, including the shoulders and arms, exceedingly terrifying, more than those twenty-four faces. (*Lad. Jac.* 1:1–6)

Here, Jacob's dream has undergone a radical transformation. Instead of a ladder with angels, what Jacob sees here are human heads—a fiery head at the very top of the ladder, and then human faces to the left and right side of each of the ladder's twelve steps. Such a ghoulish display might indeed explain why Jacob was frightened when he awoke—but what is the point of it all? The head at the very top of the ladder seems to have been generated by the biblical text itself. It says of the ladder that "its top reached up to heaven," but the Hebrew word for "top" (*rō'š*) can also mean "head." Taken in this sense, the biblical text would seem to be saying that the ladder had an actual head on it—hence, the fiery head in our text. But what of the twenty-four faces?

The author leaves us to wonder about these things until chapter 5, when the angel Sariel comes to tell Jacob the meaning of his visionary dream:

Then he [the angel] said to me [Jacob]: "You have seen a ladder with twelve steps, each step having two human faces which kept changing their appearance. The ladder is this age, and the twelve steps are the periods of this age, and the twenty-four faces are the kings of the lawless[22] nations of this age. Under these kings the children of your children and the generations of your sons will be tested;[23] they [the foreign kings] will rise up because of[24] the wickedness of your offspring. And they [the foreign kings] will make this place empty by four ascents because of the sins of your offspring. And upon the property of your forefathers a palace will be built, a temple in the name of your God and your fathers' [God], but in anger against your children it will be made deserted, until the fourth descent of this age.[25] For you saw earlier[26] four figures, the ones who happened upon[27] the steps (the ascending and descending angels [were][28] the figures in the middle of the steps). The Most High will raise up kings from your brother Esau's children's children, and they will *succeed*[29] all the rulers of the peoples of the earth who have done evil to your descendants. And they will be given over into his power and *they* will suffer *him* against their will. He will hold them by force and rule over them, and they will not be able to oppose him until the day he *decrees*[30] upon them to serve idols and to offer sacrifices to the dead. And he will command that all people in his kingdom be forced to do this. And *there will be some* who will be guilty of such an offence; some of your family will serve the Most High, and some will worship idols.[31] Know, Jacob, that your descendants will be exiles in a strange land, and they will afflict them with slavery and inflict wounds on them every day. But the Lord will judge the people for whom they slave." (*Lad. Jac.* 5:1–17)

It is not hard to see a certain similarity between the very beginning of this explanation of Jacob's dream and the last rabbinic motif examined above, "Ensnared on the Staircase of History." In both, the steps of the ladder are taken to represent successive stages in the history of Israel. Here, however, the climb is not from one empire to the next, Babylon through Rome; instead, the ladder's twelve steps represent the "twelve periods of this age," while the two faces adorning each step, twenty-four in all, are the twenty-four "kings of the lawless nations of this age." If so, what Jacob sees is a vision of his descendants' future, an age of foreign domination divided into twelve periods. This foreign domination, the text says, will come about as a result of the "wickedness" of Jacob's offspring—it is, in other words, a divine punishment.

That much is clear. At this point, however, the text goes off in another direction and we hear no more about the staircase of history. Instead, there is a mention of "four ascents" and the destruction of the Jerusalem temple ("And . . . a palace will be built, a temple in the name of your God and your fathers' [God], but in anger against your children it will be made deserted"). The temple will remain deserted until the "fourth descent." The "four ascents" and the desolation that will last until the "fourth descent" are reminiscent of another midrashic motif examined above, "Rise and Fall of Empires," in which the four ascending and descending angels represent the four kingdoms or empires that will rule over the Jewish people. The last of the four empires is Rome, and only its final descent will bring to an end the period of foreign domination revealed to Jacob in his dream. Having mentioned these four ascents, our text then goes on to describe Israel's suffering under Roman domination in greater detail. Esau, typologically Rome, may have been the biblical Jacob's brother, but it is from his progeny that will arise evil kings who will oppress the Jewish people. Ultimately they will even force some Jews to give up the worship of their God and serve idols instead. This will be the final outrage, to be followed soon, apparently, by Rome's downfall.

The text of the *Ladder of Jacob* is rather difficult, but if I have understood it correctly, it appears to be an amalgam of two quite separate motifs (very much as two different approaches were combined in the passage from *Targum Pseudo-Jonathan* seen earlier). The **basic motif** "Staircase of History"—or at least a version of it, which we might call "The Twelve Steps of the Staircase," in which each step represents a different period and its two kings—seems to have been the original basis of this text. At some point, however, an editor or copyist familiar with the "Rise and Fall of Empires" motif resolved to insert it in this text. This was done in a rather sloppy manner. The angel in chapter 5 refers to the "four ascents" in Jacob's dream—in fact, he goes out of his way to remind Jacob twice that that is what he saw, "For you have seen the fourth figure . . . ," "For you saw earlier four figures . . . ." *But* *these reminders are just a bluff*. In fact, there was no mention of four ascents or a "fourth figure" in the original account of the dream in chapter 1, since the interpolator has apparently limited himself to tampering with chapter 5 alone. There could thus be no clearer announcement that this whole section about the Romans and the "four ascents" was stuck in after the original text had been composed. The lack of agreement between what the dream itself contains (chapter 1) and what the angel says it contained (chapter 5) makes this obvious.

There is another indication that, indeed, the whole section about Rome is an insertion. The last two sentences in the passage quoted are apparently an allusion to the enslavement of the Israelites in Egypt: "Know, Jacob, that your descendants will be exiles in a strange land, and they will afflict them with slavery and inflict wounds on them every day. But the Lord will judge the people for whom they slave." This is a nearly exact quote of Gen. 15:13–14. It certainly cannot refer to the period of Jewish suffering under the Romans—the subject of the insertion that just precedes it—because by no stretch of the imagination could it be said that the Jews were "exiles in a strange land" under the Romans: they were at home in their own land, but being ruled by foreigners. In other words, it bears no connection to the sentence that precedes it; it does, however, continue the theme of Israel's future oppression that was being discussed before the section about Rome began. Indeed, if we cut out the whole section about Rome, we get a fairly smooth interpretation of Jacob's dream as it was presented in chapter 1:

Then he [the angel] said to me [Jacob]: "You have seen a ladder with twelve steps, each step having two human faces which kept changing their appearance. The ladder is this age, and the twelve steps are the periods of this age, and the twenty-four faces are the kings of the lawless nations of this age. Under these kings the

children of your children and the generations of your sons will be
tested; they [the foreign kings] will rise up because of the wickedness of your offspring. . . . Know, Jacob, that your descendants will
be exiles in a strange land, and they will afflict them with slavery
and inflict wounds on them every day. But the Lord will judge the
people for whom they slave."

The verses that follow these continue the theme of Egyptian slavery and ultimate redemption, but the subject of Roman domination does not return.[32]

When were the "four ascents" and the description of Roman
domination inserted in the original text? It is difficult to say for
sure, but this part of the text must certainly postdate the revolt
against Rome and the destruction of the temple in 70 C.E. Indeed,
it is not difficult to imagine how the insertion came to be made.
At the time of the temple's fall, the original text of the *Ladder of
Jacob* had presumably been around for some years, but although
this text contained vague predictions of a dire future for Israel, it
made no clear reference to the cataclysmic destruction of God's
own house. If the *Ladder of Jacob* were to continue to enjoy its
prophetic reputation, some specific reference to the Romans and
the destruction had to be made. And so one was inserted: an allusion to the "Rise and Fall of Empires" motif—in which Rome
features prominently as the fourth empire—was stuck into the existing text.

THE TWELVE STEPS OF THE STAIRCASE

The material about Rome and the destruction of the Jerusalem
temple was thus added to a text that already contained its own,
rather different, explanation of Jacob's dream-vision. What can
be deduced about this original exegetical motif? As was already
observed, it bears a fundamental similarity to the "Ensnared on

the Staircase of History" motif described earlier. In fact, both that rabbinic text and the original version of the *Ladder of Jacob* are, as mentioned, **variants** of the same basic motif, "Staircase of History."

In order to understand how this motif was first created, we must return to the biblical text. Jacob sees a ladder in his dream and is frightened. What is frightening, this motif asserts, is the *ladder itself*. In this respect it bears some resemblance to Philo's explanation of Jacob's dream, with which we began. The difference is that, while Philo wished to relate the "irregular course" symbolized by the ladder to Jacob's own life, the "Staircase of History" motif relates it to the life of Jacob's descendants, the people of Israel: the ladder represents the coming ages of history, and Jacob sees the terrible things that lie in store for his offspring. No wonder he says, "How fearsome is this place!" In thus explaining Jacob's dream as foretelling what will happen to his descendants, the "Staircase of History" motif seems to be suggesting a connection between Jacob's dream-vision at Bethel and Abraham's dream-vision in the "covenant between the pieces," narrated in Genesis 15. There Abraham is warned that his descendants will be enslaved in Egypt—and, in later, midrashic elaborations of this passage, he is warned about the subsequent domination of his offspring by other foreign powers.[33] The "Staircase of History" motif seems designed to suggest that Jacob, Israel's immediate ancestor, received at Bethel a similar warning about his descendants' future oppressors.

In both variants of this basic motif, the fact that the Bible mentions certain angels ascending and descending on the ladder is relatively unimportant: their traveling up and down the ladder of future ages probably holds no particular significance for Jacob, save perhaps that, in the hard times to come, his progeny will be watched over and protected. But the whole point is the frightening display of the ladder and the domination of Jacob's descendants that it foretells, domination by foreign kings.

Why does the version of this motif in the *Ladder of Jacob* specify that the coming ages are divided into twelve steps? The whole idea of the display of future history does have certain obvious affinities with other Second Temple texts, many of which likewise conceive of time as divided up into a certain number of periods or units (usually ten, but sometimes twelve).[34] It seems to me unlikely that any more precise significance be attributed to the number twelve in context, especially since, for this original version of the text, the tribulations of Jacob's progeny will start with the period of slavery in Egypt and not with the Babylonian exile (as per the rabbinic motifs); twelve is simply a great many difficult periods for the Jewish people to live through before the messiness of history will be resolved.[35] In short, I do not think the twelve steps offer any clue as to when, precisely, the *Ladder of Jacob* was written.

Other clues, however, do exist. The first has already been mentioned: the very fact that the material about the Roman destruction of the temple has been added to an earlier version suggests that the original *Ladder of Jacob* must go back to before the great Jewish revolt of 68–70 C.E. How much earlier is difficult to guess. The twelve equal steps and the twenty-four faces on them highlight the fact that, for this author, Jewish history consists of an unbroken series of foreign oppressors. It is difficult to imagine someone holding such a view during the period of the revolt of the Maccabees or that of their immediate Hasmonean successors; whatever the author's opinion of them might have been, he would probably not have depicted them as *foreign* rulers, the "kings of the lawless nations." If this bit of evidence is to be taken seriously, then the *Ladder of Jacob* might well be thought to have originated in a pre-Maccabean text. This is certainly possible; if so, the interpolator's reluctance to retouch chapter 1 may represent not sloppiness so much as an unwillingness to make more than a minimum number of changes in a text that was already an old classic and whose opening sentences, therefore, might not easily be tampered with. On the other hand, the absence of any reference to the *Ladder of Jacob* elsewhere in Second Temple writings—as well as the fact that it survived only in the Slavonic *Paleya*—make such an early date of composition problematic. Alternately, it might be possible to assign to this work a date in the early to mid–first century C.E., at a time when Maccabean nationalism had faded into dim memory and when the later Hasmoneans seemed so linked to Hellenism and foreign powers—indeed, subsequently, to the Romans themselves—as to be classifiable as foreign rulers, even if homegrown.

AN OVERVIEW

The case of Jacob's dream provides a good example of how ancient biblical interpreters sometimes sought to reckon with a text that, on the one hand, was potentially puzzling but, on the other, afforded interpreters an opportunity to put a particular "spin" on the Bible's words. At first glance, of course, the image of the ladder and the ascending and descending angels could not have been particularly troubling. It must have seemed to be a visual embodiment of the special connection between heaven and the particular spot on which Jacob was sleeping—a spot that, as Jacob goes on to say, is the very "house of God" and the "gateway of heaven." As for the angels, their going up and down must have simply been a way of showing that this connection with heaven was active and ongoing; if their presence on the ladder served any other purpose, was it not to symbolize the divine protection that God went on to promise Jacob directly when He spoke to him in his dream? But precisely because all these things are subsequently *spoken*, the visual image itself must also have appeared somewhat unnecessary. Was its purpose simply to be some kind of illustration of God's words? Or was this image intended to make some other point?

This question about the purpose of the image apparently stands behind the motifs "Changing of the Guard," "Exiled Angels," and "Angels Descended to Admire Jacob." All of these, we have seen, took a minimalist approach to the dream, excluding the angels and the ladder from its content and seeing in its words only a confirmation of the divine grant of land to Jacob and his descendants. The ladder, according to common approach of these motifs, was thus a real ladder and *not* part of the dream, and the angels who went up and down on it were quite unrelated to God's words of encouragement. Such an approach required, however, a separate explanation for the ascending and descending angels. "Angels Descended to Admire Jacob" took what seems like the most direct approach, asserting that the purpose of these (multiple) ascents and descents was to permit the angels to take a look at the sleeping Jacob in the flesh. That such a motif is reflected relatively early—in John's Gospel—suggests that it preceded the other two not only in simplicity but chronologically as well. In this motif, because it envisages myriads of angels ascending and descending on a single ladder, the order "ascending/descending" was unimportant: clearly, some angels must have been going up, returning to heaven, while other angels were going down. But this basic scheme came to be elaborated at a certain point: the originally separate midrashic motif of "Jacob's Face Engraved on the Heavenly Throne" was eventually combined with this one, so that the angels now descended to see Jacob and ascended to see his image on the heavenly throne. In fact, we saw how the targumic tradition succeeded in blending *three* originally distinct motifs—"Exiled Angels," "Angels Descended to Admire Jacob," and "Jacob's Face Engraved on the Heavenly Throne"—into a single whole.

It is also noteworthy that interpreters of this school used the occasion to assert what was hardly evident in the biblical text itself: even at this early stage of his life, they say, Jacob was a paragon of virtue. Thus Jacob is called "Jacob the righteous," and it was precisely his righteousness that caused the exiled angels to wish to accompany him on his journey, or caused the heavenly angels to wish to go down and see this remarkable human being in person.

Meanwhile, other interpreters had taken the opposite tack and included the ladder and the angels in the dream itself. What did these signify? As mentioned, they seemed, on the face of things, altogether positive. At a relatively early stage, however, some interpreters wished to find in Jacob's dream the equivalent of Abraham's dream-vision in Genesis 15, where it had been foretold to him that "your offspring will be strangers in a land not theirs, and they will be enslaved and oppressed four hundred years" (Gen. 15:13). If such a glimpse of the future was afforded to Abraham, ought not Israel's more immediate ancestor, Jacob, have been shown the same thing—or more? Out of such considerations developed the basic motif "Staircase of History": Jacob saw at Bethel the steps or stages through which his descendents would have to climb in future centuries. This motif is first attested in a text to which was added, in rather clumsy fashion, a new section describing Roman oppression and the destruction of the Jerusalem temple. This fact alone argues that the "Staircase of History" is a fairly old motif, certainly antedating 70 C.E., and possibly even going back to pre-Maccabean times.

At some point, this motif came to be combined specifically with the theme of the four empires that will oppress the Jews—a theme attested in the book of Daniel and elsewhere (though the identity of the four was apparently somewhat different there).[36] Now the ladder came to have only four rungs: Babylon, Persia-Media, Greece, and Rome, each of which constituted an obstacle to the ascent of the ladder: thus was created the daughter-motif, "Ensnared on the Staircase of History." To this scheme was added the punch-line from Jer. 30:10, "Do not fear, my servant Jacob, and *don't go down*, Israel." Citing this biblical verse added an element of hope to the old staircase motif: Keep the faith, Israel, and keep on climbing!

Probably at a somewhat later date was created a **rival motif**, "Rise and Fall of Empires." This was a midrashic triumph in two respects: It accounted perfectly for the angels in the dream as well as the ladder (whereas "Staircase of History" had essentially omitted the angels). Moreover, it had an even more specific message of hope: God had promised to end the rise of Edom/Rome, even though it looked like their climb would never end (Obad. 1:4). This motif's precise chronological relation to the staircase motif cannot be determined for sure, but since a better midrash usually tends to circulate more freely and eventually drives out a lesser one (a kind of anti–Gresham's law), it seems to me probable that "Rise and Fall of Empires" came about *after* "Staircase of History" even in its four-empires configuration; indeed, the element of the four empires in the staircase motif may well have served as a direct inspiration for the "Rise and Fall" motif. The fact that rabbinic texts attribute the "Staircase of History" motif to R. Meir, a *tanna* of the second century C.E. and "Rise and Fall of Empires" to an *amora* who lived more than a century later might support this relative dating.

Meanwhile, what of the biblical Jacob? According to the Genesis account, after his vision of the ladder he continued his journey to his uncle Laban's house, where he met and eventually married his two cousins, Leah and Rachel, and fathered his twelve sons, the future twelve tribes of Israel. He also had a daughter, Dinah— and it is the story of her rape by Shechem, the son of Hamor, that constitutes the background of our next examination of ancient biblical interpretation.

Chapter Three

THE RAPE OF DINAH,
AND SIMEON AND LEVI'S REVENGE

he story of Jacob's only daughter, Dinah, is contained in chapter 34 of Genesis. The narrative begins with brutal frankness:

Dinah, the daughter that Leah had borne to Jacob, once went out to visit the [other] girls of the land. But she was spotted by Shechem, the son of Hamor the Hivite, chief of that country, and he seized her and forced her to lie with him.[1] [Afterwards,] being taken with Dinah, Leah's daughter, he acted lovingly towards her and spoke to her tenderly. Then he said to his father Hamor, "Get this girl for me as a wife." (Gen. 34:1–4)

What happens in the ensuing verses does not seem to reflect very well on *any* of the figures involved. The rapist's father, Hamor, does indeed approach Jacob and seek to contract a marriage, but Dinah's brothers are enraged at the proposal. Instead of simply refusing, however, they tell Hamor that the marriage proposal will be acceptable only if the bridegroom and all the other males of the city first undergo circumcision. They agree, and all are circumcised in a single day. Three days later, when the men of the city are at the height of their disablement and pain, Dinah's two brothers, Simeon and Levi, enter the city stealthily and kill all the men. Jacob, apparently taken aback at their action, reproves them, but they reply, "Should our sister be treated like a whore?"

Ancient interpreters were therefore puzzled by the very existence of this narrative: it seemed to have no particular purpose, and certainly no lesson to impart. Nothing happens as a result of it: Jacob and his family do not end up taking over the city of Shechem (same name as the rapist) and settling there, nor does the violent revenge end up involving Jacob in an all-out war with the neighboring Canaanites, as he apparently had feared. The Bible says nothing of any pregnancy or birth that might have resulted from the rape; Dinah's subsequent life is never evoked. What, then, was the connection of this incident with the rest of Scripture? Any moral or ethical teaching was hard to discern in it: as already mentioned, no one involved seemed to have behaved in exemplary fashion. The brothers lie about being willing to give Dinah to Shechem as a bride; in fact, they use the sacred rite of circumcision to trick their victims and then punish a whole city for the act of a single one of its citizens. For his part, Jacob seems particularly ineffectual. What is more, the story itself is told with striking detachment; there is no way to know if the events recounted were approved or disapproved by God. The story ends, quite literally, with a question mark.

If the story itself is enigmatic, it was the task of ancient interpreters to make it less so, indeed, to supply an interpretation of its various particulars that might also suggest some sort of overall purpose, or lesson, behind its inclusion in sacred Scripture. As we have already seen with the Slavonic *Ladder of Jacob*, ancient interpreters did not generally write biblical commentaries in the modern fashion, citing the text verse by verse and then providing their own explanation. Instead, they *retold* the text in their own words, inserting in their retellings explanations of any difficulties found in the biblical version.[2] Such retellings abound in the literature of the late biblical period, starting from the third century B.C.E. and extending into the first or second century of the common era. The story of Dinah is thus retold or alluded to in a number of texts from this period.

In the following, I would like examine in detail several of these retellings. My starting point will be the *Testament of Levi* section of the *Testaments of the Twelve Patriarchs*, a work generally believed to have been written in the first century B.C.E.[3] Although this text contains one fairly continuous retelling of the biblical story, its retelling, no less than that of Jacob's dream at Bethel, is best analyzed in terms of the exegetical motifs of which it is composed.

Weapons from Heaven

There is a brief reference to the Dinah incident at the beginning of the *Testament of Levi* (2:2), but the main discussion of this biblical story is found in chapters 5 and 6. According to this text, the virtuous Levi prays to God to be relieved from his grief over the sad state of humanity; he then falls asleep and, in his dream, he is ushered into heaven by an angel. At the culmination of this heavenly ascent, the subject of vengeance for the rape of Dinah is mentioned:

> And the angel opened the gates of heaven to me, and I saw the holy Temple and the Most High upon a throne of glory. And He said to me: "To you, Levi, have I given the blessing of the priesthood, until I come and dwell in the midst of Israel." Then the angel brought me to earth and gave me *a shield and a sword* and said: "Take revenge on Shechem because of Dinah, and I will be with you, for the Lord has sent me." (*T. Levi* 5:1–3)

This passage's mention of the "shield and a sword" given to Levi is certainly puzzling. After all, the biblical account mentions no such thing; on the contrary, it says that the two brothers "each took up *his* sword and they came upon the city" (Gen. 34:25). Why should the author of the *Testament of Levi* say that the weapons came from an angel?

While I do not know of any such tradition in rabbinic writings, two slight **variants** of this **basic motif** are to be found elsewhere in the literature of the Second Temple period. In the first, Judith, heroine of the book of Judith, alludes to the same Shechem incident in her prayer to God in these words:

> O Lord God of my ancestor Simeon, to whom *You gave a sword* in hand to take revenge on the strangers who had loosed the adornment of a virgin [Dinah] to defile her . . . (Jth. 9:2)

Here it is a sword, rather than a sword and shield, that the angel provides to carry out the vengeance on Shechem, and the sword is given to Simeon rather than to Levi. Nevertheless, the fundamental similarity between these two narrative expansions is clear; the motif of heaven-sent weaponry in the Dinah episode seems to have been known to more than one author. Indeed, another evocation of this same motif may be found as well in the first-century Hellenistic romance *Joseph and Aseneth*:

> And Simeon and Levi drew their swords from their sheaths and said, "Behold, have you seen these swords? With these two swords the Lord God punished the insult of the Shechemites [by] which they insulted the sons of Israel, because of our sister Dinah, whom Shechem the son of Hamor had defiled. And the son of Pharaoh saw their swords drawn and was exceedingly afraid and trembled over his whole body, because *their swords were flashing forth like a flame of fire*. (*Jos. Asen.* 23:14)

While this text does not say where the swords (note the plural) came from, it asserts that through them *God* had punished the Shechemites (whereas in the biblical narrative Simeon and Levi act completely on their own initiative). This in itself may reflect some underlying tradition of the divine origin of their weapons. What is more, the swords seem here to have some supernatural quality to them, since they flash like fire. This too may suggest that they were not ordinary human swords.

Where did the **basic motif** of the heaven-sent weapons come from? Its origins are no doubt diverse. To begin with, the very idea that two men, Simeon and Levi, were able to overcome the entire city of Shechem and slay all its males (Gen. 34:25) must have seemed, to say the least, curious. How could they have accomplished such a feat? The effects of circumcision, however painful, would hardly have prevented the Shechemites from defending themselves in time of danger! Thus, the story itself might have seemed to suggest that Simeon and Levi employed some unusual means to carry out their conquest and slaughter—that, in other words, they were not armed with ordinary weapons.

Such a notion would seem to be confirmed by another curious detail in the narrative. The Hebrew of Gen. 34:25 says that the two brothers came upon the city בטח (usually translated in modern Bibles as "securely" or "in safety").[4] This word was similarly understood by ancient interpreters: thus, the Old Greek translation of the Pentateuch, the Septuagint, translates this word as ἀσφαλῶς, "in safety" or "with certainty." Rabbinic exegetes specifically sought to account for this feeling of safety by suggesting that Jacob too participated in the attack.[5] But since the verse says that Simeon and Levi "each took his sword and came upon the city בטח," the most straightforward explanation would appear to be that their feeling of security came *as a direct result* of the preceding action, their taking up their swords. Here again was a possible indication that these swords were unusual: armed with them, the two brothers could then proceed to take on an entire city, confident of victory.[6]

Finally, it is to be noted that Jacob's blessing of Simeon and Levi in Gen. 49:5 seems specifically to allude to the swords they used in the incident at Shechem: "Simeon and Levi are brothers, tools of violence are מכרתיהם." The significance of this last word is still obscure today (modern translations include "their weapons," "their swords," and "their spades"), but it is noteworthy that some rabbinic sources understood it as meaning "their swords," connecting the word with the similar-sounding Greek μάχαιρα, "small sword" or "dagger"[7] (the same word was used to refer to the brothers' swords in the Septuagint version of Gen. 34:25). That their father Jacob should thus seem to have specifically mentioned their weapons—perhaps in the word מכרתיהם, and in any case in the phrase "tools of violence"—could only highlight the possibility that it was *because of their swords* that these two men were able to prevail over an entire city.

For some or all of these reasons, then, the idea seems to have developed that Simeon and Levi had managed the conquest of Shechem with special weaponry provided for the occasion by God or an angel. (It is not clear from which biblical **site** this motif arose, whether from בטח in Gen. 34:25 or from "tools of violence are מכרתיהם" in Gen. 49:5, or perhaps from a contemplation of both verses simultaneously.) This motif, "Weapons from Heaven," was known to the author of the *Testament of Levi* and thus found its way into his retelling; it is likewise reflected, in somewhat different form, in Jth. 9:2 and in *Jos. Asen.* 23:14. But Levi's divine weaponry is only the first of a number of exegetical motifs found in the *Testament of Levi*.

One Son Dissented

One of the big problems that interpreters faced in the story of Dinah is the fact that Jacob's sons lie: first they say that they cannot allow Dinah to marry Shechem unless he and all his countrymen are circumcised; then—after the mass circumcision is performed—they take advantage of the weakened condition of the Shechemites in order to slay all the males of the city. That the proposal of a mass circumcision was just a trick is plainly stated in Scripture: "The sons of Jacob answered Shechem and his father Hamor *with guile*, because they had defiled their sister Dinah" (Gen. 34:13).

Yet such obvious duplicity was problematic to ancient interpreters, who liked to hold up scriptural heroes as models of proper conduct. It is therefore not surprising that both the brief retelling of this incident found in Judith (9:2–4) and the somewhat lengthier one in *Jubilees* (30:1–25) gloss over this element of the brothers' guile. Indeed, Judith makes no mention of circumcision whatsoever—a striking fact!—and *Jubilees* only mentions it after its retelling is concluded, cleverly converting the brothers' words from their original function in the narrative (a means of deceiving the Shechemites) into a divine teaching about the evils of intermarriage:[8]

> [The angel of the presence speaks to Moses on God's behalf:] That is why I have written for you in the words of the Torah everything that the Shechemites did to Dinah, and how Jacob's sons said, "We will not give our daughter to a man who has a foreskin, because for us that would be a disgraceful thing." [Indeed,] it *is* a disgraceful thing, for the Israelites who give [their own daughters to foreigners] or who take in marriage one of the foreign women, because it is impure and despicable for Israel. (*Jub.* 30:12–13)

In similar fashion, the ancient Aramaic targums change the expression "with guile" in Gen. 34:13 to "with wisdom,"[9] as if to say: Whatever their reason, the brothers spoke the truth when they said an Israelite daughter can only be given to one who is circumcised. A lie, in other words, can sometimes be true. Philo (*On the Migration of Abraham* 224) went the way of Judith and simply skipped any mention of circumcision, as, somewhat later, did Josephus and the anonymous author of the *Liber Antiquitatum Biblicarum*.

Not so the *Testament of Levi*: the matter of circumcision is indeed mentioned in its retelling. The precise significance of this mention, however, depends on how one interprets a crucial difference in the extant manuscripts of the Greek text. Most manuscripts read as follows:

[Levi says:] I advised my father and my brother Reuben that he should tell the sons of Hamor to be circumcised, because I was zealous because of the abomination which they had done in Israel. (*T. Levi* 6:3)

The above is the reading followed by H. W. Hollander and M. De Jonge in their commentary (indeed, they do not even mention the existence of a variant reading in their text-critical notes). R. H. Charles, however, basing himself on the Vatican manuscript (Codex Graecus 731), which he considered "the most important of all the MSS," had offered a different translation:

And after this I counseled my father and Reuben my brother to bid the sons of Hamor *not* to be circumcised; for I was zealous because of the abomination which they had wrought on my sister.

The difference between these two readings is obviously of great importance. According to the first, Levi is *in favor of* circumcision; he apparently urges it (as in the biblical story) as a deception that will leave the Shechemites vulnerable to attack, for, he says, he was "zealous" because of his sister's rape. According to the second reading, on the contrary, Levi *opposes* circumcision; his remark about being "zealous" would then appear to explain why he, apparently *unlike his father and Reuben*, did not accept the idea of intermarrying with the Shechemites and becoming one people. That is, if Levi is "zealous" and wishes to kill the Shechemites, and *therefore* opposes circumcision, then presumably those who supported circumcision had no intention of killing the Shechemites but, rather, were willing to intermarry with them.

Which reading is correct? De Jonge and others have labored mightily on the textual history of the *Testaments of the Twelve Patriarchs*, and it may well be that their reconstruction of the relationship between the extant textual witnesses is correct. However, in a question like this, text-critical grounds alone may not be sufficient to decide the matter. Even the oldest manuscripts are still many centuries away from the putative Urtext. That a single word, *not*, might have been dropped over the course of this text's transmission is hardly beyond the realm of possibility, especially since its omission would bring this retelling of the story of Dinah into conformity with the biblical text (where the brothers do indeed tell the Shechemites to be circumcised).[10] It therefore seems unwise to seek a decisive answer to this question through an assessment of the existing manuscripts alone. Indeed, perhaps an understanding of the *Testament of Levi*'s exegetical underpinnings will prove helpful in this matter.

A SINCERE PROPOSAL

Here it is important to mention a striking detail in the biblical text. In the Bible, while Simeon and Levi apparently overcome the city of Shechem alone, the earlier proposal to the Shechemites that they be circumcised does not come specifically from these two brothers: "The *sons of Jacob* answered Shechem and his father Hamor with guile, because he had defiled their sister Dinah" (Gen. 34:13). This is a slight, but important, discrepancy, since it seems to say that the idea of a mass circumcision came from Jacob's sons as a whole. If those who proposed circumcision (or at least most of them) were *not* those who attacked the city, then perhaps that proposal really was sincere. Indeed, if it were otherwise, why did Jacob's other sons let Simeon and Levi do the attacking *alone*? That is, if circumcision had from the beginning been a deception, proposed by the "sons of Jacob" (all of them, apparently, for Simeon and Levi have not yet been singled out by the text) as a means of deceiving the Shechemites, then all the brothers should have joined the attack.[11]

It is apparently for this reason that the idea developed that in fact the proposal of circumcision was completely separate from the decision to attack the city, and that the latter was the result of Simeon and Levi's "zeal" and not a family-wide plot. If so, the original proposal to circumcise the entire male population was indeed a sincere proposal; this idea is a fundamental part of the basic motif of a dissenting brother opposing circumcision ("One Son Dissented"). One other ancient text preserves this basic motif: the retelling of the story of Dinah found in Theodotus, the Hellenistic author of a poem dealing (among other things) with this biblical episode, fragments of which are cited, via Alexander Polyhistor, in Eusebius's *Praeparatio evangelica*:

> But when Sychem [= Shechem] the son of Hamor saw her [Dinah], he loved her; and after seizing her as his own, he carried her off and ravished her. Then, coming back again with his father to Jacob, he asked for her in the partnership of marriage. Jacob said that he would not give her until all the inhabitants of Shechem were circumcised and became Jews. Hamor said that he would persuade them. . . . As Hamor went into the city and encouraged his subjects to be circumcised, one of the sons of Jacob—Simeon by name— decided to kill Hamor and Sychem, since he was unwilling to bear in a civil manner the violent attack upon his sister. When he decided this, he shared it with his brother [Levi]. (Theodotus, frag. 4, 6, cited in Eusebius, *Praep. ev.* 9.22:5–6, 8)

Here, the family is in favor of circumcision and intermarrying; in fact, the paterfamilias himself, Jacob, is the one who proposes this to Shechem and Hamor—apparently quite sincerely. It is only afterward that one of Jacob's sons, Simeon, decides on his own to kill Hamor and Shechem and thus not to permit things to go forward as planned. If so, then the circumcision and the slaughter were not only unrelated, but those who eventually undertook the latter (Simeon and Levi) must have been from the start opposed to circumcision as a means of allowing intermarriage between the two groups.

This same basic motif, "One Son Dissented," seems to underlie the *Testament of Levi*, except that there it is Levi who apparently initiates the dissent from the family's position: Levi is opposed to circumcision because he is "zealous" (*T. Levi* 6:3) and will thus hear nothing of intermarriage with the Shechemites. (In our terminology, we would thus say that "Levi Dissented" and "Simeon Dissented" are two variants of the same basic motif, "One Son Dissented.") For this same reason, our passage in the *Testament of Levi* (in all versions) continues:

> And I killed Shechem first, and Simeon [killed] Hamor. And after that the brothers came and smote the city with the edge of the sword. And [our] father heard of it and was angry and distressed, because they had accepted the circumcision and had been killed after that, and in his blessings he did otherwise.[12] Indeed, we *had* sinned, because we did this against his will, and he became ill on that day.[13] (*T. Levi* 6:4–7)

What had they done against Jacob's will? If the correct reading of our crucial verse were (as Hollander and De Jonge suggest) "I advised my father and Reuben my brother that he should tell the sons of Hamor *to be circumcised*," then the proposal to circumcise had originated with Levi and came about because, as he tells us, he was "zealous because of the abominations which they had wrought," namely, the rape of Dinah. If so, then circumcision was (as in the biblical story) from the beginning part and parcel of a plan to kill the Shechemites. Now, if such was Levi's advice to his father and Reuben, then they apparently followed it, for of course the Shechemites did undergo circumcision. In other words, Jacob and Reuben cooperated with Levi's planned deception. But then afterward Jacob hears of it and is angry, "because we had done this thing against his will." If it was against his will, why did he go along with it and urge the Shechemites to be circumcised? This makes no sense.

There is one way to salvage the reading of Hollander and De Jonge. One might understand the text to mean that Levi deceived not only the Shechemites but his own father as well. In other words, Levi wished to kill the Shechemites but was afraid his father would not go along with the idea. He therefore pretended to be reconciled with Shechem's deed and suggested a mass circumcision. Jacob agreed with the suggestion and, along with Reuben, passed it on to the Shechemites. They underwent circumcision. Levi and Simeon then nevertheless went ahead and led the attack on Shechem. Jacob then "heard of it and was angry and distressed, because they had accepted the circumcision and had been killed after that."

Such an understanding of the *Testament of Levi* has a few drawbacks, however. To begin with, the *Testament of Levi* never mentions that Levi deceived Jacob, and Jacob (as we have just seen) is said to be angry not because he had been tricked and lied to but because the Shechemites had been killed. Moreover, this is said to have happened "against his will." In other words, Jacob's will was that the Shechemites be circumcised and live. But if so, then why had the suggestion to circumcise originally come from Levi? What was Jacob's "will" before Levi suggested circumcision—simply to walk away? Finally, it seems most unlikely that the author of the *Testament of Levi* should go out of his way to make Levi into a deceiver of his own father. After all, Levi is otherwise a great hero in this text, the recipient of divine revelation, nay, a journeyer to heaven and God's choice for the priesthood forever. Why make him the perpetrator of a fraud on Jacob, especially when the biblical text implies nothing of the kind? It makes much more sense for the *Testament of Levi* to have singled out Levi in order to praise him, that is, to make him the lone dissenter from the other brothers' (sincere) suggestion of circumcision and intermarriage. And so, as it says in the biblical account, the (other) "sons of Jacob" proposed circumcision, quite sincerely, but the "zealous" Levi could not go along with this and so tried to persuade his father and oldest brother to withdraw the suggestion.[14]

Thus, it seems to me altogether likely that the original text of the *Testament of Levi* is the same as that found in Codex Graecus 731: "And after this I counseled my father and Reuben my brother to bid the sons of Hamor *not* to be circumcised." It was Jacob and his other sons who proposed circumcision and intermarriage with the Shechemites and the "zealous" Levi who was against the idea. The *Testament of Levi* goes out of its way to tell us that Levi tried to persuade his father and Reuben to withdraw the offer of circumcision, since the virtuous Levi certainly would not want to use circumcision as a trick. The Shechemites, however, are circumcised despite his objections and, zealot that he is, Levi cannot let this plan go ahead; he and Simeon go out and slaughter the Shechemites anyway. *That* is what upsets Jacob: "And [our] father heard of it and was angry and distressed, because they had accepted the circumcision and had been killed after that." Killing the Shechemites was indeed, according to this scenario, "against his will."[15] Not only does this reading, and this reading alone, make sense of the crucial passage as a whole in the *Testament of Levi*, but it is in basic agreement with another early retelling of the Dinah episode, that found in Theodotus.[16] But if so, how did Levi's original urging that the Shechemites "not be circumcised" turn into "be circumcised" in most of the textual witnesses? It seems that this must have come about as a result of some copyist(s) "adjusting" the *Testament of Levi* to fit the biblical story. For, in the biblical narrative, of course, circumcision is a trick designed to allow Jacob's sons to overcome the Shechemites. An editor or copyist, knowing this but failing to understand the exegetical tradition that separated circumcision and the attack into two different and diametrically opposed positions, simply amended Levi's urging from "not to be circumcised" to "be circumcised."[17]

All this might appear to be a relatively minor matter, yet much depends upon it. If indeed the proposal of circumcision was sincere, then the whole biblical story must be viewed in a new light. Jacob and his other sons were, according to such a view, quite willing to allow Shechem to marry Dinah, indeed, willing to intermarry with the people of Shechem as a whole and to become "one people" (Gen. 34:17).[18] It was only Levi's "zeal" that thwarted this plan. His zealotry thus had the precise purpose of overthrowing a decision to intermarry and was not an act of revenge. In addition, it should be remarked that the interpretation presented in the *Testament of Levi* has another happy result, namely, the elimination of the problem of duplicity inherent in the biblical story. Now no one is a liar—not Jacob, not the other sons, and not Levi. This certainly was an interpretive coup! There remained, however, the matter of the killings themselves, and the motive that lay behind them.

Killed One Each

In the brief account of the slaughter in the *Testament of Levi* that was cited above, there is another striking deviation from the biblical version:

And I killed Shechem first, and Simeon [killed] Hamor. And after that the brothers came and smote the city with the edge of the sword. (*T. Levi* 6:4–5)

Once again, the author of the *Testament of Levi* seems to be taking great liberties with the biblical account. After all, the matter of who killed whom does not appear to be particularly complicated in the Bible. According to the biblical account, Simeon and Levi "killed all the males" (Gen. 34:25). The next verse goes on to relate how, in particular, "they slew Hamor and his son Shechem with the sword." Should one suppose, however, that this statement conflicts with the former and indicates that Simeon and Levi really only killed these two, the next verse (Gen. 34:26) clearly indicates otherwise, for it states that the (other) sons of Jacob "came upon the slain and plundered the city." In other words, when *these* sons of Jacob entered, the "slain" were already slain, and all that was left to do was plunder the city.

Quite different is the account presented in *T. Levi* 6:4–5. Here Levi kills only one person, Shechem, while his brother Simeon similarly kills only Shechem's father, Hamor. As for the rest of the city's inhabitants, they are killed by the (other) brothers: "And after that the brothers came and smote the city with the edge of the sword." Why should the account in the *Testament of Levi* so flagrantly contradict that of the Bible itself? And why should it specify (as the Bible does not) that in killing Shechem and Hamor, Simeon and Levi each killed one of the two (rather than having both brothers kill the two together)?

Once again, there is a parallel to the version of the *Testament of Levi* in a passage attributed to Theodotus:

Thus then Simeon rushed upon Hamor himself and struck him upon his head; he seized his throat in his left hand, then let it go still gasping its last breath, since there was another task to do. At that time Levi, also irresistible in might, seized Sychem [= Shechem] by the hair; the latter grasped his knees and raged unspeakably. Levi struck the middle of his collarbone; the sharp sword entered his inward parts through the chest; and his life thereupon left his bodily frame. When the other brothers learned of their deed, they assisted them and pillaged the city; and after rescuing their sister, they carried her off with the prisoners to their father's quarters. (Theodotus, frag. 8, cited in Eusebius, *Praep. ev.* 9.22.10–12)

The reader will notice that, here too, Simeon has killed Hamor and Levi, Shechem. What of the remaining Shechemites? On this point our source is not clear: Theodotus says that the other brothers "assisted" Simeon and Levi (presumably, in subduing the city), but he does not mention any further killings; indeed, he even speaks of "prisoners."[19] Elsewhere, however, it appears that Theodotus attributed at least *some* other killings to Simeon and Levi, for the summary found in an earlier section of Eusebius (*Praep. Ev.* 9.22.10) says that Simeon and Levi "slew those that they happened to meet" on the way to finding Shechem and Hamor.

Commentators in the past have noticed the agreement between the *Testament of Levi* and Theodotus on the matter of who killed Shechem and Hamor, as well as the fact that both avoid saying what the biblical account clearly asserts, namely, that Simeon and Levi "killed *all* the males" (Gen. 34:25). I am not aware, however, of any explanation that has been given for this peculiarity, and especially for the fact that *T. Levi* 6:4–5 plainly asserts that Simeon and Levi killed only one man each, the rest of the males having been killed by the other brothers. There is, however—apart from any desire to apologize for the violent behavior of Jacob's two sons—a good biblical reason for this assertion. It is to be found, once again, in Jacob's blessing of these two sons in Gen. 49:5–7, a passage that ancient interpreters generally held to refer to the incident at Shechem:

Simeon and Levi are brothers, tools of violence are their weapons. Let me not enter into their counsel, nor rejoice in their assembly: for in their wrath they can kill a man, and when feeling kindly, they hamstring an ox! Cursed be their wrath, so fierce, and their

anger—how unyielding! I will divide them in Jacob and scatter
them in Israel. (Gen. 49:5–7)

The above is my own attempt at a faithful rendering of this difficult
passage. On close inspection, it is evident that the passage makes no
clear reference at all to the Shechem incident. Instead, these words
seem to constitute a general description of the *tribes* of Simeon and
Levi (just as the other "blessings of Jacob" in Genesis 49 similarly
refer to tribes), whose violent nature is being highlighted. The
Simeon and Levi tribes are "brothers" in violence: when these people are angry, they will not flinch at murder, and even when they are
in a good mood, what do they do? Hamstring an ox!

Ancient interpreters, of course, did not read these words in this
way. Instead, the very conjunction of the names of Simeon and
Levi in this "blessing" was understood to mean that its subject
was the violent cooperation of these two brothers in the Shechem
incident. Therefore, the general assertion "they can [or "would"]
kill a man" (הרגו איש) was now understood as a statement of past
fact: it was in the attack at Shechem that these two individuals
did indeed "kill a man." Now, of course, this assertion need not
be taken literally as meaning *one single man*. In fact, it was apparently in order to clarify this point that the Septuagint translators changed this "man" into "men," ἀπέκτειναν ἀνθρώπους,
implying that Simeon and Levi killed *some men* there (or are *in
general* capable of murder). But this very change indicates a certain discomfort among ancient interpreters with the singular form
"man"—if Jacob literally says that Simeon and Levi killed *a man*,
how is that compatible with the Genesis narrative?[20]

It is to answer this question that the motif "Killed One Each"
found in the *Testament of Levi* (and Theodotus as well) first arose.
Yes, it asserts, Jacob did say "they killed a man," and by this he
meant quite literally that *each brother killed a man:* Simeon killed
Hamor, and Levi killed Shechem (or, conceivably, vice versa). For

the same reason, Gen. 34:26 specifies that Simeon and Levi killed (presumably only) "Hamor and his son Shechem." As for the statement in Gen. 34:25 that the two brothers "killed all the males," it is indeed in conflict both with the specification that follows it and with Jacob's words in Gen. 49:6. But given the very fact of this apparent conflict, the line of interpretation represented by the *Testament of Levi* chooses the path of leniency and understands that Simeon and Levi had in fact committed only one killing each: Simeon killed Hamor, and Levi killed Shechem; hence, "in their wrath they [each] killed a man." If so, then the Bible's statement in Gen. 34:25 must mean something different. Perhaps instead of "they killed all the males," the verb ויהרגו was construed as a passive ("and all the males were killed"—equally possible in an unpointed text). In any case, these words must have been understood as some sort of general assertion about *what happened* in the attack on Shechem—a general assertion clarified by what immediately follows it: since Simeon and Levi killed Hamor and Shechem, the rest of the killing had to have been done by someone else, presumably, the other brothers.[21]

Shechem Killed because a Foreigner

Thus, in the account of the *Testament of Levi*, Simeon and Levi each "killed a man" as asserted in Gen. 49:6. But the question remained, Why? Was it right that even the rapist himself (not to speak of his father and countrymen) ended up being punished by death? It is interesting that the law of rape contained in the Book of Deuteronomy presents a case strikingly similar to that of Shechem and Dinah:

> If a man meets a virgin who is not betrothed, and seizes and lies with her, and they are found, then the man who lay with her shall give to the father of the young woman fifty pieces of silver, and she

shall be his wife as a result of his having violated her; he may not divorce her all his days. (Deut. 22:28–29)

Here, as in the case of Shechem and Dinah, a man rapes a young woman who is neither married nor engaged. In fact, the two texts use the same terms to describe the crime: "lie with" (שכב) and "violate" (ענה). Yet the law in Deuteronomy says that the man in such a case should be treated rather leniently. He is simply required to pay a fine and to marry the young woman himself,[22] and he must remain married to her "all his days." If so, interpreters could not help wondering why Shechem had been killed by Simeon and Levi.[23] After all, he *wanted* to marry Dinah, just as the law later prescribed; he even wanted to pay her father an extravagant amount of money (Gen. 34:12), doubtless in excess of the fifty pieces of silver required by the law. Why did the brothers kill him instead of accepting the offer?

The answer proposed by many interpreters was that Shechem was a *foreigner*. For the only way in which Shechem's case seemed to differ from that described in Deuteronomy was that the perpetrator here was "the son of Hamor *the Hivite*" (Gen. 34:2), that is, a Canaanite, a foreigner living in the land that God had given to Jacob and his descendants. Now, according to Deuteronomy, such Canaanites were not only not to intermarry with the Israelites (Deut. 7:3), they were to be destroyed utterly (Deut. 7:2). Perhaps that was why Scripture, after mentioning Shechem's crime, went on to describe it as a "disgrace *in Israel*"—as if the national honor itself had been violated—and to stress repeatedly that Shechem had in fact "defiled" Dinah (Gen. 34:5, 13, 27).

It is not surprising, therefore, to find that early interpreters highlighted Shechem's foreignness in retelling the story:

Then Judith . . . cried out to the Lord with a loud voice, and said: "O Lord God of my ancestor Simeon, to whom You gave a sword to take revenge on the *strangers*." (Jth. 9:2)

And you, Moses, command the children of Israel and exhort them not to give their daughters to the gentiles and not to take any of the daughters of the gentiles [for their sons], because that is abominable before the Lord. That is why I have written for you in the words of the Torah everything that the Shechemites did to Dinah, and how Jacob's sons said, "We will not give our daughter to a man who has a foreskin, because for us that would be a disgraceful thing." [Indeed,] it *is* a disgraceful thing, for the Israelites who give [their own daughter to foreigners] or who take in marriage one of the foreign women, because it is impure and despicable for Israel. And Israel will not be free from this uncleanness if it has a wife of the daughters of the gentiles, or has given any of its daughters to a man who is of any of the gentiles. (*Jub.* 30:11–14)

When Shechem, the son of the king Hamor, saw her, he stole her away and lay with her, and, being now enamored of her, asked his father to take the girl for his wife. Hamor, agreeing, went to Jacob to request that Dinah now be legally joined to his son Shechem. Jacob, having no way to gainsay because of the standing of the person asking, still thought it unlawful to marry his daughter *to a foreigner*, and asked permission to hold a council on the subject of his request. (Josephus, *Jewish Antiquities* 1:331–38)

Against such a background, it is striking that the *Testament of Levi* makes nothing of Shechem's foreignness. Indeed, neither Shechem nor his father is ever described as a "foreigner," "gentile," or "stranger," as in the texts cited above. Then why, in the view of the *Testament of Levi*, did God allow Shechem to be killed? If, according to the understanding of *T. Levi* 6:3 presented above, Jacob and his others sons had been quite willing to have the Shechemites circumcised and then intermarry with them, should not Levi have gone along with them? Was not Levi's "zeal" in killing this potential "convert" a case of gross overzealousness?

Shechemites Died for Other Crimes

The answer that the *Testament of Levi* gives to this question is surprising. It is found in the continuation of its narration of the episode (partially cited above):

> And [our] father heard of it and was angry and distressed, because they had accepted the circumcision and had been killed after that, and in his blessings he did otherwise. Indeed, we *had* sinned, because we did this against his will, and he became ill on that day. But I saw that God's sentence upon Shechem was for evil; for they had sought to do the same thing to Sarah that they did to our sister Dinah, but the Lord had stopped them. And in the same way they had persecuted our father Abraham when he was a stranger, and they had acted against him to suppress the flocks when these had become big with young; and they had mistreated Ieblae, his homeborn slave. And in this way they treated all strangers, taking their wives by force and banishing them. But the anger of the Lord against them had reached its term. And I said to my father: "Do not be angry, lord, because through you the Lord will reduce the Canaanites to nothing, and He will give their land to you and your seed after you." (*T. Levi* 6:6–7.1)

Levi's sin, according to his account, was not that he had actually killed someone, but only that he had done so against his father's will and had thus caused him to become ill. But as for the killing itself—not only the killing of the perpetrator, Shechem, but of his father, Hamor, and the other Shechemites—it was simply a carrying out of the divine will. For Levi "saw" what Jacob had not yet perceived: that, because of the Shechemites' past crimes, God had already found this whole people to be guilty and had sentenced them to death. Indeed, he had perceived that *all* the Canaanites (of whom the Shechemites were but one part) were eventually to be killed or banished and their land given to Jacob's descendants.

In other words, the *Testament of Levi* does not mention Shechem's foreignness as the reason for his crime being such an abomination, because foreignness *as such* is irrelevant. What matters is that, because of the sinfulness evident in crimes like the rape of Dinah or the "abduction" of Sarah at Gerar (Genesis 20), the Canaanite tribes as a whole had been sentenced to death. This is quite in keeping with what is said elsewhere in the Pentateuch, and in particular with the sentence pronounced against Canaanites in Deut. 7:2, as well as with the justification of their banishment in Lev. 18:24–30 specifically on grounds that they committed sexual "abominations."

Here again, it is most significant that the interpretation of the *Testament of Levi* is uniquely in agreement with that of Theodotus as preserved by Eusebius, which also contains the motif "Shechemites Died for Other Crimes":

Seizing [Levi], he [Simeon] urged him to agree to the act by producing an oracle which said that God had determined to give ten peoples [that is, the Canaanite tribes listed in Gen. 15:19–21] to the descendants of Abraham. Simeon says the following to Levi: "For I have indeed learned the word from God, for of old He said He would give ten peoples to the children of Abraham." (Theodotus, frag. 6, cited in Eusebius, *Praep. ev.* 9.22.8–9)

For Theodotus, too, it is because God had decided (as the *Testament of Levi* says) to "reduce the Canaanites to nothing" and had already promised to "give their land to you and your seed" that the slaughter of the Shechemites can proceed. It was all in keeping with God's will.

Other Shechemites Participated

Shechem is thus killed not because he is a foreigner per se but because he is a member of one of those particular peoples on whom "God's sentence . . . was for evil" (*T. Levi* 6:8). If this is the case, then the killing of the other Shechemites needs no further justification: they had *all* been sentenced by God to die. This interpretation of the *Testament of Levi* is in stark contrast to that found elsewhere among ancient interpreters, who are at pains to suggest that the Shechemites were somehow all involved in the crime against Dinah:

> [The continuation of Judith's prayer:] O Lord God of my ancestor Simeon, to whom You gave a sword to take revenge on *the strangers* [plural!] who had loosed the adornment of a virgin to defile her, and uncovered her thigh to put her to shame, and polluted her womb to disgrace her[24]—for You said, "It shall not be so," and [yet] they did so. Therefore You gave up *their* rulers to be slain, and *their* bed, which was ashamed of the deceit they had practiced, to be stained with blood, and You struck down slaves along with princes, and princes on their thrones; and You gave their wives as prey and their daughters to captivity, and all their booty to be divided among Your beloved sons, who were zealous for You, and abhorred the pollution of their blood, and called on You for help— O God, my God, hear me also, a widow. (Jth. 9:2–4)

> But Jacob and his sons were angry at the men of Shechem because *they* defiled Dinah, their sister. And so they spoke treacherously with them and deceived and misled them. And Simeon and Levi entered Shechem unexpectedly. And they executed judgment upon all the men of Shechem and killed all the men they found there and did not leave a single one alive. They killed them all painfully because *they* had dishonored their sister Dinah. (*Jub.* 30:3–4)

I have not seen it pointed out previously, but such attempts at attributing to the Shechemites a collective role in the rape are not an ad hoc invention of these interpreters. They are in fact based on a small detail in the biblical text. In describing how the brothers plundered the city of Shechem after the slaughter, the Bible notes in passing: "And the sons of Jacob came upon the slain and plundered the city, because *they* had violated their sister" (Gen. 34:27). It was apparently this biblical "they" that provided the warrant for later writers to assume that the other Shechemites had in fact participated in the crime against Dinah.

THE SHECHEMITES' OTHER CRIMES

In any case, it is thus interesting to contrast the position presented in these other texts with that seen in the *Testament of Levi*. While the former justify the collective punishment of the Shechemites by supposing that they were jointly guilty of the rape of Dinah, the *Testament of Levi* understands the Shechemites to have been guilty of a whole host of crimes of which the rape of Dinah was but one example. It was this multitude of sins that caused them— indeed, all Canaanite tribes—to be condemned collectively.

There is only one other ancient interpreter who mentions the Shechemites' other crimes, and he is, not surprisingly, Theodotus:

> God smote the inhabitants of Shechem, for they did not honor whoever came to them, whether evil or noble. Nor did they deter-mine rights or laws throughout the city. Rather, deadly works were their care. (Theodotus, frag. 7, cited in Eusebius, *Praep. ev.* 9.22.9)

It is striking how Theodotus's justification matches that of the *Testament of Levi*, for "not honor[ing] whoever came to them" indeed corresponds to the latter part of the indictment in the *Testament of Levi*, which mentions the persecution of Abraham "when he was a stranger" and concludes, "And thus they did to all strangers."

Shechemites Persecuted Strangers

As for the exact crimes mentioned in *T. Levi* 6:9— "And in the same way they had persecuted our father Abraham when he was a stranger, and they had acted against him to suppress the flocks

when these had become big with young; and they had mistreated
Ieblae, his homeborn slave"—the first part seems to be an elaboration of an earlier verse in Genesis:

> And there was strife between the herdsmen of Abraham's livestock
> and the herdsmen of Lot's livestock, and *the Canaanite and the Per-*
> *izzite were then in the land*. And Abraham said to Lot, "Let there
> be no dispute between me and you, or between my herdsmen and
> your herdsmen, for we are kinsmen." (Gen. 13:7–8)

One question that has intrigued commentators of all periods is the
relationship between this family quarrel involving Abraham and Lot
and the mention of the Canaanites and Perizzites in the text.[25] Why
bring them into it? The interpretive tradition represented by the *Tes-*
tament of Levi apparently reasoned as follows: Since the strife involved the "herdsmen" of the two men, it must obviously have been
a dispute over the livestock (מקנה) itself—perhaps Lot's men were en-
vious of the bounty of Abraham's flocks and herds (contrast Gen.
13:2 and 5). If the Canaanites and Perizzites are then mentioned, it
must be that they *became involved* in this family squabble. Perhaps,
indeed, they joined with Lot's herdsmen and began trying, as the
Testament of Levi suggests, to reduce the size of Abraham's livestock in any way they could. For this same reason Abraham next
suggests that the dispute be ended, "for we are kinsmen"—that is,
"Let's keep the Canaanites and Perizzites out of this." And, if it is
Abraham who says this, that would tend to confirm the supposition
that these outsiders had intervened *against Abraham*.

But why is this passage relevant to the past history of the Shechemites? Because these same "Canaanites and Perizzites" are
mentioned by Jacob after the slaughter is over: "You have
brought trouble on me to make me odious to the land's inhabitants, *the Canaanite and the Perizzite*" (Gen. 34:30). The clear
implication is that the Canaanites and Perizzites are somehow the

Shechemites' close kinsmen, part of the same tribal group, and hence the ones most likely to be upset by the slaughter. For this reason, the suggestion that the Shechemites—or, rather, the larger grouping to which they belong—had sought to "suppress" Abraham's flocks seems clearly to be based on Gen. 13:7–8.[26]

As for "Ieblae," Abraham's slave mentioned in this same catalog of abuse, his identity is unknown; the name occurs in various Greek manuscripts as Eblae, Iekblae, etc. It seems to me that the name may be based on Gen. 24:2, where Abraham addresses "his slave, the eldest of his household, who was in charge of all his possessions." Rabbinic tradition identified this slave as Eliezer, Abraham's servant mentioned in Gen. 15:2, but it need not necessarily have been so. "His slave" (עבדו) might—given the fact that this person is immediately given the further description of "eldest of his household"—have been taken as a proper name, 'Abdo or something similar;[27] the distance from that to Ieblae, Eblae, etc. is not far to travel.[28] I do not know, however, how he may have been mistreated.

"We Disgraced Them"

Thus, according to the *Testament of Levi*, the Shechemites and other Canaanites had a history of both sexual misconduct and mistreating foreigners,[29] and for this reason—and not because they were *all* guilty specifically in the matter of Dinah—their collective punishment at the hand of Jacob's sons was entirely justified. Yet it is interesting that the idea that the Shechemites were collectively guilty of the rape of Dinah (as hinted in Gen. 34:27) is also found in the *Testament of Levi*. For, having advanced the idea of the Shechemites' past crimes, the text then moves to another matter:

And I said to my father: "Do not be angry, lord, because through you the Lord will reduce the Canaanites to nothing, and He will give their land to you and your seed after you. For from this day on Shechem will be called a city of imbeciles; for as someone mocks a fool, so we mocked them; because also they had wrought folly in Israel to defile our sister." (*T. Levi* 7:1–3)

To say that "*they* had wrought folly"—putting the Shechemites in the plural—is clearly to adopt the explanation of the motif "Other Schechemites Participated," whereas until now the *Testament of Levi* had endorsed the position of that motif's rival, "Schechemites Persecuted Strangers." What is more, the assertion that "from this day on" Shechem will be called a city of imbeciles does not really fit with the sentence immediately preceding. For if God is giving the land of Canaan to the Israelites, then the future inhabitants of Shechem will be Israelites. Why should the place be called a city of imbeciles if the imbeciles are no longer there? And indeed, on reflection, it may be shown that this last sentence has to do with an entirely separate bit of biblical exegesis, one referring not to the *original* Shechemites involved in the story of Dinah but to the inhabitants of that city in a later period.

Shechem the Non-People

In order to understand this remark in the *Testament of Levi*, we must go back to God's words in Deut. 32:21, "So I will make them [the Israelites] jealous with a non-people, with a foolish nation I will anger them." Who are the "non-people" to whom God was referring? Apparently, ancient exegetes held that the reference here was to the Samaritans. Such an identification was no doubt based on the biblical report that the cities of Samaria, the inhabitants of which had been exiled by the Assyrian king, were repopulated by a conglomeration of different nations (2 Kings 17:24–31). As a result, the Samaritans came to be thought of as, quite literally, not a people but a mishmash of different peoples.

Therefore, when Deut. 32:21 speaks of a "non-people," exegetes concluded that the reference had to be to Samaria.

A reflection of this ancient exegesis is found in Ben Sira:

With two nations (גוים) my soul is vexed, and the third is not a people (עם); Those who live in Seir, and Philistia, and the foolish nation (גוי נבל) that dwells in Shechem. (Sir. 50:25–26)

Here, the identification of Deuteronomy's "nation-that-is-not-a-people" with the Samaritans is clear enough. Moreover, Ben Sira picks up the second part of Deut. 32:21, "with a foolish nation I will anger them," by repeating the same phrase: the Samaritans are "the *foolish* nation that dwells in Shechem."[30]

But this second part of Deut. 32:21 raised an obvious question: why were the Samaritans said to be *foolish*? The "non-people" part was certainly clear in view of their composite origins, but what was *foolish* about them?

It was to answer this second question that another midrashic motif was devised, that found in *T. Levi* 7:3. For at some point it was noticed that the crime of the Shechemites in the Dinah story had been referred to with a term that sounded similar: "The sons of Jacob came in from the field when they heard of it; and the men were indignant and very angry, because he [Shechem] *had wrought a folly in Israel by* lying with Jacob's daughter" (Gen. 34:7). If what the Shechemites had done with regard to Dinah was described as a "folly" (נבלה), then this might explain why Deut. 32:21 had referred to the later inhabitants of Shechem, the Samaritans, as a "foolish" people (גוי נבל); this was a subtle allusion to the sort of conduct that had always been associated with that place.

Yet even that did not answer the question satisfactorily. Certainly rape is no mere "folly"; why then had the Bible called it that in the case of Dinah? To modern scholars, of course, the word נבלה does not just mean "folly." While this word can sometimes

refer to the conduct of a נבל, a fool (see, e.g., Isa. 9:16; 32:26), it
is most often found in connection with grave sexual offenses
(Deut. 22:21; Judg. 19:23-24; 20:6, 10; 2 Sam. 13:12; Jer. 29:23;
cf. Hos. 2:12) and should be translated in such cases as "outrage"
or the like.

Apparently, however, this usage puzzled ancient interpreters,
who sometimes mistakenly saw the root for "fool" in the word
even when the context was inappropriate. (Thus, while the Septuagint translates נבלה in our verse as ἄσχημον, "shame," it translates
the nearly identical usage in Deut. 22:21 as ἀφροσύνη, "folly.")
And so, the motif represented in the *Testament of Levi* comes to
explain the association of the root נבל, "fool," with the rape of
Dinah. The latter was termed a נבלה *not* because it was mere
"foolishness"—it was much worse than that!—but because, as a
result of the rape, the sons of Jacob "mocked" the Shechemites.
The Hebrew or Aramaic verb underlying "mocked" was no
doubt the D-form (*pi'el*) of the same root נבל, which, however,
truly means not "mock" but "disgrace." Indeed, that is the whole
point of this exegetical motif: the rape of Dinah was called a נבלה
because, as a result of it, the sons of Jacob *disgraced* (נבלו) the Shechemites, and even today Shechem is known as a "city of fools"
in memory of this event.

The *Testament of Levi*, aware of this tradition, has tacked it on
to the end of its retelling of the Dinah story. But in so doing, the
author of this text inadvertently included a reflection of the interpretive expansion of Gen. 34:27, seen above in Judith and *Jubilees*, to the effect that the Shechemites as a group were guilty of
the rape of Dinah: "For as someone mocks a fool, so we mocked
them; because also they had wrought folly in Israel to defile our
sister" (*T. Levi* 7:2–3). The fact that this explanation of the
collective punishment of the Shechemites conflicts with the main
one presented in the *Testament of Levi* should not be surprising,
for, as was noted earlier, double explanations for the same

thing—through the inclusion of **rival motifs**—occur frequently in interpretive texts. This case of **overkill** in particular should not seem surprising, since it comes in the midst of a remark which, as I have suggested, was tacked on later to a text that originally sought to explain the Shechemites' punishment in quite a different fashion.

God Ordered the Shechemites' Death

One final exegetical motif that the *Testament of Levi* shares with a number of early sources deserves mention, namely, the idea that the slaughter of the Shechemites had in fact been ordered by God. Once again, this is an exegetical idea that, at first glance, seems to counter the biblical narrative, which gives no indication of divine approval for the brothers' action, still less of divine sponsorship. Yet this idea that God commanded the slaughter is clearly stated by the *Testament of Levi* in some of the passages already seen:

> Then the angel brought me to earth and gave me a shield and a sword and said: "Take revenge on Shechem because of Dinah." (*T. Levi* 5:3)

> But I saw that God's sentence upon Shechem was for evil. . . . The anger of the Lord against them had reached its term. (*T. Levi* 6:8, 11)

The same idea may be found in a number of the other early texts that we have been examining:

> O Lord God of my ancestor Simeon, to whom You gave a sword to take revenge on the strangers . . . for You said, "It shall not be so," [yet] they did so. Therefore You gave up their rulers to be slain . . . and You struck down slaves along with princes, and princes on their thrones; and You gave their wives as prey and their daughters to captivity. (Jth. 9:2–4)

God smote the inhabitants of Shechem, for they did not honor whoever came to them, whether evil or noble. (Theodotus, Frag. 7, cited in Eusebius, *Praep. ev.* 9.22.9)

And let it not be done thus henceforth again that a daughter of Israel shall be defiled. For the verdict was ordered in heaven against them [the Shechemites], that they [the brothers] might annihilate with a sword all of the men of Shechem because they committed a disgrace in Israel. And *the Lord* delivered them into the hands of the sons of Jacob, so that they might exterminate them with the sword and execute judgment upon them. (*Jub.* 30:5–6)

Simeon and Levi drew their swords from their sheaths and said, "Behold, have you seen these swords? With these two swords *the Lord God punished* the insult of the Shechemites, by which they insulted the sons of Israel. (*Jos. Asen.* 23:14)

The idea that it was God who was ultimately responsible for the death of the Shechemites thus appears to have been broadly established. No doubt it was generated by a strong desire to explain (or apologize for) the apparent savagery of Jacob's sons' retribution in the biblical story. What is more, it fit well with some of the other motifs examined above, for example, "Weapons from Heaven" or "Shechemites Died for Other Crimes." Yet it would be wrong to conclude that such factors alone were responsible for the existence of this theme; it too seems to be an *exegetical* motif, arising from a biblical verse not yet examined in our discussion.

The verse in question describes the reaction of Jacob's sons upon hearing news of the rape:

The sons of Jacob came in from the field when they heard of it; and the men were indignant and very angry, because he [Shechem] had committed a disgrace in Israel by lying with Jacob's daughter, and *such a thing ought not to be done*. (Gen. 34:7)

What does the biblical narrative mean by adding this last phrase? To begin with, it should be pointed out that the Hebrew words used here, וכן לא יעשה, apparently carried a tone of moral outrage not immediately apparent in the English translation. Thus elsewhere in Genesis, when Abimelech wishes to reproach Abraham for almost leading him to commit adultery, he says: "What have I done against you, that you would have brought a great sin upon me and my kingdom? *Things that ought not to be done* you have done with me" (Gen. 20:9). Abimelech's actual words here seem to have the force of, "What you did is absolutely wrong and outrageous!" So similarly with regard to Dinah, it seems that the phrase "such a thing ought not be done" is not merely an observation about the proper workings of a well-ordered society but a heartfelt expression of revulsion at the act in question: it was an outrage!

Yet—especially if what seems like a biblical idiom came to be, in time, no longer idiomatic—the words "and such a thing ought not to be done" could take on a new coloring. They might now indeed seem prescriptive, "This is not how things should go on," or even predictive, "This thing will not be allowed to stand as is." Such an understanding of the Hebrew words seems to underlie the Septuagint translation of this verse:

> And the men were indignant and very angry, because he [Shechem] had committed a disgrace in Israel by lying with Jacob's daughter, and it *shall not be thus.* (Gen. 34:7)

The wording "and it shall not be thus" (καὶ οὐχ οὕτως ἔσται) indeed suggests that the original meaning has been slightly, but significantly, altered. This phrase now seems to be quite detached from what precedes it and has become a *judgment* about what has taken place and/or a prediction about what will follow: it shall *not* be thus!

And who said these words? In the context, "and such a thing
ought not to be done" (= "This is an outrage!") seems to be what
literary critics call "implied direct speech." That is, the text, in reporting the brothers' reaction, presents what they said to one
another—"Shechem has committed a disgrace in Israel by lying
with Dinah; this is an outrage!"—without actually saying, "Here
is what they said." It simply states their thoughts as though from
the narrative's own point of view.

From a certain angle, however, these words can take on (or
purposely be given) a different meaning. For if the Bible adds
"and such a thing ought not to be done," might not an ancient
interpreter—one who regarded this story as sacred writ, nay, the
word of God—have concluded that these were God's own words,
expressing, therefore, divine disapproval of Shechem's action?
Especially if they are understood in a prescriptive or predictive
way, as the Septuagint apparently understands them ("it shall not
be thus"), these words might easily seem to represent what is
otherwise quite lacking in the biblical story, God's own *prise-
de-position* with regard to the events. Here the divine narrator,
having reported the anger of the brothers at Dinah's rape, adds
his own editorial judgment: it shall not be thus.

This is precisely how these words were interpreted in the passage from Judith examined above:

> O Lord God of my ancestor Simeon, to whom You gave a sword to
> take revenge on the strangers who had loosed the adornment of a
> virgin to defile her, and uncovered her thigh to put her to shame,
> and polluted her womb to disgrace her; *for You said, "It shall not
> be so"*—and [yet] they did so. (Jth. 9:2)

Here, the expression of outrage originally intended to be attributed to the brothers now is specifically attributed to God: He said
"It shall not be so," and *as a result* He gave a sword to Simeon in

order that he avenge this dastardly crime. The same interpretation seems also to underlie the beginning of the passage from *Jubilees* cited above:

[The angel tells Moses:] And *let it not be done thus henceforth* again that a daughter of Israel be defiled; for judgment was ordained in heaven against them [the Shechemites]. (*Jub.* 30:5)

Here too, "such a thing ought not to be done" has been converted from implied direct speech by the brothers into divine speech, put by *Jubilees* into the mouth of the "angel of the presence" who is the book's narrator.

In this way, these two ancient texts present a specific scriptural warrant for the idea that God had actually condemned Shechem's action and that this condemnation was causally related to the rest of the story. It is not hard to see that this interpretation of the words "and such a thing ought not to be done" must have played a crucial role for other interpreters as well (even when the verse was not directly cited). It supported the idea that revenge for the rape of Dinah had actually been commissioned or (indirectly) carried out by God, an idea represented in some form by *all* the early interpreters whom we have been discussing.

SIMEON NOT INVOLVED

Having thus examined a number of exegetical motifs associated with the *Testament of Levi* and other ancient texts that retell the rape of Dinah, we might now conclude by seeking to answer one final question: What is the relationship of the *Testament of Levi's* understanding of the story to that found elsewhere within the *Testaments of the Twelve Patriarchs* itself, and specifically the testament attributed to that other major figure involved in the biblical revenge, Levi's brother Simeon?

The answer to this question is striking. One would think from the *Testament of Simeon* that the Bible had not mentioned Simeon in connection with the Dinah incident, since nowhere in this testament is that episode even alluded to. This is certainly remarkable when one considers how elsewhere in the *Testaments* the author seizes on whatever scant details can be found in Scripture concerning Jacob's various sons and elaborates upon them in his homiletic discourse. Why is not a large segment of the *Testament of Simeon* devoted to the Dinah incident, just as a large part of the *Testament of Levi* was?

Equally striking, and not unrelated, is the fact that the *Testament of Simeon* contains an allusion to the "blessing" Jacob gave to Simeon and Levi, also mentioned in *T. Levi* 6:6. But what a difference! Here is what Simeon says to his children:

> For I have seen in a copy of the book of Enoch that your sons after you will be brought to ruin by fornication, and they will do harm to Levi with the sword, but they will not prevail against Levi, because he will fight the war of the Lord and will conquer your hosts. And they will be few in number, divided among Levi and Judah, and there will be none from you to [attain] sovereignty, *as also my father Jacob prophesied in his blessings.* (T. Sim 5:4–6)

What Simeon has seen in the "book of Enoch" (which here seems to mean the preexistent Torah) is that the tribe of Simeon will suffer heavy losses because of "fornication" and will become "few in number." This is indeed what happens later in the Pentateuch: while the tribe of Simeon is numbered at the beginning of the desert wanderings at 59,300 (Num. 1:23), by the time of the second census they are down to 22,200 (Num. 26:14). Where did they all go? An obvious possibility was that they perished in the plague that befell Israel after Zimri's sin with the Midianite woman, the "sin of Baal Peor" (Numbers 25). Zimri was, after all, a Simeonite; his tribesmen doubtless also sinned with other Midianite women, and as a consequence many Simeonites must have been "brought to ruin by fornication" in this plague.

Even if *all* those who died in the plague were Simeonites, however, that still would not account for their population loss, for "those that died in the plague were twenty-four thousand" (Num. 25:9), leaving another 13,100 Simeonite dead to be accounted for in some other fashion. It is apparently for this reason that the *Testament of Simeon* adduces another catastrophe that further diminished the Simeonite population: there was some sort of armed conflict between the tribes of Levi and Simeon, and it was that conflict, fiercely fought on both sides, that resulted in Levi's victory (for theirs was the side of justice, "the Lord's war") and Simeon's reduction to "few in number."

The War between Simeon and Levi

Whence did the author of the *Testament of Simeon* deduce the existence of such a war between Simeon and Levi? It seems that this idea was generated by none other than Jacob's "blessing" of Simeon and Levi in Genesis 49. (Simeon seems to say as much at the end of the passage cited above: what I have just described, he says, is "as also my father prophesied in his blessings.") Apparently, this author chose to understand Jacob's opening words, "Simeon and Levi are brothers, tools of violence are their weapons" (Gen. 49:5) as meaning, "They are brothers, *yet* tools of violence are their weapons." That is, even though they are brothers, they will eventually come to blows: the tribe of Simeon will attack Levi at swordpoint, but Levi will eventually triumph, and Simeon will be diminished and dispersed. For why else (according to this view) did Jacob decide to join Simeon and Levi together in the same blessing—the only two brothers to be so joined? Certainly not because their fates were similar! Levi went on to inherit the priesthood, whereas Simeon fell into obscurity and was passed over entirely by Moses in *his* blessings (Deuteronomy 33). Thus, if Jacob joined them together in Gen. 49:5–7, all the while referring to their "tools of violence," bloodshed, and fierce anger, it must have been because he foresaw that these two tribes would be joined in battle.

In fact, it was apparently this war between the tribes of Simeon and Levi that would determine their very different fates, for according to the *Testament of Simeon*, Levi "will fight the war of the Lord and will conquer your [Simeon's] hosts. And they will be few in number, *divided among Levi and Judah*, and there will be none from you to [attain] sovereignty" (*T. Sim.* 5:5–6). The indicated phrase appears likewise to be an allusion to Jacob's blessing, specifically, to its last line: "I will divide them in Jacob and I will scatter them in Israel" (Gen. 49:7). Here too, however, a radical transformation has taken place, for the "them" of Gen. 49:7 now no longer refers to the tribes of Simeon and Levi together, but only to the former: the *Simeonites* will be divided in Israel, not only territorially, but with regard to their future functions. For one might have expected that Simeon, Jacob's second son and hence next in line after (the discredited) Reuben, would have inherited one or both of the two great hereditary prizes, priesthood and kingship. Yet, mysteriously, he was passed over for both. This came about, according to the *Testament of Simeon*, at least in part because of the war with Levi; it seems that these prizes were likewise "divided among Levi and Judah," leaving neither priestly nor political dominion for Simeon, "and there will be none [from you Simeonites] to [attain] sovereignty."[31]

What can be learned from both this passage in particular and from the fact that the *Testament of Simeon* throughout avoids mentioning the rape of Dinah or the subsequent revenge? The answer is obvious. The *Testament of Simeon* seeks to deny, or at least pass over in silence, Simeon's role in the affair. The incident

itself is not mentioned, and Jacob's blessing of Simeon and Levi—
which other texts (including the *Testament of Levi*) explain as
talking about the events at Shechem—is instead interpreted in
such a way as to have it refer to some unknown war between Levi
and Simeon. And why is that? It seems likely that the author of
the *Testament of Simeon* (like the authors of Judith and *Jubilees*)
viewed the revenge on Shechem as entirely a good thing. As *Jubilees* observes:

> And on the day when the sons of Jacob slew Shechem, a writing
> was recorded in their favor in heaven that they had executed righ-
> teousness and uprightness and vengeance on the sinners, and it was
> written for a blessing. (*Jub.* 30:23)

As far as *Jubilees* is concerned, not only was the act of revenge
"on the sinners" (plural) justified, but it constituted an act of
righteousness to be recorded to Jacob's sons' credit in heaven. Indeed, *Jubilees* elsewhere maintains that it was in part for this act
that Levi was granted the priesthood (*Jub.* 30:17–18).

Now, the position of the *Testament of Simeon* on the same issue
must be deduced from its silence, a risky procedure at best. Yet the
silence is almost deafening. For, as has been pointed out, the great
theme of the *Testament of Simeon* is ζῆλος, both "zeal" and
"envy." What would have been easier than to have Simeon, in his
confessional mode, bemoan the overzealous slaughter of the Shechemites as another instance of ζῆλος gone wild? Or the *Testament of Simeon* could have adopted the somewhat equivocal
position found in the *Testament of Levi*. Simeon could have admit-
ted that Jacob condemned the revenge in his blessings because
what Simeon had done was indeed against his father's will, and another instance of zeal unrestrained; on the other hand, the slaughter turned out to be ultimately justified because the Shechemites
had been destined by God to extinction for their evil ways.

These obvious possibilities are passed up in the *Testament of Simeon*, and it even interprets Jacob's "blessing" in Gen. 49:5–7 so as *not* to have it refer to the Shechem incident at all but to some unknown future battle between the tribes of Simeon and Levi. Apparently, even Jacob's condemnation of his two sons' "wrath" in the incident was too much for the author of the *Testament of Simeon* (or the originator of this interpretation) to bear. He could not stand the slightest implication that there was anything wrong with the brothers' revenge, and so he converted Jacob's words into a condemnation of Simeon alone for some otherwise unknown battle between his descendants and those of Levi.[32] (In similar fashion, *Jubilees* avoids mentioning the substance of Jacob's blessings, dismissing them in a single, broad reference in *Jub*. 45:14.) Since Simeon's own fate hardly turned out favorably—he was passed over for the priesthood and kingship and omitted entirely from Moses' blessings—the author of the *Testament of Simeon* likewise found it necessary to suppress any connection between Simeon and the revenge elsewhere in the text. The attack on Shechem might as well not have happened, for any role that Simeon played in the incident would have (as in *Jubilees*) accrued to his credit and would thus call into question the later fate suffered by Simeon and his descendants.

All this is to say that the *Testament of Simeon* and the *Testament of Levi* seem to present rather different views of the incident at Shechem. Underlying the *Testament of Simeon* seems to be the conviction that the brothers' act of revenge was altogether good; that is why this text went through the contortions we have seen. The *Testament of Levi* took a more balanced view, accepting Jacob's condemnation at face value, while offering one slight justification for Levi's role, namely, that Levi had from the beginning opposed circumcision. At the same time it suggested that what happened was ultimately in keeping with God's decision to destroy the Canaanites in general. The *Testament of Simeon's* view is thus in harmony with that of *Jubilees* and (apparently) Judith, whereas the *Testament of Levi's* once again inclines more in the direction of Theodotus's account, which, at least in the fragmentary form in which it has come down to us, contains no indication that the deed was one of "righteousness" or "uprightness." The contrast of these two testaments on this point is potentially significant for our understanding of the evolution of the *Testaments* as a whole.

SUMMARY AND CONCLUSIONS

We have examined a number of individual exegetical motifs concerning the story of Dinah as interpreted in various Second Temple documents: "Weapons from Heaven," "One Son Dissented," "Killed One Each," "Shechem Killed because a Foreigner," "Shechemites Died for Other Crimes" (and two related motifs: "Shechemites Persecuted Strangers" and "God Ordered the Shechemites' Death"), "Other Shechemites Participated," "We Disgraced Them," "Shechem the Non-People," and "War between Levi and Simeon." Each of these, we have seen, originated in an ancient interpreter's fixing on some little detail in the biblical text—Jacob's assertion that Simeon and Levi killed *a man*, the apparent connection of נבלה to נבל, or the phrase "and such a thing ought not to be done"—in order to assert that something not evident from the biblical narrative did in fact take place or was in fact the case.

Apart from the inherent interest of these motifs because of what they show about how this biblical story was interpreted in Second Temple times, they can tell us something in particular about the presentation of the story in the *Testament of Levi*. To begin with, the *Testament of Levi's* version of the events at Shechem is an interweaving of different exegetical motifs found as well in other ancient texts. Indeed, almost all of the motifs studied in the *Testament of Levi* were attested in similar form elsewhere: "Weapons from Heaven" (found in Judith and apparently alluded to in *Joseph and Aseneth*), "Killed One Each" (Theodotus), "Shechemites Died for Other Crimes" (Theodotus), "Other Shechemites Participated" (Judith, *Jubilees*), "Shechemites Persecuted Strangers" (Theodotus), and "God Ordered the Shechemites' Death" (Judith, Theodotus, *Jubilees*, and *Joseph and Aseneth*). At the same time, two other motifs, "Levi Dissented" (a variant of the basic motif "One Son Dissented") and "We Disgraced Them," are uniquely attested in the *Testament of Levi*. (The motifs "Shechem Killed because a Foreigner" and the "War between Levi and Simeon" were found in other documents but not in the *Testament of Levi*.)

That the *Testament of Levi*'s retelling is an interweaving of different interpretations is suggested not only by this list of shared sources but by the fact that sometimes, as we have seen, these different motifs duplicate or even conflict with one another and have at times been somewhat clumsily combined or reconciled. Moreover, the fact that the *Testament of Levi* differs in at least some points of interpretation from *all* the other texts mentioned may support the notion that no direct *literary* dependence exists between the *Testament of Levi* and any of the others.

At the same time, the resemblance between the interpretation of the Dinah incident underlying the *Testament of Levi* and that attributed to Theodotus in Eusebius is most striking. It seems likely that they represent a common source or tradition. Particularly when viewed in contrast to the other early retellings studied, these two show a communality of thought that is undeniable. Moreover, the agreement between *Jubilees* and Judith, while perhaps less striking, is nonetheless impressive. Is it not possible to distinguish two broadly different approaches, the *Testament of Levi*–Theodotus line and the *Jubilees*–Judith line, the latter distinguished by its somewhat more bloodthirsty quality and a certain xenophobia withal?

THE QUESTION OF INTERMARRIAGE

Our overall concern has been with exegesis, how the *Testament of Levi* and other texts from the same general period interpret the story of Dinah and Simeon and Levi's revenge. It must be observed, however, that interpretation is *never* utterly divorced from the world in which it takes place, and certainly not when it comes to the interpretive works of Jews in the Second Temple period.[33] Ancient biblical interpreters always have an axe to grind. At the very least, they are out to show their readers something nonobvious, something new, which other readers have not understood: "Read it my way and you will gain insight into the real meaning of the text." But often they have a particular program or position they wish to put forth, a stand on some issue that they wish to back up and support with their interpretation of this or that part of the Bible.

In the case of the story of Dinah, one issue that is clearly being invoked is that of intermarriage between Jews and non-Jews, that is, exogamy (and its opposite, endogamy). Our various texts' pronouncements on this subject have been examined in recent years by historians of the Second Temple period, and it might not be inappropriate to mention some of their findings here.

One relatively recent treatment of intermarriage concludes that, while no blanket prohibition of it appears anywhere in the Hebrew Bible, the situation had changed dramatically in the latter part of the Second Temple period: by then, "[i]ntermarriage and other violations of fundamental norms were deemed worthy of capital punishment."[34] In support of this contention, *Jubilees*, Theodotus, the *Testament of Levi*, and other documents are cited. In the light of the foregoing pages, however, such a characterization seems in need of more nuance. For, as just noted, the surviving texts seem to divide into two schools. *Jubilees* is indeed vehement in its denunciation of exogamy, as is Judith as well (though the passage is admittedly quite brief). But Theodotus and the *Testament of Levi* tell a different story. As we have seen, the *Testament of Levi* does not stress the foreignness of Shechem or his Hivite origins, nor (unlike Judith and *Jubilees*) does it speak of him as a gentile or stranger. Moreover, if I am correct in preferring the reading of Codex Graecus 731, then Jacob and Levi's brothers were all in favor of intermarriage with the Shechemites and even overruled Levi's vehement objections. Indeed, whichever manuscript one chooses, it is clear from the *Testament of Levi* that Jacob *accepted the idea* that Shechem and his countrymen would be circumcised and intermarry with his descendants. The same is true of the view expressed in Theodotus. In other words, the material examined herein hardly supports the picture of a blanket condemnation of exogamy.

Another recent study seems closer to the mark in distinguishing "two opposing approaches to intermarriage" in Second Temple times, one of which viewed it as "unthinkable" and a "second, permissive trend that placed no impediment on intermarriage."[35] This does indeed correspond to the evidence examined in the foregoing pages (although that evidence is, oddly enough, not cited by this author);[36] indeed, the two approaches that we have identified as already present at a relatively early period (starting in the second century B.C.E.) seem to have continued their career, as the author of this study documents, on into rabbinic writings.

But was exogamy truly a social reality in the second century B.C.E.? Another recent study on the subject seeks to claim that it was not: the apparent silence of Ben Sira and the authors of 1 and 2 Maccabees on the subject of exogamy is taken as evidence of its not having been a real issue.[37] Of course, arguments *ex silentio* are not as strong as other evidence, and it seems to me difficult to maintain such a claim in the face of the vehemence of *Jubilees* and other ancient texts on the subject. This study, however, concludes that what seems like a condemnation of intermarriage in the *Aramaic Levi Document* is actually a condemnation of "priests' failure to marry women from priestly families," whereas *Jubilees'* stance is explained as a kind of literary construct rather than a reflection of any social reality: *Jubilees* says what it says "in accordance with *Jubilees'* characteristic idea of Israel as a kingdom of priests."[38] While this proposal is intriguing, it seems in the end to founder on a lack of conclusive evidence. The silence of ben Sira is a bit puzzling, but it may simply reflect the social reality of his own upper-crust circles rather than that of most Jews in the early second century B.C.E. As for 1 Maccabees, it is almost superfluous to observe that this is a book of Maccabean propaganda whose main focus is on political and military history, not social issues. Nevertheless, at one point it does mention (as this author notes) Jews "being joined with (ἐζευγίσθησαν) the Gentiles" (1 Macc. 1:15). The original Hebrew text (not preserved) appears to have used the same verb as Num. 25:3 (ויצמד), and perhaps in the same sexual sense; even if not, it would be hard to exclude exogamy from the sorts of "being joined" condemned by this verse. The date and provenance of the *Testaments of the Twelve Patriarchs* is sometimes disputed, but certainly its evidence deserves consideration in this context. Quite apart from its treatment of the story of Dinah in the *Testament of Levi*, it contains a few quite unambiguous injunctions against exogamy (see, for example, *T. Levi* 14:5–6, *T. Jud.* 13:6–8, *T. Dan* 5:4–5).[39]

In regard to the overall attitude of the *Testaments* toward exogamy, I have already observed that the *Testament of Levi*'s view of the Dinah story is in marked contrast to that found in the *Testament of Simeon*; the strange silence of the latter might well be explained if its author subscribed to the Judith-*Jubilees* school of thought. In any case, the apparent disagreement of these two testaments on the meaning of the Dinah story supports the idea, already put forward by others, that the *Testament of Levi* is rather different in form and origin from the other testaments. It would be difficult, however, on the basis of its interpretation of the biblical story of Dinah to say anything about the date of the *Testament of Levi* vis-à-vis that of the *Testament of Simeon* or the other testaments. For if the *Testament of Levi*'s views are partially mirrored in those attributed to Theodotus, whose poem may go back to the second century B.C.E., the view of the incident identified in the *Testament of Simeon* seems to be at least as old, finding its echo in *Jubilees* and, to a lesser extent, in Judith.

One conclusion that ought to be resisted, in my opinion, is that the *Testament of Levi*'s rather tolerant views on foreigners and its apparent contemplation of some sort of conversion and intermarriage are to be connected specifically with the editorship or editorial preferences of the early Christian whose hand is visible in the final form of the *Testaments*. Everything seen above underlines the *traditional* character of the interpretations of the Dinah story found in the *Testament of Levi*, and its internal contradictions as well as its resemblances to other documents would suggest that the *Testament of Levi*, like so many other instances of early biblical interpretation, is a patchwork put together by an author or editor who was familiar with various exegetical traditions of long-established authority and who, in seeking to combine them into his own account, did not always weed out elements that conflicted with ideas or interpretations presented elsewhere in the same work. In any event, the story of Dinah is merely one of numerous biblical passages interpreted within the *Testaments*. An assessment of the implications of its interpretation can no doubt be aided by a consideration of other exegetical motifs found elsewhere in the *Testament of Levi* and in the *Testaments* as a whole.

Chapter Four

REUBEN'S SIN WITH BILHAH

*T*he book of Genesis contains a passing reference to a sin committed by Jacob's firstborn son, Reuben: "When Israel dwelt in that land, Reuben went and lay with Bilhah, his father's concubine; and Israel [= Jacob] heard of it" (Gen. 35:22). If this verse was originally part of some longer narrative, the words cited are, in any case, all that remains; the text then immediately turns to a genealogy of Jacob's descendants. This fact is surprising in and of itself. For surely one would expect some further details and, in particular, an account of what *happened* after Jacob "heard of it." After all, the crime of a son having relations with his father's wife (or concubine) is condemned no fewer than four times in the Pentateuch, suggesting that this offense was considered among the most serious of all (Lev. 18:7, 21:10; Deut. 22:30, 27:20). It was also subject to severe punishment: both the son and the woman were to be put to death (Lev. 21:10).

Despite this, the Genesis narrative says nothing of Reuben's punishment. He certainly was not killed; he goes on to play a principal role in the later story of Joseph's enslavement and all that follows. Nor is there any mention of Bilhah being punished. It is true, of course, that this infraction took place before the revelation of divine law at Sinai. Still, one would expect some mention of *what happened* as a result of this sin—all the more so because similar, indeed lesser, offenses recounted in Genesis are sometimes accompanied by vivid accounts of the consequences suffered by the offenders.[1]

Reuben's Punishment

Early interpreters of Hebrew Scripture did, however, have a solution to this apparent difficulty: if Reuben was not killed, they reasoned, he was punished nonetheless. For Reuben was the firstborn, and, as such, he ought to have received the בכורה, the special inheritance due the firstborn; according to Deut. 21:15, the firstborn's portion consisted of twice the normal share of the father's possessions. Yet, in the Pentateuchal narrative, Reuben gets no double portion. Instead, it is his younger brother Joseph who seems to have been given the firstborn's share, since, at the end of his life, Jacob "adopts" Joseph's two sons Ephraim and Manasseh for purposes of inheritance, in effect doubling the amount that Joseph's descendants will receive after his death (Gen. 48:5–6).

Clearly, then, Reuben is passed over: not only does he *not* get the double portion, but someone else, Joseph, does. It is true that the Genesis account nowhere actually says that Reuben's double portion was taken away because of his sin with Bilhah. However, Jacob's final "blessing" of Reuben does seem to imply as much:

> Reuben, you are my firstborn, my might and the beginning of my strength, preeminent in pride and preeminent in power. Unstable as water, you shall not have preeminence, because you went up to your father's bed; then you defiled it—you went up to my couch. (Gen. 49:3–4)

This text as a whole is notoriously difficult in Hebrew, but the allusion to Reuben's sin with Bilhah, "you went up to your father's bed," seems clear enough. As for the phrase in the preceding line, אל תותר, "you shall not have preeminence," its verbal root basically means "leave over, remain, be extra." In context, this passage might thus be interpreted as Jacob's assertion that Reuben was not to acquire (or pass on) the firstborn's extra allotment *because of his sin with Bilhah*. If so, then Reuben *was* punished: the birthright that should have been his was allotted to Joseph instead.

The first reflection of this interpretation is found within the Bible itself, in a parenthetical remark at the beginning of the book of Chronicles:

> The sons of Reuben, the firstborn of Israel (for he *was* the firstborn; but because he *defiled his father's couch*, his birthright was given to the sons of Joseph the son of Israel, so that he is not enrolled in the genealogy according to that birthright). (1 Chr. 5:1)

This text states outright that Reuben had lost his birthright because of the Bilhah episode—indeed, "defiled his father's couch" is a direct allusion to the words of Jacob's blessing cited above.

And so, interpreters ever afterward understood that Reuben's punishment for his sin with Bilhah was the transfer of his double portion of the inheritance to his younger brother Joseph. Yet that hardly answered all the questions interpreters might raise in connection with this incident. For, given the severity of his offense (at least as reflected elsewhere in the Pentateuch), was not Reuben being let off rather lightly with such a punishment? Or had there perhaps been extenuating circumstances? And what had happened to Bilhah? Was not her guilt equally great? It was in part in answer to such questions as these that various expanded retellings of the incident appeared in the literature of the Second Temple. I will here focus on two ancient retellings, those of the book of *Jubilees* and the *Testament of Reuben* section of the *Testaments of the Twelve Patriarchs*, using the latter as my point of departure.

Saw Bilhah Bathing

The *Testament of Reuben* version of the Bilhah episode contains a number of remarkable features, but perhaps none so striking as its explanation of the circumstances which led Reuben to commit his sin. For, in his recollection of the incident, Reuben reports as follows:

> For had I not seen Bilhah bathing in a covered place, I would not have fallen into this great iniquity. But my mind, clinging to the thought of the woman's nakedness, would not allow me to sleep until I had done the abomination. (*T. Reub.* 3:11–15)

Reuben, according to this account, did not simply *decide* to sin with Bilhah but was inadvertently led to do so by catching sight of her in her bath. If so, then Reuben's sin was a little like that of David and Bathsheba, which likewise began with David glimpsing Bathsheba bathing (2 Sam. 11:2). This hardly exonerated Reuben, but the implied comparison might indeed serve to make his crime seem a little less repugnant. Indeed, the same motif is found in the book of *Jubilees*:

> And Reuben saw Bilhah, Rachel's maid, the concubine of his father, bathing in water in a secret place, and he desired her. (*Jub.* 33:2)

Given the fact that such extenuating circumstances make Reuben's sin seem somewhat more understandable—and his relatively light punishment by Jacob somewhat more justifiable—one might well conclude that the motif of Bilhah's bathing was strictly the apologetic invention of one of these two texts (or of their common ancestor). Is not this expansion of the too-brief biblical narrative simply the result of the imposition of a "universal" literary motif onto the biblical story?[2]

But perhaps it was not *simply* that. For in Jacob's blessing of Reuben, cited above, there is one particularly problematic phrase that aroused the curiosity of early interpreters:

> Reuben, you are my firstborn, my might and the beginning of my strength, preeminent in pride and preeminent in power. *Unstable as*

water, you shall not have preeminence, because you went up to your father's bed; then you defiled it—you went up to my couch. (Gen. 49:3–4)

"Unstable as water" (פחז כמים) is problematical on a number of counts. To begin with, the translation "unstable" itself, commonly found in modern versions, is probably true neither to the original sense of the word here nor, more importantly, to the way this word was understood by the ancient interpreters who lived toward the end of the Second Temple period. For, as a recent study has documented, this word, although hardly a common one, is found in various contexts—within the Hebrew Bible itself and in Ben Sira, at Qumran, and in several rabbinic texts—*all in the sense of "wanton" or "lewd."*[3] Thus, the phrase פחז כמים was most likely understood in the late and postbiblical periods as "wanton as water." (Indeed, the Septuagint translates פחז here with the verb ἐξυβρίζω, "to become riotous or wanton.") But this is only to highlight the problem that then confronted early biblical interpreters. For how can someone be "wanton as water"? What is *wanton* about this vital substance?

A number of early translators and commentators struggled with this problem. *Targum Onqelos*, for example, paraphrases the Hebrew as "since you followed your own direction [?] just like water."[4] Here, the comparison to water has been creatively combined with the lack of restraint suggested by פחז: just as water follows its own direction and flows without respecting boundaries or borders, so was Reuben's behavior unbounded. A somewhat different idea underlies the rendering in *Targum Neophyti*:

I compare you, Reuben, my son, to a small garden, into which rushing streams of water have poured, and you were unable to withstand them and were overcome by them; just so, my son Reuben, were you overcome despite your wisdom and good deeds.[5]

Once again, the odd mention of *water* in the original has shaped the translation. But here, Reuben is *overcome* by water—that is, by passion—just like a little garden flooded by rushing streams. (Much the same translation is found in one version of the *Fragment Targum* [MS Vatican Ebraicus 440] as well as in *Targum Pseudo-Jonathan*.)[6]

Such was not, however, the only solution to the puzzle of "wanton as water." Indeed, behind the motif of Bilhah bathing as found in the *Testament of Reuben* and *Jubilees* seems to stand an attempt at an alternate solution to this problem. This interpretation apparently takes the phrase פחז כמים as פחז במים, "wanton *in* water" or "*with* water," and concludes, therefore, that Reuben's sin must have involved some *wantonness in or with water*. But of what could that wantonness have consisted? The sin itself is described starkly enough in the next verse: "you went up to your father's bed; then you defiled it—you went up to my couch." There was thus little possibility of associating water directly with the defiling of Jacob's "couch." And so, an interpreter might naturally conclude that the wantonness in or with water took place *before* the sin itself, indeed, had been a contributing factor to it: Reuben was wanton in or with water, Jacob says, and after that he defiled his father's couch. From such basic observations as these there might easily have developed a story to the effect that Reuben had wantonly observed Bilhah bathing in water and was thereby led to have relations with her.

There is one bit of evidence from a rabbinic text that may support such a hypothesis. It is a remark cited in *Genesis Rabba*:

> Our rabbis said: You [Reuben] sinned in water, let one who is drawn up from water [Moses] come and bring you back, as it is said, "Let Reuben live and not die" [Deut. 33:6]. (*Genesis Rabba* 98:4)

This remark cleverly connects Reuben's sin with the words attributed to Moses in Deut. 33:6, "Let Reuben live." For if Reuben is described as having been "wanton as water" with regard to his sin with Bilhah, then there is a certain sense in the Bible's having Moses, who was drawn up "out of the water" by Pharaoh's daughter (Exod. 2:10), pray for him later on. But note that, in presenting this interpretation, this text clearly understands פחז כמים as "wanton *in* [or 'with'] water," for it says explicitly, "You [Reuben] sinned in [or 'with'] water (במים)." In other words, here is another interpretation that understands this cryptic phrase in the same way as the *Testament of Reuben* and *Jubilees* had: that is, Reuben had somehow sinned in or with water. (Indeed, it seems entirely plausible that this remark in *Genesis Rabba*, with its vague attribution to "our rabbis," may in fact be a reminiscence of this same exegetical motif that presented Reuben as wantonly observing his father's concubine in her bath—it was *thus* that Reuben "sinned in water.")[7]

It should also be noted that this whole idea that Reuben *saw* Bilhah bathing was probably influenced, consciously or otherwise, by the fact that the second syllable of פחז is reminiscent of the Hebrew חזה, "see, behold." Given the difficulties raised by a phrase like "wanton as water," interpreters pondering it may have been led to hypothesize Bilhah's bath (on the model of Bathsheba's) not only because it offered a way of combining wantonness and water, but because the -חז part of פחז further suggested the element of *seeing*. In fact, trying to break פחז down into smaller units is not without parallel elsewhere among early exegetes: a number of rabbinic texts seek to do precisely that, via the interpretive process known as *notariqon*:[8]

You [Reuben] lost them [the firstborn's two portions]. What brought this about? [You were] פחז כמים. . . . This is a *notariqon.* R. Eliʿezer said [it stands for] פחזת [you were wanton], חטאת [you sinned], זנית [you committed fornication]. (*Midrash Tanḥuma, Vayyeḥi,* 9)

Such attempts to break פחז down into components (of which this *Midrash Tanḥuma* passage is but one example)[9] may bolster the idea that some still more ancient exegete had in similar fashion broken down פחז and gone on to suggest that Reuben was "wanton as water" because he had sinned (פשע) and had beheld (חזה) his father's concubine when she was bathing.[10]

Poured Out like Water

Thus, the *Testament of Reuben* and *Jubilees* both seem to contain an exegetical motif designed to account for the cryptic phrase פחז כמים in Jacob's blessing of Reuben (Gen. 49:4). But the *Testament of Reuben* may also contain another allusion to this phrase. For, at the beginning of his testament, Reuben admonishes his sons in these words:

> And see, I call the God of heaven to witness to you this day, that you not walk in the youthful ignorance and lewdness *in which I indulged myself* and defiled the bed of my father Jacob. (*T. Reub.* 1:6)

That this author is thinking of the words of Jacob's blessing seems to be apparent from the phrase "defiled the bed of my father Jacob," which is patently "you went up to your father's bed: then you defiled it" (Gen. 49:4). It is therefore interesting that this text speaks of the "lewdness in which I indulged myself," for in Greek this verb literally means "in which *I was poured out* [ἐξεχύθην]." While ἐξεχύθην is sometimes used in Greek for giving oneself over to an emotion, it may be that the author of *the Testament of Reuben* (or its Vorlage) chose specifically this expression because "poured out" was another way of explaining the cryptic description of Reuben as "wanton as water" in this passage: Reuben was *poured out like water* when he indulged himself with his father's concubine.

An interpreter might easily conclude that the "water" part of פחז כמים was indeed intended to suggest being "poured out" into passion, for a similar expression is to be found in the book of Psalms. Referring likewise to turbulent emotion (here, apparently, fear), the psalmist says, "I have been *poured out like water*, and all my bones are pulled apart" (Ps. 22:15). If "poured out like water" here means "given over to uncontrollable emotions," an interpreter might reason that perhaps this was the significance of Reuben's being "wanton *as water*" in Gen. 49:4: he was "poured out" into wantonness. (It is noteworthy that the Septuagint translation of Ps. 22:15 renders "poured out" with the same Greek word, ἐξεχύθην used by the *Testament of Reuben*.)

But the existence of such an interpretive tradition is not merely hypothetical. It is attested in the Vulgate translation of Gen. 49:4. There, פחז כמים is rendered as *effusus es sicut aqua*, "you were poured out like water"—precisely the Latin equivalent of the *Testament of Reuben*'s ἐξεχύθην. Moreover, it should be pointed out that this interpretation is not very far from that seen above in *Targums Onqelos* and *Neophyti*, which saw in the mention of water the image of unrestrained emotion, emotion that follows its own inclination or overwhelms its victim like rushing waters flooding a little garden. Thus, if, in the *Testament of Reuben*, Reuben warns against being "poured out" (ἐξεχύθην) into lewdness, this is most likely not merely an interesting turn of phrase in the Greek but the reflection of another (perhaps long-established) explanation of the cryptic פחז כמים. Nor should it be at all surprising that, if this is indeed the case, then two different explanations of this phrase coexist in the *Testament of Reuben* (that is, פחז כמים means both "wanton *in* water"—with the whole story of Bilhah's bath created to explain how this could be—yet also "poured out like water"). As we have already glimpsed, this phenomenon of exegetical reduplication within a single text—called **overkill**—is extremely common in all manner of documents from the Second Temple period and afterwards.[11]

Bilhah Was Asleep

In any case, the *Testament of Reuben*'s version of the events contains, as we have seen, one potentially mitigating circumstance with regard to Reuben's sin: he had first caught sight of Bilhah bathing. But what of Bilhah's role in the affair? Did she happily cooperate with Reuben's designs? Indeed, had she perhaps desired this union as much as he did, even seeking to arrange things so that Reuben would be led into temptation?

To such questions the terse biblical account gives no answers whatsoever. But the *Testament of Reuben* does have a definite position on the issue of Bilhah's guilt, and we have already seen one brief indication of it in Reuben's previously cited words: "Had I not seen Bilhah bathing *in a covered place*, I would not have fallen into this great iniquity" (*T. Reub.* 3:11). The indicated words seem clearly designed to rule out the possibility that Bilhah had consciously sought to arouse Reuben's passions; unlike Bathsheba, this text seems to be saying, Bilhah had bathed in a *covered* place and thus bore no responsibility whatever for Reuben seeing her nakedness. Indeed, the same assertion is found in the previously cited words from the *Jubilees* account: "And Reuben saw Bilhah, Rachel's maid, the concubine of his father, bathing in water *in a secret place*" (*Jub.* 33:2). Here too, Bilhah is utterly without blame.

But what about the events on the night in question? the *Testament of Reuben* resumes its account in these words:

> For while our father Jacob was away at his father Isaac's when we
> were in Gader, near to Ephratah, house of Bethelehem,[12] Bilhah

became drunk and went to sleep naked, lying in her room. And I, having entered and seen her nakedness, did the impiety, and leaving her sleeping, I went out. (*T. Reub.* 3:13–14)

Here again, the *Testament of Reuben* seems to have arranged everything so as to argue Bilhah's innocence. For, in the Genesis account, the incident with Bilhah is *followed by* the mention of Jacob's trip to visit his father Isaac at Hebron (Gen. 35:27). But if Jacob had been home at the time of Reuben's sin, then that would strongly imply that Bilhah had herself been an active participant— otherwise, under what circumstances could this tryst have taken place? And so this account moves Jacob's trip backward so as to have it *precede* Reuben's sin: with Jacob away, Reuben can then have sought out Bilhah without her knowing beforehand of his intentions or cooperating with them in any way.

And indeed, the rest of the passage in the *Testament of Reuben* makes explicit Bilhah's noninvolvement in the affair: she is drunk and asleep when Reuben enters and (apparently, still) asleep when he leaves. Although drunkenness did not speak very well for Bilhah's character and is elsewhere in the *Testaments* the subject of extended parenesis (*T. Jud.* 14:1–8), it was apparently necessary here to have Bilhah drunk in order to make clear that she was not even conscious of the sin in which she was involved—not when it happened and not afterward.

It is interesting that the *Jubilees* account concurs with the *Testament of Reuben* in some, but not all, of these details:

And he [Jacob] went to his father Isaac, he and Leah his wife, on the new moon of the tenth month. And Reuben . . . hid himself at night, and he entered the house of Bilhah [at night] and found her sleeping alone on a bed in her house. And he lay with her, and she awoke and saw, and behold, Reuben was lying with her in the bed, and she uncovered the border of her covering and seized him, and

cried out when she discovered that it was Reuben. And she was
ashamed because of him, and released her hand from him, and he
fled. And she lamented because of this thing exceedingly, and did
not tell it to anyone. (*Jub.* 33:1–6)

Here too, Jacob's trip to visit his father preceded the incident in
question, and, here as well, Reuben entered Bilhah's room while she
was asleep. She was not, however, drunk in this account. Instead,
she apparently seized Reuben unconsciously, in her half-sleep—or
perhaps, as some have suggested, the text here is garbled and should
instead present Reuben as seizing her.[13] In any case, when "she discovered that it was Reuben," Bilhah cried out—another clear indication that she was not, in this author's view, in any way a willing
participant. Her subsequent shame and lamentation argue as much.

It is, of course, convenient for these authors to have Bilhah
completely innocent, for this would explain Scripture's silence
about her: for, not only (as noted earlier) does Scripture fail to
mention her punishment, but Jacob's later reflections on the incident in Gen. 49:3–4 make no allusion to Bilhah's role whatsoever.
What better explanation than that she was a completely passive,
nay, unconscious, victim of Reuben's lust? And, of course, this
would likewise reflect a little better on the woman who was, after
all, the ancestress of two of Israel's twelve tribes.

Here as well, however, it would be wrong to assume that apologetics alone are responsible for this imaginative reconstruction of
the events. Both the *Jubilees* and the *Testament of Reuben* versions
seem to be based, however obliquely, on Scripture—once again, on
Jacob's words to his son Reuben at the end of his life. "Unstable as
water, you shall not have preeminence, because you went up to your
father's bed; then you defiled it—you went up to my couch" (Gen.
49:4). The language of this verse is intentionally modest: "went up
to your father's bed" or "couch" is obviously a polite way of saying
"had sexual relations with your father's concubine." And yet, if
these expressions are taken *au pied de la lettre*, they virtually invite

the scenario underlying the *Testament of Reuben* and *Jubilees*. For how could Reuben have literally *gone up to his father's bed* if Jacob were in it? The use of this expression almost required later interpreters to assume that Jacob was *not* in his bed—although it was *his* bed, and not Bilhah's (separate) bed somewhere else—and that, by implication, he must not have been home at the time but away on some journey. What easier solution than to conclude that Jacob's trip to visit Isaac actually took place before the Bilhah incident, although Scripture does not mention it till afterward?

Bilhah, on the other hand, *was* in the bed. For Jacob speaks of *Reuben* going up to his father's bed and not, therefore, of Reuben and Bilhah both going up to bed together. Again, if one takes Jacob's words as a precise statement of the facts, the only conclusion that one can draw is that when Reuben, *alone*, went up to his father's bed, Bilhah was already lying in it. Indeed, in Gen. 49:3–4, *Reuben does everything*, and Bilhah is not mentioned or even alluded to. What could seem more obvious than that she was an utterly passive participant, passed over in the text because *she did nothing of significance*? And so our interpreters interpret: both *Jubilees* and the *Testament of Reuben* maintain that, when Reuben entered to do his misdeed, Bilhah was already in bed, in fact, fast asleep and thus quite unconscious of what was about to happen. No wonder her punishment is never mentioned: a careful reading of the biblical text disclosed to interpreters that she was in all likelihood an innocent victim.

An Angel Told Jacob

How did Jacob learn of Reuben's sin? In the *Testament of Reuben*, Reuben continues his narrative of the events in these words:

> And immediately an angel of God revealed my impiety to my father Jacob, and when he came he mourned over me, and he touched her no more. (*T. Reub.* 3:15)

In this account, Jacob learns at once of the affair from an angel, and upon his return he mourns for Reuben and separates himself forever from Bilhah. The *Testament of Reuben* here is quite at odds with the account in *Jubilees*:

> And she [Bilhah] lamented because of this thing exceedingly and did not tell it to anyone. And when Jacob returned and sought her, she said to him, "I am not clean for you, for I have been defiled with regard to you; for Reuben has defiled me and has lain with me in the night, and I was asleep, and did not discover it until he uncovered my skirt and slept with me." And Jacob was exceedingly angry with Reuben because he had lain with Bilhah, because he had uncovered his father's skirt. And Jacob did not approach her again because Reuben had defiled her. (*Jub.* 33:6–9)

In *Jubilees*, contrary to the *Testament of Reuben*, it is Bilhah herself who tells Reuben. (Note also that here, while Bilhah is, as in the *Testament of Reuben*, spurned ever after, Jacob's attitude to Reuben in *Jubilees* is not nearly so forgiving as in the *Testament of Reuben*: there is no talk of mourning here; instead, Jacob is said to be "exceedingly angry.")

Now, with regard to *how* Jacob learned of the affair, one might say that *Jubilees* follows a rather naturalistic course. That is, having Bilhah tell Jacob what had happened is, in view of Scripture's own silence on the matter, more or less what one would expect; after all, *someone* must have informed Jacob, since he obviously knows about the affair when he speaks the words of Gen. 49:3–4, and Bilhah certainly was a likely choice for the informer, especially given her apparent innocence in the whole episode. But then, why does *Jubilees* stress that Bilhah told *no one* but Jacob? There is no indication that she acted thus in the biblical story—and Jacob, after all, mentions Reuben's "defil[ing] my couch" in the presence of Reuben's brothers in Gen. 49:4, so certainly they eventually all knew of it. Why then does *Jubilees* go out of its way to assert that Bilhah kept it a secret? The passage cited above is quite specific: Bilhah "lamented because of this thing exceedingly, and *did not tell it to anyone*," but "when Jacob returned and sought her, she said to him, 'I am not clean for you.'"

This narrative expansion in *Jubilees* seems aimed at accounting for a single cryptic phrase in Gen. 35:22, "While Israel [= Jacob] dwelt in that land, Reuben went and lay with Bilhah, his father's concubine; and *Israel heard of it*." Why does the text add these last words and then simply stop? That is, normally one would expect that Jacob's hearing of the affair would be mentioned because his finding out had some immediate consequences—"Jacob heard of it and at once did such-and-such," or even merely, "Jacob heard of it and was very angry."[14] But simply to say that he heard of it and leave it at that—this might seem to imply that there was something special or significant about the very fact that he did hear of it, or the way that he heard of it. And so, *Jubilees* apparently interprets this phrase to mean that Jacob *alone* heard of it, that is, "and *Israel* heard of it" but no one else did. In this way, an apparently pointless phrase acquired a certain sense.

The *Testament of Reuben* does not follow *Jubilees* in this matter; instead, it maintains that Jacob heard from an angel. Now, the *Testament of Reuben* may do this, as others have suggested,[15] in order to allow Bilhah to sleep through the entire episode. For, if she was unconscious the whole time, then Jacob would have to have heard about what happened from someone other than Bilhah. What could be more convenient than having an angel tell Jacob?

And yet, I am not entirely convinced that such is the angel's raison d'être. After all, in the *Testament of Reuben*, Reuben is most contrite after his misdeed (see below). What better way, from the standpoint of the *Testament of Reuben*'s author, for Jacob to learn of the crime than from Reuben's own lips as he tearfully confesses his sin? This would still allow Bilhah to be an unconscious participant and would make Jacob's reaction in the *Testament of Reuben* (*not* anger, but sadness: "he mourned over me," Reuben says) far more understandable. In other words, the angelic informer was hardly necessary in order to maintain that Bilhah had been asleep the whole time.

But if the angel was not necessitated by Bilhah's unconsciousness, why then was it created? The answer, it seems to me, might well lie in that same problematic phrase, "and Israel heard of it." For if its significance is *not* to be, à la *Jubilees*, "and Israel *alone* heard of it," then perhaps Scripture added these apparently pointless words in order to indicate that there was indeed something unusual about *the way* that Jacob learned of what happened, that is, "and Israel *heard* of it"—*heard* but not in the manner of ordinary hearing: he heard from an angel.

No other ancient text suggests that Jacob heard from an angel, so one should be cautious about attributing too much significance to this detail. It seems clear, however, that the insistence in *Jubilees* on Bilhah's having told *only* Jacob was designed to explain the problematic "and Israel heard of it." Perhaps one ought to consider a similar function for the angelic informer in the *Testament of Reuben*.

Bilhah Spurned Forever

We have seen that the major consequence of Reuben's sin with Bilhah was his loss of the firstborn's double portion. But what of Bilhah? Apparently, both *Jubilees* and the *Testament of Reuben* hold her to have been an innocent victim: she was asleep and perhaps drunk at the time and had no idea what was happening to her. But then one might well ask why it is that Jacob subsequently spurns Bilhah. For so both texts maintain: the *Testament of Reuben* says that Jacob "touched her no more," and *Jubilees* says

that Jacob "did not approach her again because Reuben had defiled her." Note that they do not say that Jacob "sent her away"
or divorced her; he simply no longer had relations with her. But
why was that?

Once again, these texts are seeking to draw out the full meaning of the biblical narrative. Let us look at Gen. 35:22 in its
broader context:

> While Israel [= Jacob] dwelt in that land, Reuben went and lay with
> Bilhah, his father's concubine; and Israel heard of it. And the sons
> of Jacob were twelve. The sons of Leah: Jacob's firstborn, Reuben,
> and Simeon and Levi and Judah and Issachar and Zebulun [etc.].
> (Gen. 35:22–23)

The apparent lack of transition between the brief account of
Reuben's sin and the list of Jacob's sons that follows is most striking: what does the one have to do with the other? What is more,
for reasons we have just examined, the words "and Israel heard
of it" seem to be missing something, some statement about what
happened as a result of Jacob's hearing of it. The abrupt transition therefore seems all the more jarring.

Unless . . . unless this list of Jacob's descendants *is* what happened as a result of Jacob hearing about it. That is to say, under
normal circumstances, Jacob might well have had more children.
Leah, of course, may have by then been too old to bear children,
and Rachel had just died in childbirth (Gen. 35:19), but Jacob's
two concubines, Bilhah and Zilpah, might still have been of child-
bearing age. If, therefore, after Scripture says that Jacob "heard
of" Reuben's misdeed, it immediately adds, "And the sons of Jacob
were twelve," could it not mean that, *as a result of what Jacob
heard*, he had no further children? In other words, the idea that
Jacob had no further relations with Bilhah—something that is neither specifically asserted by Scripture nor in keeping with biblical

law or later legal practice—may have originated as an attempt to establish a causal connection between the phrase "and Israel heard of it" and the genealogical list that follows it in the text.[16]

It is interesting that, according to the Masoretic accents, this particular verse constitutes a rare Pentateuchal example of the phenomenon known as פיסקא באמצע פסוק ("break in the middle of the verse"). That is to say, the entire unity—"While Israel dwelt in that land, Reuben went and lay with Bilhah, his father's concubine; and Israel heard of it. And the sons of Jacob were twelve"—is treated in two different ways by the Masoretic accents, as if it were a single verse on the one hand, and as if it were actually two separate verses on the other. This schizophrenic attitude is epitomized in the irregular break (represented in the Masoretic accents by the anomalous combination of the accents סילוק and אתנח under a single word, ישראל, and as well by the blank space which, by convention, is left after this word) which is introduced just before the last words of the verse, "And the sons of Jacob were twelve." The accent סילוק is used to mark the *end* of a biblical verse—like a period in Western punctuation—while אתנח indicates the major syntactic pause *within* the verse, usually somewhere near its middle—like a semicolon. It is thus as if the Masoretic scribes were trying to say "stop" and "go" at the same time. The existence of such mid-verse breaks has, not surprisingly, given rise to various explanations and has challenged the ingenuity of numerous scholars.[17]

Some scholars have sought to find a unified explanation of this phenomenon that will cover all occurrences, but I personally agree with those who feel no single explanation will fit all cases. With regard to Gen. 35:22, however, the reason for the פיסקא באמצע פסוק seems less than utterly opaque. *For what is being presented as a single verse here is clearly a combination of two quite unrelated matters.* The question one should ask is thus *not* why this rare scribal pause comes before "And the sons of Jacob were twelve," for these words have nothing to do with what precedes them! The question, on the contrary, is why the words "And the sons of Jacob were twelve" had ever have been considered *connected* to the preceding sentence and, consequently, were *not* separated off and treated as the beginning of the next verse (to be followed immediately by "The sons of Leah, Jacob's firstborn [etc.]").

The answer to this question, it seems to me, lies before us: an ancient interpretive tradition, represented by *Jubilees* and the *Testament of Reuben*, found the words "and Israel heard of it" strangely anticlimactic. This tradition therefore interpreted "And the sons of Jacob were twelve" as a biblical statement of what came about as a result of Jacob's hearing of the affair. Such a tradition, although it was later rejected by rabbinic interpreters bent on clearing Reuben of any crime, was nonetheless preserved in the division into verses, which treated "And the sons of Jacob were twelve" as an integral part of what preceded it. And so Gen. 35:22 corresponds exactly to another recent study's conclusion regarding the פיסקא באמצע פסוק: it is a unit composed of two different verses— verses which, in this case at least, were joined together in keeping with an ancient exegetical tradition about their relationship: Jacob heard, and *as a result* his sons were (only) twelve in number.[18]

Reuben Punished with Illness

If Bilhah, who was innocent, ends up being spurned by Jacob, should not Reuben's punishment have been more severe than merely the loss of the firstborn's double portion? This problem, which occupied rabbinic exegetes,[19] was obviously likewise of concern to both the *Testament of Reuben* and *Jubilees*. The latter text does not address the unfairness per se, but stresses instead that, by later standards, Reuben and Bilhah both got off rather lightly:

[The angel tells Moses:] And let them [the Israelites] not say, "Reuben was allowed to live and [have] forgiveness after he lay with his father's concubine while she had a husband, and her husband—his father Jacob—was still alive." For the ordinance and punishment and law had not been completely revealed for everyone, but in your days [it is] like the law of times and days and an eternal law for everlasting generations. And this law will not expire, nor is there any forgiveness for it, but both of them should be uprooted from the midst of the people. On the day when they have done this they shall be killed. (*Jub.* 33:15–17)

This passage is quite striking, since, in order to explain why Reuben and Bilhah were not killed for so grave an offense, *Jubilees* is obliged to state here that later Pentateuchal law had not been revealed in the days of Reuben as binding on everyone, and as a result neither he nor Bilhah received the full sanctions of the law.[20] If so, then presumably one ought not to wonder that Reuben was punished relatively lightly—both he *and* Bilhah could have fared far worse.

The *Testament of Reuben* follows a different tack, specifying that Reuben did indeed suffer an additional punishment:

For I tell you that God afflicted me with a great affliction in my loins for seven months, and if our father Jacob had not prayed for me to the Lord, the Lord would have killed me. I was thirty years old when I did the evil thing before the Lord, and for seven months I was sick to the point of death. (*T. Reub.* 1:7–8)

Reuben is stricken with a grave illness, one so severe that he would have died were it not for Jacob's prayerful intervention. The nature of this illness is not specified, other than that it struck Reuben "in the loins." This detail is no doubt in keeping with the principle of "Let the punishment fit the crime" or, as it is known in rabbinic texts, "measure for measure,"[21] a principle which, as others have pointed out, is in evidence elsewhere in the *Testaments* and the other literature of the period.[22]

This illness of Reuben's may indeed be an ad hoc invention by the author of the *Testament of Reuben*; elsewhere in the *Testaments*, Gad and Simeon are likewise physically stricken for their moral flaws. However, there are two exegetical points of interest in connection with this idea. The first is the wording of Moses' blessing at the end of Deuteronomy, "Let Reuben live and not die, and may his numbers be many" (Deut. 33:6). These words troubled ancient interpreters, for why should Moses be asking for Reuben (the person, not the tribe since, as they saw it, tribes do not "die") *to live* long after he had in fact died? It is thus possible that some interpreters thought that these words of Moses were in fact an allusion to some time when Reuben was *still alive but in danger of dying*—that Moses was in fact quoting a prayer that had been uttered at a time when Reuben was deathly ill, "Let Reuben live and not die." If that were the case, then such a prayer—especially since it turned out to be efficacious—might well have been prayed by Reuben's own father, Jacob.[23]

It is interesting, in this connection, to note that Philo attributes the words "Let Reuben live and not die" to *Jacob*, in spite of the fact that they appear in Deuteronomy:

> And while Abraham prays, as we have said, that the grace of hearkening to the holy words and learning holy truths may live, *Jacob*, the Man of Practice, prays for the life of natural goodness, for he says "Let Reuben live and not die." (Philo, *On the Change of Names* 210)

This may not be a lapse of memory of Philo's part, but a reflection of just such an explanation, one that held that the words "Let Reuben live . . ." were *not* spoken for the first time by Moses himself but were being quoted by him from an earlier prayer of

Jacob's.[24] If such a traditional interpretation of this verse was indeed known to the author of the *Testament of Reuben*, this would help explain not only the fact of Reuben's illness but also this author's insistence in the passage cited above on the fact that Jacob's prayer saved Reuben *from death*—for the prayer was "Let Reuben live *and not die*." Similarly, the precise wording of Jub. 33:15 cited above is also noteworthy: "And let them not say: to Reuben was *granted life and forgiveness* after he had lain with his father's concubine." For, as we have just seen, *Jubilees* elsewhere says nothing of Reuben being *forgiven*, either by God or by Jacob. But if "Let Reuben live and not die" was originally a prayer that Jacob prayed on Reuben's behalf for forgiveness from a God bent on killing him, then Reuben was indeed granted both life and forgiveness.

It is noteworthy that rabbinic exegetes likewise understood these words as a prayer on behalf of *Reuben himself*, rather than the tribe of Reuben; more importantly, one widely disseminated interpretation also seems to imply that this prayer—or part of it, at least—was spoken *during Reuben's lifetime*:

> Let Reuben live in this world and let him not die the death by which the wicked die in the world to come. (*Targum Pseudo-Jonathan* Deut. 33:6)

> Let Reuben live in this world; and may he not die a second death, by which the wicked die in the world to come. (*Fragment Targum* Deut. 33:6)

> Said Raba: How can it be shown that the resurrection of the dead is alluded to in the Torah? It is said: "Let Reuben live and not die." *Let Reuben live*—in this world—*and not die*—in the world to come. (b. *Sanhedrin* 92a)

All these interpretations seek to distinguish the meaning of "Let Reuben live" from "and not die": if the former applies to life in this world, then the latter applies to life in the world to come. But if "Let Reuben live" indeed applies to life in this world, it follows that, when these words were first spoken, Reuben must have still been alive *in this world*. In other words, this well-known rabbinic interpretation of Deut. 33:6 might further support the idea that when "Let Reuben live and not die" was first said, Reuben was still living—perhaps indeed gravely ill and near death, as the *Testament of Reuben* reports.[25]

Finally, it is to be noted that Jacob's prayer is sufficiently important to the author of the *Testament of Reuben* for him to return to it later on:

> But my father consoled me, for he prayed for me to the Lord, that the Lord's anger might depart from me, as the Lord showed me. (*T. Reub.* 4:4)

Clearly, then, Jacob's prayer for Reuben was rather significant to the author of the *Testament of Reuben*. It seems to me strange that this author would twice mention this prayer if it were simply his own concoction. Especially in view of the evidence just cited from Philo, *Jubilees*, and rabbinic sources, it certainly seems possible that both the existence of Jacob's prayer itself in the *Testament of Reuben* and the illness that it is said to have cured were initially inspired by "Let Reuben live . . ." in Deut. 33:6.

Joseph Heads the List

A related point found in the above-cited passage from the *Testament of Reuben* concerns the timing of the whole incident. For in *T. Reub.* 1:7 (cited above), Reuben says that he was thirty years old when he committed his sin with Bilhah. This is in contrast to *Jubilees*, which holds that he was twenty-one at the time.[26] Now, according to the chronological framework of the *Testament of*

Reuben, Reuben was exactly thirteen years older than Joseph (*T. Reub.* 1:1–2). In other words, Joseph was seventeen at the time of Reuben's sin. But seventeen is precisely the age of Joseph when, according to Scripture, he was shepherding with his brothers:

> These are the generations of Jacob: Joseph was seventeen years old when he was shepherding the flock with his brothers; he was a lad with the sons of Bilhah and Zilpah, his father's wives. (Gen. 37:2)

Now, there was one particular aspect of this verse that bothered exegetes, and that was the fact that the words "These are the generations of Jacob" are not followed (as one would normally expect) by a genealogical list, starting with the name of Jacob's firstborn, Reuben. Instead, the text jumps to Joseph, and begins the story of how his brothers sold him into slavery. This anomaly was responsible for a number of different motifs found in rabbinic exegesis, all of which sought to explain why the name of Joseph appears here instead of Reuben.[27]

It may be that the *Testament of Reuben*'s specification of Reuben's age as thirty at the time of his sin was likewise designed to explain this same anomaly. For if Reuben's sin with Bilhah occurred when Joseph was seventeen, then precisely at the time when Scripture said, "These are the generations of Jacob: Joseph . . .", Reuben had just lost his firstborn status, at least with regard to the double portion, which was now to go to Joseph—and so *that* is what Scripture meant by "These are the generations of Jacob: Joseph . . ." Indeed, if (according to the chronology of The *Testament of Reuben*) Reuben was now just recovering from his deathly illness, these words in Scripture may have represented to the author of *The Testament of Reuben* a kind of final settlement of Reuben's case. He is, because of Jacob's prayer, to be allowed to live, but he will not get the double portion originally intended for him, for, as far as the division of property is concerned, "These are the generations of Jacob: Joseph . . ." The new firstborn—in terms of inheritance—will be Joseph, the firstborn of Jacob's other legitimate wife, Rachel; henceforth he will head the list of Jacob's descendants, if not in birth order, then at least with regard to Jacob's legacy.

Reuben's Penitent Abstinence

The *Testament of Reuben* further relates that, after recovering from his illness, Reuben went on to repent for a period of seven years:

> And in the resoluteness of my soul I repented before the Lord for seven years. Wine and strong drink I did not drink, and meat did not enter into my mouth, and I did not taste any dainty food, mourning over my sin, for it was great, and such a thing shall not happen in Israel.[28] (*T. Reub.* 1:9–10)

Reuben's repentance in the *Testament of Reuben* is hardly surprising. After all, it was virtually a necessity for *any* early exegete to assert that Reuben deeply regretted his sin with Bilhah; otherwise Scripture would seem to be presenting the spectacle of an unrepentant sinner who basically gets off with a slap on the wrist (the loss of the firstborn's double portion). And yet, Scripture said nothing openly about Reuben's remorse for what he had done.

There were nevertheless one or two dark hints that Reuben had indeed repented. To begin with, the prayer "Let Reuben live" certainly seems to imply that Reuben had been forgiven by whoever is speaking these words. If Jacob or Moses were asking that Reuben's life (in this world and/or the world to come) be spared in spite of his sin with Bilhah, did that not mean that the stricken Reuben had himself expressed regret over the incident and had therefore been forgiven by the speaker of these words? And so indeed this text was interpreted: "What is the meaning of *Let*

Reuben live and not die? It indicates that Reuben repented"
(*Sifrei Debarim* 347).

But there was another biblical passage that seemed to indicate
as well that Reuben had repented, and this one may be more
closely related to the specification in the *Testament of Reuben* that
Reuben's penance took the particular form of *abstaining from
pleasant food and drink*. The passage comes later on in Genesis,
toward the beginning of the Joseph story. For, when Joseph is first
seized by his brothers, the other brothers wish to kill him (Gen.
37:20), but Reuben intervenes on his behalf, and they instead cast
him into a pit (Gen. 37:24). The text then says that "they"—the
brothers—*sat down to eat*, and, seeing a passing caravan, decided
to sell Joseph as a slave. After this, "Reuben returned to the pit
and saw that Joseph was not in the pit" (Gen. 37:29). Obviously,
then, Reuben had *not* "sat down to eat" with his brothers; otherwise he would have known what had ensued. But where was he?

> "And Reuben returned to the pit": Where had he been? R. Eli'ezer
> said: he was occupied with his sackcloth and fasting, and when he
> turned from his sackcloth and fasting, he went and peered into the
> pit, as it is said, "And Reuben *returned* to the pit." (*Genesis Rabba*
> 84:19)
>
> And Reuben returned to the pit, for he had not been eating with
> them when they sold him [Joseph], since he was fasting because he
> had upset his father's bed [in the sin with Bilhah]. (*Targum Pseudo-
> Jonathan* Gen. 37:29)[29]

Thus, the fact that, according to the plain sense of the biblical narrative, Reuben did not sit down to eat with the other brothers suggested to rabbinic exegetes that there must have been a reason for
this strange behavior. Since the last thing to be said about Reuben
was the brief mention of his sin with Bilhah in Gen. 35:22, they
combined these two bits of information and concluded that

Reuben was purposely *abstaining* from food and drink because he was repenting for his sin. In view of this rabbinic tradition, it may not be stretching things to suppose that similar exegetical thinking underlies the motif of Reuben's repentance in the *Testament of Reuben*, and specifically his abstinence from wine and pleasant food, for a vow of penitent abstinence would well account for Reuben's strange absence from his brothers' meal.[30]

Watchers Looked Continually

There is a final bit of biblical interpretation that is relevant to the *Testament of Reuben*'s presentation of the Bilhah episode. One of the lessons to be learned from this episode, Reuben maintains, is that of the evils of womankind, for, "having no power or strength over man, they use wiles, trying to draw him to them by their outward bearing, and she who cannot overcome by strength overcomes by craftiness" (*T. Reub.* 5:1–2). Continuing on in this vein, he then cites a famous incident in history to support his contention, namely, the fact that the heavenly "Watchers" were drawn to mate with the "daughters of men" (Gen. 6:1–2), thus ultimately bringing about the cataclysmic flood in the time of Noah. Alluding to this story, Reuben observes:

> Therefore, flee from wantonness, my children, and command your wives and daughters that they not adorn their heads and faces, for every woman who resorts to such wiles is destined for eternal punishment. For thus they [that is, the "daughters of men"] bewitched the Watchers before the flood; these looked at them continually, and so it was that, in their lust for them, they thought of the deed in their minds. (*T. Reub.* 5:5–6)

Here, the *Testament of Reuben*'s explanation seems to contrast with that of other ancient exegetes, who generally attribute guilt

for what ensued only to the Watchers themselves and do not mention the role of the women:

> And the angels, the children of heaven, saw and *lusted* after them.
> (1 *Enoch* 6:2)
>
> [Hear me] so that you are not taken in by the designs of the inclina-
> tion to evil and by lustful eyes. . . . The Watchers of heaven fell
> because of this; they were taken because they did not keep the com-
> mandments of God. (*Damascus Document* 2:16–21)

A similar note is sounded in other early retellings. In Sir. 16:7,
1 *Bar.* 3:26–28, *Jub.* 5:1–5, 3 *Macc.* 2:4, and 2 *Enoch* 34:1–2,
there is no mention of the women "bewitching" the Watchers or
of the women being guilty in any way. Where, then, did the *Testament of Reuben* get this idea?

It seems to have been suggested to him by the very wording of
Gen. 6:1–2:

> And so it was, as men came to increase over the face of the earth,
> that daughters were born to them. And the sons of God saw the
> daughters of men, that they were beautiful, and they took wives for
> themselves from all those whom they chose. (Gen. 6:1–2)

Why does the text say that the sons of God *saw* that the daughters of men were beautiful? If they indeed *were* beautiful, why did
Scripture not simply say that? The author of the *Testament of
Reuben* thus apparently perceived in this turn of phrase a hint
about female "wiles": the daughters of men must have specially
adorned themselves to attract the attention of the sons of God.
They caused the Watchers' eyes to return to them again and
again, so that, in the *Testament of Reuben*'s phrase, "these looked
at them *continually*." It was this continual contemplation that ultimately led to lust.

SUMMARY

In the foregoing we have concentrated on ten different narrative expansions of the biblical narrative of Reuben's sin with Bilhah as it is retold in the *Testament of Reuben* and the book of *Jubilees*. The exegetical motifs underlying these expansions included: "Saw Bilhah Bathing," "Poured Out like Water," "Bilhah Was Asleep," "An Angel Told Jacob," "Bilhah Spurned Forever," "Reuben Punished with Illness," "Joseph Heads the List," "Reuben's Penitent Abstinence," and "Watchers Looked Continually." Each of these motifs, it was suggested, was fundamentally *exegetical*; that is, each was connected with, or developed out of, something that *was* present in the biblical text, a difficult word or phrase or some little anomaly in the sequence of events.

From the foregoing it is clear that the account of Reuben's sin presented in the *Testament of Reuben* bears a particularly close relationship to that found in *Jubilees*. Can one conclude that the author of the *Testament of Reuben* had the *Jubilees* version in front of him when he composed this work? Such questions are not susceptible to easy answers. Indeed, all too often in the past, scholars have been inclined to assume that, when two retellings of a biblical story share some feature not found in the Bible itself, then one of the two retellings is dependent on the other, or that, at the very least, the two are based on some other *text* which served as their common ancestor. An understanding of the exegetical basis for many such motifs should suggest that greater caution is appropriate. For if a given motif was created in response to some little irregularity in the biblical story, then that motif's appearance in more than one retelling may simply demonstrate that that particular way of accounting for the irregularity had gained wide currency.

Nevertheless, I think that there is some evidence in this case to argue that a direct, *literary* relationship exists between the accounts in *Jubilees* and the *Testament of Reuben*. To begin with, almost all the motifs from the *Testament of Reuben* listed above, if they are paralleled at all, are paralleled in *Jubilees*. Surely this is a striking datum. Beyond this, however, a number of particulars shared by the two texts argue their close relationship. Especially significant, in my opinion, is the fact that both texts, in incorporating the "Saw Bilhah Bathing" motif in their retellings, specify that Bilhah was in a "covered" or "secret" place. This element, as we have seen, is motivated by a desire to make Bilhah utterly innocent, but it in itself serves no directly *exegetical* function: the phrase פחז כמים does not particularly suggest that Bilhah was bathing in secret. Of course, it is not impossible that the element "in secret" came to accompany this motif in its travels, but it seems more likely to me that the author of *Jubilees*, who otherwise stresses Bilhah's innocence, introduced this detail in his retelling and that it was simply copied by the author of the *Testament of Reuben*. (Indeed, if the Hebrew text of *Jubilees* read בסתר, which means both "in secret" and "in a sheltered [or 'covered'] place," it is easy enough to imagine how this could become ἐν σκεπεινῷ τόπῳ in the Greek of the *Testament of Reuben*.)

Another detail that may indicate that the *Testament of Reuben* copied directly from *Jubilees* is the fact that both retellings contain the motif "Bilhah Spurned Forever." Now, in the severe view of *Jubilees*, this motif has a certain logic: Reuben's sin was one for which "there is no consummation of days, and no atonement for it, but they must both be rooted out in the midst of the nation" (*Jub.* 33:17), so it makes sense that, despite her innocence, Bilhah suffered *some* punishment. In the *Testament of Reuben*, however, this motif makes very little sense: here, after all, even *Reuben* is forgiven by Jacob. Why should Bilhah, who was apparently unconscious during the entire episode, be spurned by Jacob ever after? Thus it seems that the author of the *Testament of Reuben* incorporated this motif without really considering its implications—and this too might suggest that he simply had the text of *Jubilees* very much in mind.

But if so, then it is interesting as well to consider those items in the *Testament of Reuben* not paralleled in *Jubilees*. Where did they come from? We saw that the status of "An Angel Told Jacob" is somewhat in doubt: it may be an *exegetical* motif, designed to account for the anticlimactic "and Israel heard of it" (in which case it parallels the exegetical function of "Bilhah Told Only Jacob" in *Jubilees*), or it may simply be an ad hoc creation of the *Testament of Reuben*. My own guess is that, if the author of *the Testament of Reuben* had *Jubilees* before him, he had little reason to deviate from *Jubilees* in this matter; certainly Bilhah could wake up or regain consciousness after the sin was accomplished (as she apparently does in *Jubilees*) without compromising her innocence in any way. And if, nevertheless, this author wished to maintain that Bilhah slept through the entire episode, he still might (as suggested earlier) have *Reuben* be the one to tell Jacob afterward; this would, if anything, bolster the *Testament of Reuben*'s picture of the penitent Reuben and make more understandable Jacob's instant forgiveness of his son. The fact that these options were not taken leads me therefore to suspect— although, I admit, without direct corroborating evidence—that this angelic informer represents another, independent explanation of "and Israel heard of it." The author of the *Testament of Reuben*, aware of such a motif, might have decided to adopt it (and thereby deviate from the *Jubilees* account) precisely because it would allow Bilhah to remain asleep in his version.

In any case, it seems that the author of the *Testament of Reuben* adopted two other motifs also absent from *Jubilees*, "Reuben Punished with Illness" and "Reuben's Penitent Abstinence." Were these indeed adoptions, or were they instead made up out of whole cloth by the author of the *Testament of Reuben*? I do not believe that "Reuben's Penitent Abstinence" could simply be the creation of the author of the *Testament of Reuben*: the same motif is found in rabbinic sources, where it serves to explain Gen. 37:29. The case of "Reuben Punished with Illness" is somewhat less clear. But the fact that the *Testament of Reuben* specifies that Reuben was sick *to the point of death* and that he was only saved *because of a prayer of Jacob's*, a prayer in fact mentioned twice in the *Testament of Reuben*, suggests that this author may have been aware of some tradition to the effect that Deut. 33:6, "Let Reuben live and not die . . . ," was a prayer uttered during Reuben's own lifetime, at a moment when he was sick and at death's door. The existence of such a motif may be inferred from the passages I have cited from both Philo and rabbinic texts.

In addition to these two motifs that appear in the *Testament of Reuben* but not in *Jubilees*, there is another. It should be recalled that the *Testament of Reuben*'s use of the word ἐξεχύθην, "poured out," may reflect yet another exegetical motif, the explanation of פחז כמים as "poured out like water." This motif was found to exist in the Vulgate translation *effusus es sicut aqua* and to be reflected as well in the expansive translations of the targums. Once again, the *Testament of Reuben* seems to have been aware of traditional explanations of the Reuben-Bilhah episode apart from those found in *Jubilees*.

In sum, the *Testament of Reuben* demonstrates a detailed familiarity with *Jubilees*, so detailed that it is indeed likely that its author had a copy of *Jubilees* at hand (or in memory) when he composed his own retelling. At the same time, he was apparently also familiar with exegetical motifs not found in *Jubilees*, and he incorporated some of these as well.

What can be said about *Jubilees'* sources? This is a far more difficult question, but it seems that the version of Reuben's sin with Bilhah found in *Jubilees* likewise contains elements drawn from already traditional motifs. One sure sign of such a situation is the presence in a given retelling of two different motifs, each of which was originally designed to account for the same detail in the biblical text—the phenomenon of **overkill**. In *Jubilees*, there are two different explanations of the significance of "and Israel heard of it": on the one hand, Bilhah told *only* Jacob (that is, "and *Israel* heard of it [but no one else did]," but on the other, Bilhah was spurned (that is, "And Israel heard of it and [as a result] Jacob's sons were [only] twelve"). The idea of Bilhah being spurned was certainly consonant with *Jubilees'* view, so why should this author have also *created* the motif "Bilhah Told Only Jacob"? I therefore suspect that at least the latter motif had been traditional by the time of *Jubilees'* composition.

The same may well be true of other motifs in *Jubilees*. "Saw Bilhah Bathing" may be attested as such only in the *Testament of Reuben* and *Jubilees*, but that hardly proves that the author of *Jubilees* created it. Indeed, the rabbinic motif to the effect that Moses, the one "drawn up from water," had intervened for Reuben, who had sinned *in* or *with* water, is predicated on Reuben having been guilty of some water-related "wantonness." What form of wantonness could be invented save one that involved Bilhah and bathing? If this rabbinic tradition is thus predicated on a scenario similar to that of *Jubilees*, that scenario must have been widespread and may go back to a time before *Jubilees'* composition, for it is unlikely that a motif found only in this heretical (in rabbinic eyes) text served rabbinic exegetes as a source of direct inspiration. (If it is not widespread in rabbinic sources, the reason is clearly that another motif triumphed over it there, namely, the one that held Reuben to have been guilty only of upsetting beds.)[31] Similarly: "Bilhah Spurned Forever" is an interpretive motif designed to explain the abrupt juxtaposition of "and Israel heard of it" with "And the sons of Jacob were twelve" by claiming that the latter came as a result of the former. But the idea that these two statements are allied in meaning is likewise reflected in the Masoretic tradition of including them in a single verse, albeit one with a break preserved in the middle (פיסקא באמצע פסוק). Here again, it is unlikely that the Masoretic tradition is directly dependent on *Jubilees*.

It thus seems that even *Jubilees* had its sources—or, as I would prefer to put it, it seems that when the author of *Jubilees* sought to retell the story of Reuben and Bilhah, he did not do so in an exegetical vacuum, but was aware of, and incorporated, interpretive traditions that had been in existence for some time. Of course, the previous existence of such traditions can only be glimpsed here and there in a text like *Jubilees*, one of our earliest specimens of ancient biblical interpretation outside of the Bible itself. (Indeed, in *Jubilees*, preexistent traditions can usually be divined only when, as in the instance just discussed, the text contains two explanations for the same exegetical problem.) But that exegetical traditions existed even at such an early date should hardly be surprising. After all, even the most skeptical source critic of the Hebrew Bible concedes that a great many of its older texts go back centuries before the Babylonian exile. Presumably, such texts survived to later biblical and postbiblical times only because they were carefully copied century after century. Now, it seems most unlikely that such copyists were merely human duplicating machines, or that those who sought to preserve these ancient texts did so without inquiring into their meaning until the second or third century B.C.E., at which time books like *Jubilees* began to be composed. Instead, it appears that the composition of such books constituted an act not only of creating new interpretations (in the case of *Jubilees*, sometimes highly polemical ones) but of assembling and choosing among existing interpretations as well. With care, it is possible to glimpse some of these ancient interpretations and to reconstruct their elaboration and reworking in the literature of the Second Temple period.

Chapter Five

HOW LEVI CAME TO BE A PRIEST

In ancient Israel, the tribe of Levi was deemed to have a special connection with the service of God. Numerous biblical texts speak of the Levites as *the* priestly tribe and attribute to them certain special functions connected with the worship of God. But why exactly had the Levites been selected for such honors, and how did their selection come about? Several biblical narratives appear to have been designed in order to answer this question. Thus, the selection of the Levites is at one point connected with their zealousness following the Golden Calf incident (Exod. 32:25–29), while elsewhere God's choice of the Levites seems to follow from the Levite Aaron's having served as a priest (see Deut. 10:8) or, possibly, to be the result of Moses' words in his final blessing of that tribe before his death (Deut. 33:8–10). Needless to say, all these passages locate the selection of the Levites for their priestly role sometime during the lifetime of Moses, who lived three generations after the tribe's founder, Levi.

It is a striking fact that, despite this biblical evidence, some early postbiblical texts assert that the choice of the Levites went back earlier, to the time of Jacob's son Levi himself. Indeed, they assert not only that Levi had been informed that his descendants would become the priestly tribe but that he himself had been anointed and functioned as a priest during his own lifetime, offering sacrifices to God. This idea is to be found in three ancient texts: (1) the book of *Jubilees*, composed in the second century B.C.E.; (2) an ancient text called the *Aramaic Levi Document* (*ALD*), of uncertain date, known to scholars from fragments found among the Dead Sea Scrolls[1] and in a trove of Hebrew manuscripts discovered in the storeroom of a Cairo synagogue, the "Cairo Geniza";[2] and (3) the *Testament of Levi* (*T. Levi*) section of the *Testaments of the Twelve Patriarchs*,[3] written in a slightly later period and apparently dependent on the *ALD*. Each of these texts asserts, in one way or another, that Levi was informed by God that he and his descendants would be priests in perpetuity and that, in keeping with this, Levi himself was then actually anointed as a priest and instructed in the proper priestly procedure. In the following, I would like to explore the origins of this tradition and, in particular, to examine some of the exegetical issues that, I believe, are connected to its creation and development.

JACOB'S VOW

Before actually turning to the relevant passages in *Jubilees* and the other two sources mentioned, it will be useful to identify at least one starting point for the tradition of Levi's elevation to the priesthood. This is an incident already examined in chapter 2 above: Jacob's vision at Bethel, in which he saw a great ladder stretching from the earth to the height of heaven. The next morning, it will be recalled, Jacob marked the spot of this vision with a special stone and gave the site a new name, while at the same time making a solemn vow:

> He called the name of that place Bethel; but the name of the city was Luz at first. Then Jacob made a vow, saying: "If God stays with me, and watches over me on the journey on which I am traveling, and gives me food to eat and clothing to wear, so that I return safely to my father's house, then the Lord will be my God, and this stone, which I have set up for a pillar, will be God's house; and of everything that You give me I will give a tenth to You." (Gen. 28:20–22)

It is this vow that is of particular interest to the tradition of Levi's elevation to the priesthood. For while other aspects of the story—Jacob's vision itself and its possible significance, or the etiological connection of Bethel with this narrative—tend to monopolize the attention of modern readers, Jacob's vow to give back to God a tenth (tithe) of what he receives must have seemed particularly troubling to ancient interpreters. *Nowhere in the rest of the story of Jacob's life is he ever said to have fulfilled this vow.* Now, failing to fulfill a vow was a serious matter, indeed, a grave sin (Deut. 23:22). It hardly seemed reasonable that the virtuous Jacob could have allowed himself to be guilty of such a sin. But if he had fulfilled his vow, when could he have done so—and why did not the Bible at least hint that he had? Also troubling was the "how," since, in later times, tithes were only given to members of the priestly tribe, the Levites (see Num. 18:21–28). But to what "Levite" could Jacob have given a tenth? This tribe did not yet exist!

A tradition known from rabbinic sources supplied an answer to at least the first question. Exegetes saw the later episode of Jacob's wrestling with a "man" (angel)[4] at the Jabbok ford (Gen. 32:24–32) as a consequence of Jacob's vow in Gen. 28:22. Jacob had indeed failed to keep his vow, and it was for that reason that the angel was dispatched to wrestle with him.

> Jacob wished to cross the Jabbok ford, but he was held up there. The angel said to him: "This is not as you as you had promised, 'I will give a tenth to you'" [Gen. 28:22]. (*Pirqei deR. Eli'ezer* 37)[5]

Another tradition likewise connects Jacob's payment of his vow with that particular night at the Jabbok ford, suggesting, however, that Jacob paid his vow just before the angel's appearance:

> *And he took from what had come into his possession . . . :* He separated out the tithe, and from what was left he sent a gift to his brother Esau. (*Midrash Leqaḥ Ṭob.* 32:14)[6]

The Bethel Connection

But there was another incident, somewhat later on in Genesis, which ancient exegetes also sought to connect with Jacob's unpaid vow. It comes just after Jacob's sons have taken their revenge on the inhabitants of Shechem for the rape of Dinah:

> And God said to Jacob, "Arise, go up to Bethel and dwell there, and build there an altar to the God who appeared to you as you fled from your brother Esau." (Gen. 35:1)

The injunction to "build there an altar," on the very spot where Jacob had earlier made his vow, seemed like a polite summons from God: "Pay up!" And so, for example, Josephus specifically associates this commandment in Gen. 35:1 with Jacob's previous vow:

> God appeared to him [Jacob] and commanded him to take heart, and, purifying his tents, to *perform at last those sacrifices* which he had vowed to offer after he had first set out for Mesopotamia and had had the dream vision. (Josephus, *Jewish Antiquities* 1:341)

A few rabbinic sources likewise suggest that it was at Bethel that Jacob paid his overdue vow.[7]

Now, it is this same exegetical tradition that serves as a starting point of the narrative found in *Jubilees*, the *ALD*, and the *Testament of Levi*. These sources, however, add the further specification that it was Jacob's son Levi who actually performed the sacrifices on Jacob's behalf—that he had recently been made a priest and so quite naturally exercised this function at Bethel.

Levi Was Appointed a Priest

Let us begin with the *Jubilees* account of the events at Bethel:

> And he [Jacob] stayed that night at Bethel, and Levi dreamed a dream that he had been appointed and ordained a priest of the

Most High God, he and his sons forever. And he woke from his sleep and blessed the Lord. And Jacob rose early in the morning, on the fourteenth of that month, and he gave a tenth of all that came with him, of men and cattle, of gold and every vessel and garment, and he gave a tenth of everything. And in those days Rachel became pregnant with her son Benjamin. And Jacob counted his sons from him [Benjamin] upward and Levi fell to the portion of the Lord. And his father put garments of the priesthood on him and filled his hands. . . . And he [Jacob] tithed all the clean animals and made a burnt offering, but the unclean animals he did not give to his son Levi, but he gave him all the souls of the men. And Levi served as priest in Bethel before his father Jacob, in preference to his ten brothers, and he became a priest there. (*Jub.* 32:1–9)

According to *Jubilees*, Levi is thus specially designated to officiate at the altar at Bethel: he offers the sacrifices and receives his father's vowed tithe. It will be noticed, however, that this brief passage actually presents two different accounts of *how* Levi came to be designated for this role. First, he has a dream in which he is appointed a priest, "he and his sons forever." But then the text proceeds to relate how Jacob (apparently ignorant of this dream) decides that, so long as he is now finally fulfilling his old vow, he ought to tithe not only his material possessions but his own sons as well. Counting backward from the youngest, Jacob thus designates the tenth, Levi, as a kind of human tithe, "the portion of the Lord." That this means that Levi will become a priest is made clear in the next sentence, "And his father put garments of the priesthood on him and filled his hands," the latter phrase being a technical term for consecration to the priesthood (cf. Exod. 28:41, 29:9, 29, etc.).

These two motifs are not necessarily mutually exclusive; indeed, it appears as if Levi had his dream and Jacob, knowing nothing about it, then did his counting backward and arrived at exactly the same conclusion as that indicated by Levi's dream. Still, this very fact must be considered striking. The two explanations are presented quite independently of one another—and either one of them alone would have been quite sufficient to explain how Levi came to be selected for his special role. Levi could have had his dream and, having told it to Jacob, the latter might have decided to follow its implications and name him a priest. Alternately, there could have been no dream, and Jacob could have obtained the same result simply by counting his sons backward from Benjamin. Thus, these two, side-by-side **narrative expansions** of the biblical text may actually be seen to embody two **rival motifs**, "Levi Dreamt He Was Ordained" and "Levi the Human Tithe." Each sets forth a rival set of circumstances to explain precisely how Levi came to be selected for the priesthood.[8]

Levi's Vengeance Rewarded

Still more striking, however, is the fact that, apart from Levi's dream and Jacob's decision to "tithe" his sons, *Jubilees* contains two other explanations of how Levi came to be designated for his priestly role. Both occur somewhat earlier in the narrative. The first appears as part of *Jubilees*' retelling of the story of Dinah (Genesis 34) and the zealous vengeance wrought by Levi and his brother Simeon on behalf of their sister (above, chapter 3). After narrating these events, it will be recalled, *Jubilees* asserts:

> And the seed of Levi was chosen for the priesthood and levitical [service], to minister before the Lord always, just as we [angels] do.[9] And Levi and his sons will be blessed forever, because he was zealous to do righteousness and judgment and vengeance. (*Jub.* 30:18)

Levi's priesthood, according to this passage, was apparently granted to him as a reward for his zealous action in avenging his sister.

Isaac Blessed Levi as Priest

The next chapter of *Jubilees* contains a somewhat different idea. Having arrived at Bethel (but some time before both Levi's dream and Jacob's counting backward), Jacob decides to make a quick side-trip to visit his father, Isaac; he takes his sons Levi and Judah with him. (Such a visit is not recounted in Genesis, nor, for that matter, is it found in rabbinic retellings.) Isaac sees Jacob's two sons and immediately the "spirit of prophecy came down upon his mouth." He then blesses Levi in these terms:

> May the Lord give you and your seed very great honor. May He draw you and your seed near to Him from all flesh *to serve in His sanctuary* as angels of the presence and the holy ones [serve on high]. . . . The word of the Lord they [your descendants] will speak righteously, and all of His judgments they will execute righteously. And they will tell My ways to Jacob, and My paths to Israel. The blessing of the Lord shall be placed in their mouth, so that they might bless all of the seed of the beloved. (As for) you, your mother has named you "Levi," and truly has she named you, [for] you will be joined (*lwh*) to the Lord . . . His table will belong to you, and you and yours sons will eat from it. (*Jub.* 31:14–16)

That this is a summons to priestly service is explicit in the phrase "to serve in his sanctuary" as well as in the assertion "His table will belong to you, and you and your sons will eat from it." Moreover, the "blessing of the Lord shall be placed in their mouth" alludes to the priestly blessing described in Num. 6:22–27. In short, here it is Isaac who designates Levi and his descendants to serve in the sanctuary forever.

As we have seen, the phenomenon of **overkill** is not unusual in ancient exegetical texts. It usually comes about when the author of a particular text is aware of two earlier versions of a story or two

different explanations for the same phenomenon; unable or unwilling to decide between them, the author seeks to incorporate
both into a single retelling. But in so doing, the author inevitably
ends up, one might say, killing one bird with two stones—that is,
giving two reasons for a particular event to have occurred or
two different ways in which it took place. Now, in the case at hand,
we have an extraordinary instance of "overkill," four apparently
independent explanations of how Levi came to acquire the priesthood and levitical service: (1) through a (divinely sent) dream-
vision; (2) as a result of Jacob's mechanically counting backward
from Benjamin in the "human tithe" at Bethel; (3) as a reward for
his zeal in avenging Dinah; and (4) in a prophetic blessing by his
grandfather Isaac. As noted, these four explanations are not necessarily *contradictory*: a prophetic dream granting Levi priestly status can certainly coexist with Jacob's human tithe or Isaac's
blessing. But there was no reason for *Jubilees* to assert that all four
things happened when any one of them would have been sufficient
to account for Levi's change in status. Indeed, they disagree somewhat in their tone: saying that Levi came to be a priest via "the
luck of the draw," that is, by being the tenth son (counting backward), certainly jangles with the assertion that he had earned the
priesthood as a result of meritorious deeds—was it earned or
wasn't it? And how could Levi have had a prophetic dream indicating that he was God's choice for the priesthood after he had
already learned precisely the same thing from Isaac when the
"spirit of prophecy" came over *him*? Nor, as we have seen, does
any of these four allude to the others: *Jubilees* does not say "Levi
had a dream, and it said exactly what Isaac had said in his words
of blessing"; neither does the text assert that "Jacob counted backward, and the tenth son was Levi, confirming what Isaac had said
and what had been written in the heavenly tablets concerning the
revenge on Shechem." Rather, each of the four is presented quite
independently. This is another sign of "overkill."

THE ARAMAIC LEVI DOCUMENT

Let us turn to the traditions concerning Levi's elevation to the priesthood found in the *Aramaic Levi Document*. As mentioned, this text survives only in scattered fragments. Some parts of it were discovered at the end of the nineteenth century in the Cairo Geniza, and further fragments were found among the Dead Sea Scrolls at Qumran, in caves 1 and 4. In addition, fragments of this same text seem to have been preserved, in Greek translation, in one ancient manuscript of the *Testament of Levi* found in a monastery library at Mount Athos, Greece. There is also a Syriac fragment of the text.

It was at first thought that these Aramaic fragments might simply be part of an original, Aramaic version of the *Testament of Levi*, which was then translated into Greek and survived in the ancient Greek composition known as the *Testaments of the Twelve Patriarchs*. However, it gradually became clear that the Aramaic and Greek texts, although they had much in common, were nonetheless distinct. The Aramaic text has thus come to be called the *Aramaic Levi Document* (ALD) or *Aramaic Levi*. The fact that parts of this Aramaic text were found among the Dead Sea Scrolls indicates that it is quite old—indeed, the oldest fragments from Qumran have been dated by palaeographers to the last decades of the second century B.C.E., suggesting that its actual composition probably goes back still further. It certainly seems likely that the *ALD* served as some kind of a source for the *Testament of Levi* as now known to us in the *Testaments of the Twelve Patriarchs*, since parts of the *ALD* match the *Testament of Levi* sentence for sentence and even word for word. It is clear, however, that the *Testament* is not simply a translation of the *ALD* but, at least in spots, a free reworking.

How, according to the *ALD*, did Levi come to be a priest? It is difficult to be sure of the order of the fragments, but somewhere

toward the beginning Levi seems to tell how, as a young man, he
prayed a long prayer to God, asking Him, among other things,
"to have mercy upon me and bring me close to be Your servant
and to minister properly before You." Thereafter comes a very
fragmentary report of Levi's vision:

> Then I continued on [
> to my father Jacob and [
> from Abel Mayin. Then [
> I lay down and I remained [
> Then I was shown visions [
> In what appeared in the vision, I saw the heav[ens
> beneath me, high up, till it reached the heave[ns
> to me the gates of heaven, and an angel[
>
> (*ALD* 4:1–6 = 4Q213a, frag. 1, col. 2)

Here the text breaks off. In the parallel section of the Greek
Testament of Levi, however, the angel mentioned at the very end
of the above fragment goes on to usher Levi into heaven and re-
veal to him some of the secrets of the place. He is also told of the
brilliant future that awaits him and his descendants. Levi hides
these things in his heart and tells no one. Following this, he has a
second vision involving seven "men" (angels) who anoint him as
a priest. It is at that point that the next *ALD* fragments pick up
the story:

> And those seven departed from me and **I awoke from my sleep.**
> **Then** I said: "This is a vision, and thus I am amazed that I should
> have any vision at all." And **I hid this too in my heart and** I revealed
> it **to no one.** And we went to my father Isaac, and he too [blessed]
> me thus. Then, when [my father] **Jacob tithed** . . . everything which
> he possessed in accordance with his vow (. . .) I was first at the head
> of the (. . .) **and to me of all his sons he gave** a sacrifice of (. . .) to
> God, and he invested me in the priestly garb and he consecrated me

and I became a priest of the **God of eternity**. And I offered all of his
sacrifices and I blessed my father that he might live; and I blessed my
brothers. Then all of them blessed me, and my father blessed me as
well, and I finished offering his sacrifices at Bethel. Then we went
from Bethel and stayed at the residence of Abraham our father,
along with Isaac our father. And Isaac our father [saw] all of us and
blessed us and rejoiced. When he learned that I was priest of the
Most High God, the Lord of heaven, he began to instruct me and to
teach me the law of the priesthood. (*ALD* 4:12–5:8 [4Q213b in
boldface, with surrounding text restored from Bodleian a and b:])

After the seven angels had finished with Levi, he must have realized that he had been made a priest—but, as with the first vision,
he tells no one. Instead (as in *Jubilees*), Levi travels with his father
to visit Isaac, and Isaac "blessed me thus," that is, in keeping with
Levi's vision: Levi and his offspring are designated for the hereditary priesthood. The scene next switches back to Bethel, where
Jacob now wishes to make good on his long-overdue vow and
offer his tithes. For that purpose, Jacob clothes Levi in priestly
garments and makes him "a priest of the God of eternity."

As if that were not enough to explain the circumstances of
Levi's elevation, the *ALD* then reports that Levi and his family
visited Isaac on a subsequent occasion:

And Isaac our father [saw] all of us and blessed us and rejoiced.
When he learned that I was priest of the Most High God, the Lord
of heaven, he began to instruct me and to teach me the law of the
priesthood. (*ALD* 5:7–8 [from Bodleian b])

It is strange (if not quite impossible) that only now Isaac "learned
that I was a priest"—had he not himself said as much in his previous blessing of Levi?[10] Lastly, there comes a long section in the
ALD in which Isaac actually instructs Levi in priestly procedure.

Toward the end of these instructions (in a section extant only in the Greek manuscript from Mount Athos), Isaac says to Levi,

> And now, my child, listen to my words for . . . you are a holy priest of the Lord, and all your seed will be priests. And command your sons thus, so that they may do according to this regulation, as I have shown you. For my father Abraham commanded me to do thus and to command my sons. And now, child, I rejoice that you were elected for the holy priesthood, and to offer sacrifice to the Most High Lord. (*ALD* 10:1–4 [Athos-Koutloumous Codex 39; insert at *T. Levi* 18:2 (51)])[11]

The *ALD* thus seems to suffer from the same problem of **overkill** as *Jubilees*, although it differs somewhat in the details. Here, Levi apparently has two separate visions involving his future priesthood (*Jubilees* had mentioned only one); the first involves one angel, the second seven. Isaac then blesses him "thus," in keeping with the second vision; then Jacob (apparently quite independently) chooses him for the priesthood at the time of the Bethel tithes. Finally, Isaac learns that Levi has become a priest and instructs him about offering sacrifices, at the same time asserting that "all your seed will be priests." One might therefore ask the same question of this account as of *Jubilees*: Why so many different, and independent, elements in the story—all of which seem to be serving the same purpose, that is, to tell the reader how it was that Levi came to be a priest? Would not one alone be sufficient?

In order to make sense of this tangle, it is necessary, first of all, to look at each of the different exegetical motifs—for that is what they are—separately. Let us begin with a fairly simple and easily isolated motif, that of Jacob's counting his sons backward, found in *Jub*. 32:3, a motif clearly connected with the matter of Jacob's unpaid vows, considered briefly above.

Levi the Human Tithe

The idea that Levi was chosen for his special role as a result of Jacob's tithing his sons is rather straightforward. After all, Jacob had originally pledged to give back to God "a tenth of all that you give me" (Gen. 28:22); was it not possible that, when Jacob finally made good on this pledge, he included his sons among the items to be tithed? Not only would this account for how the Levites came to have their special connection with the cultic service of God (they happened to be the tenth tribe, counting backward), but it would provide Jacob with a ready-at-hand "Levite"—Levi himself—to receive the pledged tithe on God's behalf at Bethel, just as Levites were later enjoined in cultic law to receive tithes from the people of Israel. And so there developed the motif that Levi had been chosen by Jacob to be God's special servant at Bethel, and chosen for no other reason than that he turned out to be the tenth child (counting backward, to be sure).[12]

It should be pointed out here that, in addition to the factors just mentioned, one further consideration doubtless pushed ancient interpreters to seek to connect the Levites' later role in the Temple service with Levi himself and the events at Bethel. For, from very early times, readers contemplating Jacob's final blessing of his sons before his death (Genesis 49) had come to the conclusion that Jacob had not only blessed them on that occasion but had also distributed among them in the process various hereditary prizes. Thus Reuben, as the firstborn, had been in line to gain the firstborn's double portion, but Jacob's words to Reuben in Gen. 49:3–5 were interpreted to mean that the firstborn's portion was to be taken away from him because of his sin with Bilhah (above, chapter 4) and awarded to Joseph, the firstborn of Jacob's wife Rachel. (As we have seen, this interpretation is first attested within the Bible itself, in 1 Chr. 5:1.) Jacob's blessing of Judah in Gen. 49:8–12 similarly seemed to imply that the prize of hereditary kingship was thereby being granted to Judah's descendants: "Your brothers will praise you . . . your father's sons will bow down before you. . . . The scepter shall not depart from Judah, nor the ruler's staff from between his feet" (Gen. 49:8–10). And so it was: when hereditary kingship was at last established in Israel, it was the Judahite David who was privileged to found the royal dynasty.

But what of the hereditary priesthood? Jacob's blessing of Levi makes no allusion to that prize. In fact, Levi and Simeon are "blessed" (or, rather, rebuked) together in a single blessing of Jacob's (Gen. 49:5–7); Jacob apparently reproaches these two brothers for their fierceness in avenging their sister Dinah. Here was a twofold problem for interpreters, for not only did Jacob *not* give away the hereditary priesthood along with kingship and the double portion of the firstborn on this significant occasion but (as later events confirmed) the priesthood turned out to be the property of the tribe of Levi, Jacob's third son, in apparent preference to the tribe of the second son, Simeon. Yet nothing in Jacob's last words seemed to hint at any preference of Levi over Simeon, since the two were addressed jointly in a single blessing.

The motif "Levi the Human Tithe" provides an adequate solution to both of these problems. It asserts that Jacob did indeed confer the priesthood on Levi, but long before the time of the blessings in Genesis 49: Levi had been chosen years earlier, at the time when Jacob paid off his overdue tithe. There was, therefore, no need for Jacob to mention the priesthood in his final blessings since that matter had already been settled. What is more, this motif elegantly explains why Simeon was passed over in favor of Levi. It was nothing personal and had nothing to do with the previous conduct of either brother; it was simply a matter of blind arithmetic.[13]

Although it thus answered two pressing questions with regard to Levi's selection, this motif had a number of disadvantages. To begin with, it could only work if Jacob counted backward from his youngest son, and there was no apparent justification for such a procedure. Little wonder, then, that a **variant** of this motif developed in which a different method of counting was employed. This variant is found in some rabbinic sources,[14] for example, in *Targum Pseudo-Jonathan*:

> And an angel in the guise of a man struggled with him and said: "Did you not say that that you would tithe everything that is yours? Yet here you have twelve sons and one daughter and you have not tithed them." Thereupon Jacob set aside the four first-borns of the four mothers [presumably because firstborns fall into a special category] and there remained eight [boys. After counting up to the eighth] he went back to [the beginning, that is, to] Simeon, and Levi [thus] came out the tenth. And the angel Michael said: "Lord of the world! This one will be Your servant." (*Targum Pseudo-Jonathan* Gen. 32:25)

The passage cited above from *Pirqei deR. Eliʿezer* goes on to present the same motif:

> Jacob wished to cross the Jabbok ford but he was held up there.[15] The angel said to him: "This is not as you as you had promised, 'I will give a tenth to You'" [Gen. 28:22]. What did Jacob do? he took all the livestock that he had brought from Paddan Aram, and these were five thousand and five hundred sheep. And the angel said further to Jacob: "Do you not also have sons from whom you have not given me a tithe?" What did Jacob do? He set aside the four firstborns of the four mothers, leaving eight sons. He began from Simeon and ended with Benjamin, who was then still in his mother's womb. Then he began again from Simeon and ended with Levi, and Levi thus turned out to be the tenth, holy to the Lord, as it is said, "The tenth part will be holy to the Lord" [Lev. 27:32]. R. Ishmael said: "All the firstborns while they are being guarded

must be tithed. [Therefore, Jacob's tithe was done by counting all twelve sons,] but Jacob started counting from the youngest: he began with Benjamin who was in his mother's womb, and Levi thus turned out to be holy to the Lord, and it is about him that Scripture says, 'The tenth part will be holy to the Lord'" [Lev. 27:32]. (*Pirqei deR. Eli'ezer* 37)

It is to be noted that both these passages specify the place in which Jacob tithed his sons as the Jabbok ford and not Bethel, as in *Jubilees*. This should tell us something important, if obvious: Levi's inauguration into the priesthood via the "human tithe" method need not have taken place at one particular spot or another, but it had to be connected with Jacob's paying off his other promised tithes, *since this whole motif is dependent on a still earlier motif*, namely, the idea that (despite the silence of Scripture) Jacob did indeed pay off his promised tithes somewhere, at some point. Now since, according to these rabbinic exegetes, that happened at the crossing of the Jabbok ford, it is there that Levi is consecrated to the priesthood, but since *Jubilees* holds that the same settling-of-accounts took place later, at Bethel, then that is where the "human tithe" takes place in that text.

Whichever locale was chosen, there was one further problem with the motif "Levi, the Human Tithe," and that was that Benjamin was not yet born when the tithing was done. If he was not born, how could Jacob count back ten and arrive at Levi? The solution was to count Benjamin in utero. *Jubilees* thus says, "And in those days Rachel became pregnant with her son Benjamin. And Jacob counted his sons from him [Benjamin] upward and Levi fell to the portion of the Lord." Similarly, *Pirqei deR. Eli'ezer* specifies that Benjamin "was in his mother's womb." (Interestingly, *Pseudo-Jonathan* does not mention this fact, though it is certainly implied by the Jabbok location.) Counting the infant in utero was hardly an ideal solution; how did Jacob know that the unborn child was a son? Nevertheless, this defect was apparently not felt to be so severe as to invalidate the whole motif, for we have seen that it was incorporated into the book of *Jubilees* and into some rabbinic sources.

A Chain of Priests

Thus developed the motif "Levi the Human Tithe," a simple, if mechanical, way of explaining why Levi (and not Simeon, for example) was chosen for the priesthood, and why the priesthood was not among the hereditary benefits assigned by Jacob in his "last words" in Genesis 49. But what of the other explanations for Levi's selection found in our various texts? Let us move on to consider a second, similarly uncomplicated motif, the one that seemed to connect Levi's elevation to the priesthood with a prophetic blessing given to him by his grandfather Isaac. Here too, some background is necessary in order to appreciate fully this motif's development.

Modern readers tend not to attribute any special importance to the biblical accounts of various ancient figures—Noah, Abraham, Jacob, and so forth—who offer sacrifices or build an altar at some particular spot. Were these not simple acts of piety, acts that were quite in keeping with the righteous character of these people? However, to at least some ancient interpreters such biblical accounts appeared highly significant (and potentially problematic), since they indicated that the person involved had *served as a priest*. To these interpreters it seemed as unlikely that an ancient Israelite might just go ahead and offer a sacrifice on his own as it would seem unlikely to us that any specialized, professional work—designing a bridge, for example, or performing a surgical operation—would be undertaken by someone without prior instruction or experience. Certainly Noah et al. had not simply improvised, deciding on their own what animals to sacrifice and

how to prepare them! Yet the Bible does not specifically identify
any of them as a priest, nor is there any account of their being *instructed* in the offering of sacrifices. How then could these texts
be understood?

There was thus created a tradition, well documented in a number of ancient sources, to the effect that there had in fact been a
priesthood from the time of Adam on, that special priestly
garments (a necessity of the office) had been passed on from earliest times through a succession of holders of this priesthood, and
that priestly instructions had likewise been transmitted from
generation to generation. This priestly line of succession passed,
in one version, from Adam to Noah to Melchizedek (who was
also identified with Noah's son Shem) and on to Abraham and his
descendants.[16]

One source that appears to have been particularly drawn to
this notion of an ancient priesthood is the book of *Jubilees*. In its
retelling of biblical history, *Jubilees* asserts that Adam, Enoch,
and other early figures brought priestly offerings to God even
when there is no corresponding event in the Genesis narrative (see
Jub. 3:27, 4:25, etc.). Moreover, when the biblical text does speak
of an offering having been made, *Jubilees* sometimes inserts
details from later priestly laws (again, see *Jub.* 3:27, which super-
imposes the priestly law of Exod. 30:34 on Adam's sacrifice; or
Jub. 6:3, which integrates into Noah's offering details from the
law of Lev. 2:1–4, cf. Exod. 29:40). To the author of *Jubilees*, it
was apparently important to assert that such offerings had been
made in absolute conformity with the sacred regulations spelled
out later on in the Pentateuch. Similarly, in retelling the story of
the "covenant between the pieces" (wherein God tells Abraham
to kill certain animals [Gen. 15:9]), *Jubilees* adds details not even
hinted at in the biblical text in order for Abraham's behavior
to be consistent with his priestly status: "And he [Abraham] *built
an altar* there. And he slaughtered all of these, and he *poured*

their blood on the altar" (*Jub.* 14:10–11). Understandably, when Abraham is old and ready to die, he initiates his son Isaac into the priesthood and instructs him about sacrifices (*Jubilees* 21). Isaac then takes over the priestly succession and offers sacrifices (*Jub.* 22:3).

The priesthood of Abraham, Isaac, and other figures in *Jubilees* must be understood in this exegetical context. Throughout his book, the author of *Jubilees* goes to great lengths to assert that later biblical laws and practices had in fact been known to Noah and Abraham and the other patriarchs; in fact, one major theme of *Jubilees* is that the laws that are given to the people of Israel in the books of Exodus, Leviticus, Numbers, and Deuteronomy had actually been known long before, in the time of the patriarchs, and are thus hinted at here and there in the book of Genesis. Laws concerning the priesthood were this author's parade example. As far as he was concerned, any mention in Genesis of someone "building an altar" was virtually an indication that regular, cultic sacrifice was involved; this therefore implied the presence of a priest, someone actually trained in the laws of sacrificing animals, and—since such altars are mentioned in connection with various ancient figures—a succession of priests down through the ages. It is thus hardly surprising that Abraham is part of this chain of priests in *Jubilees*, since Genesis mentions at least three separate altars built by Abraham (12:7, 8; 13:4, 18).

It is interesting, however, to observe what happens in the next two generations. As we have already glimpsed, Isaac was, according to *Jubilees*, likewise a priest; however, *Jacob was not*. Now this might appear surprising, since Jacob is, in some respects, the great hero of *Jubilees*,[17] while Isaac is certainly less than that. But *Jubilees* is in this matter quite consistent with the twin principles mentioned above: that there had been in the patriarchal period a succession of priests,[18] and that the mention in Genesis of someone building an altar or making a cultic offering was prima facie evidence of his being part of this priestly succession. As a matter of fact, *Jubilees'* conclusion that Jacob was not a priest is closely tied to its understanding of one particular incident, the very matter of Jacob's vow and the altar at Bethel discussed above.

Jacob Was Not a Priest

It would have been difficult for *Jubilees* to avoid having Isaac be a priest. After all, Gen. 26:25 was quite specific: "And he [Isaac] built an altar there, and he called upon the name of the Lord, and he established his tent there." (This not only mentions building an altar but also, in conjunction with it, "calling upon the name" and tenting. Precisely these same three elements appear in connection with Abraham in Gen. 12:8.) But what, on the contrary, of Jacob? When he first arrives at Bethel, God appears to him in the dream of the ladder and promises him great things, just as He had promised to Abraham and Isaac. But whereas, having received these similar promises, the other two patriarchs had built altars (Gen. 12:7, 13:18, 26:25), Jacob's reaction, already cited above, is, on reflection, rather strange:

> Early that morning Jacob took the stone that he had put under his head and set it up as a pillar (מצבה), and he poured oil on its top. . . . Then Jacob made a vow: "If God is with me and watches over me on the journey that I am making, and gives me food to eat and clothes to wear, so that I return safely to my father's house— then the Lord shall be my God, and this stone, which I have set up as a pillar, will be a temple of God, and *everything that You give me I will tithe back to You.*" (Gen. 28:18–22)

Why does not Jacob offer a sacrifice to God as his father and grandfather had done? Perhaps, traveling alone as a virtual fugitive, he simply did not have with him the means of offering a sacrifice. But such an answer would hardly seem adequate to an

ancient interpreter. After all, God had "seen to" a sacrificial animal miraculously appearing to Abraham when it was needed
(Gen. 22:13); certainly the same could have been done for Jacob
had God so willed. Moreover, nothing in Jacob's words even remotely reflects the idea that it was a lack of sacrificial animals
that prevented him from making an offering immediately: if that
were the problem, he ought to have mentioned it straight out in
this speech. For that matter, even if no sacrificial animal were immediately available, Jacob surely could have made a simple meal
offering at the time. But he does not; instead, he takes a vow of
future sacrifices (tithes, in fact) and sets up a special stone monu-
ment. To the author of *Jubilees*, all this could mean only one
thing: Jacob could not offer a sacrifice at the time because he was
not a priest and had not received instructions in priestly procedure from his father Isaac. (Why, indeed, should Isaac have instructed Jacob? Isaac was still a relatively young man, and the
time had not yet come for him to pass on the priesthood.) Jacob
therefore marks the spot so that *someone else*, his father or some
other priest, might later officiate at an altar to be built on that site
and so allow Jacob to fulfill his vow.

As exegesis, this was a brilliant stroke. To begin with, it explained Jacob's strange behavior at Bethel. The מצבה, that he sets
up was not (as one might otherwise think) a substitute for an
altar or the sort of idolatrous object that this same word refers to
in, for example, Exod. 23:24, 34:13, Deut. 7:5, and 12:3. Instead,
this מצבה, is merely a visible marker and its anointing an act of
consecration for the time when Jacob can return and fulfill his
vow. (*Jubilees* makes this intention explicit in its rewording of
Gen. 28:18: "And rising early in the morning, Jacob took the
stone which he had placed at his head and he set it up as a pillar
for a sign" [*Jub.* 27:26]. The phrase "for a sign" has been added
by the author of *Jubilees*; it has no correspondent in the Genesis
text.) Moreover, this explanation exonerated Jacob from any later
charge of laxness with regard to his vow: he could not fulfill it

until he was in the company of a real priest, and that occasion, according to *Jubilees*, did not come along until Jacob's own son Levi had been duly consecrated to the priesthood.

There was one outstanding difficulty with this approach, and that was the fact that another verse in Genesis must have seemed to the author of *Jubilees* to come dangerously close to representing Jacob as a functioning priest on his own. For, in recounting Jacob's treaty with Laban at Gilead, Gen. 31:54 notes: "And Jacob offered a sacrifice (ויזבח זבח), on the mountain and called his kinsmen to eat bread; and they ate bread and tarried all night on the mountain." It is all the more significant, then, that in retelling this incident, the author of *Jubilees* introduces a significant change:

> And on the fifteenth of those days Jacob *prepared a banquet* for Laban and for all who came with him. And Jacob swore to Laban on that day, and Laban also swore to Jacob . . . and they made there a heap of witness. (*Jub.* 29:7–8)

For the author of *Jubilees*, the phrase ויזבח זבח, in Gen. 31:54 does not refer to sacrifices at all; this root is used—as it is in the significant regulation of Deut. 12:15—to refer to secular slaughter, the killing of animals outside of a cultic context. And indeed, Genesis here makes no mention of Jacob *building an altar* for cultic slaughter or "calling on the name of the Lord." Hence, the author of *Jubilees* concluded that there was indeed nothing cultic involved, and, in this retelling, all that Jacob does is to "prepare a banquet." His nonpriestly status is preserved.[19]

Isaac Blessed Levi

Thus, for the author of *Jubilees*, Isaac was a priest and Jacob was not. This fact—virtually imposed by the Genesis narrative itself— furthermore worked quite well with the second exegetical motif under consideration, namely, that the great chain of the priesthood among Israel's ancestors passed directly from Isaac to Levi and that therefore it was Isaac who ushered Levi into the priesthood. The relevant passage from *Jubilees* has already been partially cited above:

> And a spirit of prophecy came down upon his [Isaac's] mouth. And he turned to Levi first and he began to bless him first, and he said to him . . . "May the Lord give you and your seed very great honor. May He draw you and your seed near to Him from all flesh to serve in His sanctuary as angels of the presence and the holy ones. May your sons' seed be like them with respect to honor and greatness and sanctification. . . . The word of the Lord they [your descendants] will speak righteously, and all of His judgments they will execute righteously. And they will tell My ways to Jacob, and My paths to Israel. The blessing of the Lord shall be placed in their mouth, so that they might bless all of the seed of the beloved. (As for) you, your mother has named you "Levi," and truly has she named you, [for] you will be joined (*lwh*) to the Lord. . . . His table will belong to you, and you and yours sons will eat from it." (*Jub.* 31:12–14)

It is to be noted that, in this passage, Isaac does not actually *instruct* Levi in priestly matters; instead, he confers on Levi the same kind of prophetic, powerful blessing he had given to Jacob years before, save that Levi's blessing, unlike Jacob's, centers entirely on the fact that he has been chosen to succeed Isaac in cultic service. "May the Lord give you and your seed very great honor," Isaac says—and it is clear from this wording that he is not merely announcing a decision that has already been made but is himself blessing-and-so-bringing-about, just as he had done with his own sons Jacob and Esau—"May He draw you and your seed near to Him from all flesh to serve in His sanctuary." This change in Levi's status is thus brought about through Isaac's words, although, to be sure, it comes ultimately from God, for the passage stipulates that a "spirit of prophecy" guided Isaac's blessing. In other words, this passage in *Jubilees* contains another, quite self-sufficient, answer to the question, "How did Levi come to be a priest?" Its answer is that he was divinely appointed to the priesthood through a special blessing pronounced by the last priest, Isaac, just as Isaac had himself been initiated into the priesthood by his father Abraham (*Jubilees* 21). In its *Jubilees* form, this motif would suffice to answer our question without reference to any "human tithe" undertaken by Jacob, and without any of the supernatural visions that our various texts attribute to Levi and Jacob.[20]

A Side-Trip to Hebron

In any case, we have now examined two independent motifs that explain the selection of Levi for the priesthood. The second motif, "Isaac Blessed Levi," embodied the notion of priestly succession dear to *Jubilees*' author. But it posed a problem as well, one of timing. For, if Jacob was not a priest, then it must have been Levi who officiated at the altar that Jacob built at Bethel. That meant that Levi had to be blessed by Isaac and initiated into the priesthood sometime before the sacrifices at Bethel. But when could Isaac even have *seen* Levi? Levi was born and grew up in Aram, where his father Jacob was working for his uncle. When Jacob and his family finally return to the land of Canaan, Levi is now a young man—but the Bible does not mention any meeting between him and the aged Isaac. Instead, Jacob, Levi, and the rest of the family seem to proceed forthwith to Bethel. The only verse that even suggests a possible meeting between Isaac and Levi is Gen. 35:27, "And Jacob came to his father Isaac at Mamre, Kiryat Arba (which is Hebron), where Abraham and Isaac dwelt." Presumably, Jacob might have taken Levi with him on that occasion, and Isaac could then have initiated him into the priesthood. But this meeting happened too late: it is mentioned long *after* Jacob and his family leave Bethel (Gen. 35:16). What to do?

It was here that the author of *Jubilees* hit upon a little detail in the biblical narrative that solved all of his problems. Let us look at the biblical text in question:

> And God said to Jacob, "Arise, go up to Bethel and dwell there, and build there an altar to the God who appeared to you as you fled from your brother Esau." . . . And so Jacob came to Luz in the land of Canaan—that is, to Bethel—he and all the people with him. There he built an altar and called the place El-Bethel, for that is where God had appeared to him when he fled from his brother. And Deborah, Rebekah's servant,[21] died there, and she was buried under an oak below Bethel; so the name of it was called Allon-bakhut ["oak of weeping"]. (Gen. 35:1, 7–8)

The purpose of the last sentence in this passage is apparently to explain, in passing, how Allon-bakhut, near Bethel, got its name. But the author of *Jubilees* had a question about this parenthetical observation: what was Rebekah's servant doing at Bethel with Jacob? Shouldn't she have been back in Hebron, where Rebekah and Isaac lived (Gen. 35:27)? This was, when one thinks about it, a very good question. For, as we have seen, there was nothing in the whole Genesis narrative to suggest that Jacob had had any contact whatsoever with Isaac or Rebekah or any member of their household since the time that Jacob first left home (alone, needless to say) as a youth. Yet here suddenly the text speaks of a member of that household, some servant of Rebekah's, being *present with Jacob* at Bethel and dying there.

It was because of this curious fact that the author of *Jubilees* felt entitled—required, really—to add something to the bare narrative frame of Genesis. For, the very mention of Rebekah's servant here seemed, as it were, to draw a dotted line between Bethel and Hebron. If Rebekah's servant was now at Bethel, then she must have journeyed there *from* Hebron, where Rebekah and Isaac had long been living (Gen. 35:27); and if she journeyed there, she certainly did not do so by chance. Thus, this dotted line between Bethel and Hebron invited our author to imagine the circumstances leading up to such a journey by Rebekah's servant: Jacob himself must first have gone *to* Hebron after arriving in Bethel, and then come back to Bethel once again, accompanied by Deborah (and presumably her mistress, Rebekah).

Now, all this could connect perfectly with the need to have Isaac make Levi a priest almost as soon as Jacob and his family arrive in Bethel. And so indeed, the author of *Jubilees* makes the connection: Jacob first arrives in Bethel and builds an altar there, as is specified in Gen. 35:7. He then invites his father *and mother*, Isaac and Rebekah, to come to Bethel for the sacrifices (*Jub.* 31:3), since he needs a priest to offer the sacrifices. But Isaac sends word that he wishes Jacob to come to him. The sacrifices are thus put off, and Jacob journeys to visit his father. There Isaac blesses Levi and announces his initiation into the priesthood (*Jub.* 31:12–17). Then the narrative resumes as follows:

> And in the morning [after Isaac had blessed Levi as a priest], Jacob told his father Isaac about the vow which he had made to the Lord and the vision which he had seen, and that he had built an altar and everything was prepared to make a sacrifice before the Lord just as he had vowed. . . . And Isaac said to Jacob his son, "I am not able to come with you because I have grown old. . . ." And he said to Rebekah, "Go with Jacob your son." And Rebekah went with her son Jacob. And Deborah [Rebekah's nurse] was with her. And they reached Bethel. (*Jub.* 31:26–30)

Jacob's earlier invitation to Isaac *and Rebekah* to come to Bethel now makes it seem quite logical for Isaac (though he himself is too old to travel) to send Rebekah, and Deborah along with her, back to Bethel with Jacob, where Deborah can then die as per Gen. 35:8. In other words, the passing mention of "Deborah, Rebekah's servant" in Gen. 35:8 allowed the author of *Jubilees* to posit an earlier trip of Jacob to visit his father and mother at Hebron, a trip which might then also serve as the occasion for Isaac to bless Levi and proclaim him his priestly successor. Without the passing mention of Rebekah's servant, such a hypothetical voyage might have appeared a gross intrusion on the biblical narrative; with it, on the contrary, the *Jubilees* reconstruction of things seems entirely justified.

This idea of having Jacob and Levi first visit Isaac at Hebron and then return to offer the sacrifices was thus a way of having Levi proclaimed a priest *by Isaac* while still maintaining that Jacob had indeed paid off his vows at the Bethel altar. Such a scenario was an exegetical coup for the author of *Jubilees*: his beloved notion of priestly succession could be reconciled with the biblical account of the Bethel altar. It should be noted, by the way, that the motif "Isaac Blesses Levi" appears in all three of our documents and follows the same sequence of events in all three: the family arrives at Bethel, then Jacob and Levi (and, in *Jubilees*, Judah as well) go to visit Isaac at Hebron, where Isaac blesses Levi. Thereafter, the party returns to Bethel and Jacob pays his vows (*Jub.* 32:1–2; *ALD* 5:1–4 [Bod. a, 8–9]; *T. Levi* 9:1–3). After this, the family has no further need to be in Bethel, so they return to Isaac and Rebekah at Hebron. It is apparently a second such trip to Hebron that is being referred to by Gen. 35:27, "And Jacob came to his father Isaac at Mamre, Kiryat Arba (which is Hebron), where Abraham and Isaac dwelt."

LEVI'S TWO VISIONS

Having investigated "Levi the Human Tithe" and "Isaac Blesses Levi," we may now turn to the visions that Levi is said to have had in our various texts. It will be recalled that *Jubilees* mentions only one vision of Levi's and passes over it in a single sentence: "And he [Jacob] stayed that night at Bethel, and Levi dreamed a dream that he had been appointed and ordained priest of the Most High God, he and his sons forever" (*Jub.* 32:1). (This was the motif we called earlier "Levi Dreamt He Was Ordained.") By contrast, both the *Testament of Levi* and the *ALD* seem to speak of two separate dream-visions. At first glance, these two visions appear to be quite similar, for in both Levi receives from an angel or angels the announcement that he has been chosen for divine service. At the same time, the two differ on a number of incidental details: the first takes place in or around Abel Maul/Abel Mayin, the second at Bethel; in the first there is a single angel, whereas in the second there are seven (apparently angelic) beings; the first involves Levi's entrance into heaven, whereas the second does not. Still more significant, the message given to Levi in each is somewhat different.

Let us begin with this last point, since at least some of the differences between the two messages have, I believe, largely escaped the attention of scholars. Most of the content of the first vision is missing in the *ALD*; if it corresponded to the first vision in chapters 2–5 of the *Testament of Levi*, it might well be called "Levi's Apocalypse," for the whole point of it seems to be that Levi is called on high (this part *is* in the *ALD*, as attested by 4Q213a, frag. 1, col. 2) to be told of the secrets of the heavens and the coming judgment to be passed on humankind (*T. Levi* 2:7–9, 3:1–10, 4:1). He is also told of the special role that he and his descendants are to play in Israel (4Q213, frag. 2, 10–18; 1Q21, frags. 1, 7; cf. *T. Levi* 2:10–12, 4:2–6). It should be further noted that the description of Levi's future role does not particularly stress the priesthood. Rather, the point seems to be his wisdom and overall preeminence: henceforth Levi will "stand near the Lord and will be His minister and will *declare His mysteries to men*," and "You will light up a bright light of knowledge in

Jacob, and you *will be as the sun* to all the seed of Israel" (*T. Levi* 2:10, 4:3).

The second vision (again, largely lost in the *ALD* but presented in the *Testament of Levi* 8), to the contrary, might well be referred to as the "Levi's Priestly Initiation" motif, for here Levi's *priesthood* is the whole point: he is twice specifically referred to as a "priest of the Lord" (8:3,10) and is, in priestly fashion, anointed, washed, and clothed in priestly garments (*T. Levi* 8:2–10). While this vision is, at least after the fact, said to have been a dream (*T. Levi* 8:18), it does not involve any journey to heaven or the revelation of heaven's secrets, as did the first vision. It takes place on earth, and its main concern seems to be the assertion that Levi himself had been personally initiated into priestly service during his own lifetime. Beyond this, there is also an interest in Levi's offspring and the promise that they will exercise the same priestly role as Levi in the future: this is reiterated three times (*T. Levi* 8:3, 11, and 16).

Apart from the contrast between these two visions with regard to their interests and emphases, it is remarkable that no connection between them is suggested within the dreams themselves. The first vision, were it written in anticipation of the second, might quite naturally have referred to what was to come: "Know, Levi, that you shall soon be purified and initiated into the sacred priesthood." Indeed, at least one of the seven mysterious strangers in the second vision might have specifically identified himself as the angel who had appeared in the previous vision. If not that, then surely the second vision might at least have harked back to the first in some fashion, asserting that now, in keeping with what Levi had been told in heaven, he would indeed be made fit for his divine service and clothed with priestly raiment. But none of this occurs; each of the two visions seems quite unaware of the other's existence. Thus, they are, on the one hand, somewhat redundant in function—in that both independently inform Levi of his future cultic role, and both do so through the intervention of an angel or angels—and, on the other, behind them seem to lie two rather contrasting sets of concerns. What is more, the visions themselves do not present the slightest evidence of coordination between them.

For these reasons, it seems to me worthwhile to explore the possibility at least that these two visions were *not* originally composed to be part of a single document (although both are included side by side not only in the *Testament of Levi* but, apparently, in the *ALD* as well). Instead, it might be that the two were in fact composed independently—each of them a first-person narrative, in which Levi talks about his life—and that each text circulated on its own for a time, only to be joined together at some later point. In this combined form they were preserved by both the *ALD* and the *Testament of Levi*.

Levi Entered Heaven

Let us return to consider both visions from another standpoint, that of biblical exegesis. Although it may not be immediately apparent, the first vision, "Levi's Apocalypse," is, at least roughly speaking, exegetical. That is, the motifs of Levi's ascent into heaven, the divine instruction he receives from an angel, and his consecration to be God's priest and "minister," all derive from a particular biblical passage, albeit one far from the patriarchal narratives of Genesis. The passage comes in the book of Malachi, when the prophet, speaking on behalf of God, rebukes the priests of his own day:

> So shall you [priests] know that I have sent this command to you, that My covenant with Levi may hold, says the Lord of hosts. My covenant with him was a covenant of life and peace, and I gave them to him, that he might fear; and he feared Me; he stood in awe of My name. True instruction was in his mouth, and no wrong was found on his lips. He walked with Me in peace and uprightness,

and he turned many from iniquity. For the lips of a priest should guard knowledge, and men should seek instruction from his mouth, for he is the messenger of the Lord of hosts. (Mal. 2:4–7 [RSV])

This passage was apparently quite significant to ancient interpreters: not only was it, as just mentioned, responsible for many of the details in Levi's first vision in the *Testament of Levi* (and, presumably, in the parallel portions only partially preserved in the *ALD*), but it also left its mark on the book of *Jubilees*.[22] In order to understand the influence of this passage from Malachi, however, a number of crucial points in the Hebrew text translated above will have to be examined closely.

To begin with, the words translated "My covenant with him was a covenant of life and peace" might, according to its syntax, more properly be rendered: "My covenant *was with him*, [a covenant of] life and peace."[23] If so, then this text seems not only to be stating that a "covenant" exists between God and the Levites, but also stressing (via the apparently emphatic "with him") that this covenant was in fact a *personal* one concluded with the individual named Levi. No wonder, then, that *Jubilees*, the *Testament of Levi*, and the *ALD* all insist that Levi himself was elevated to the priesthood (rather than the priesthood simply having been conferred at some later date upon his descendants, as might appear to be the case from such biblical passages as Exod. 32:25–29 and Deut. 10:8). For it made sense that Jacob had granted the hereditary priesthood to Levi at some point just as, at the end of his life, he granted the kingship to Judah and the birthright to Joseph; and the fact that God here seems to speak of a personal covenant with Levi further supported the idea that Levi *the individual* had been granted the priesthood during his lifetime.

Malachi speaks of a "covenant" with Levi. Now, while the Bible contains accounts of divine covenants with various figures, Noah, Abraham, David, and so forth, it says almost nothing outside of this passage concerning a covenant with Levi.[24] This fact would hardly invalidate for ancient interpreters the idea that God had made a covenant with Levi. On the contrary, it would only cause them to scrutinize the surrounding verses in the Malachi passage all the more closely for further details concerning the making of that covenant.

Such details were not hard to find. For the passage continues (translating literally from the Masoretic text) "My covenant was with him, life and peace; and I *gave them to him*; fear, and he feared Me; he stood in awe before My name." At first glance, these words might sound like a general characterization of Levi, a description of his behavior throughout his life, or at least in the period following his "covenant" with God. But perhaps not: perhaps, in particular, the words "and I gave them to him" referred to some specific event, the time when God granted Levi this special covenant and its benefits, life and peace (cf. Num. 25:12). If so, then it was, according to this passage, a momentous happening: Levi was filled with fear, "he feared Me; he stood in awe of My name." "True instruction," the text continues, "was in his mouth"; again, this might mean that *at the time of the making of this covenant* God filled Levi's mouth with true instruction. Might not this whole section, therefore, seem to refer to some kind of great revelation, a particular occasion on which Levi actually entered into God's presence and received divine instruction? Moreover, "he *walked with Me* in peace and uprightness" might, by the same logic, refer to this same incident, a time when Levi actually *walked with* God in heaven.

An Angel Opened the Gates

In short, an interpreter who wished to read it in this fashion might claim that the whole passage in Malachi actually describes a specific event, the making of a covenant between God and

Jacob's third son, Levi. Levi's entrance into this covenant was, by
the passage's own testimony, a visionary happening, in which he
entered into God's presence and was at once filled with awe. And
such a reading of Malachi, it seems clear, must stand behind all
three of the Second Temple texts that we have been examining:
their authors did not *invent* the idea that Jacob's son Levi had
had some sort of divine vision binding him and his descendants
forever to God's service. This idea owes its origin to the passage
in Malachi—if that passage is interpreted more or less along the
lines suggested.

But we can be still more precise in tracing the influence of this
passage. For, it will be recalled, Levi's first vision in both the *Testament of Levi* and the *ALD* speaks specifically of "an angel" and
the "gates of heaven" through which Levi is ushered, and these
details, too, come from Malachi. The last sentence cited above
(again, translated a bit more literally) reads: "For the priest's lips
will keep knowledge, and people shall seek instruction from his
mouth, for he is [or: "it was"] *an angel of the Lord of hosts.*" To
whom could this last phrase be referring? Certainly not to Levi—
he was no angel, but a mere mortal.[25] Ancient interpreters must
therefore have thought it obvious that the angel mentioned here
was indeed a real angel, one who had somehow been involved in
Levi's visionary acceptance of God's covenant. It is for that reason that the *Testament of Levi* (and apparently, though the evidence is somewhat fragmentary, the *ALD* as well) stipulated that
it was an angel who initiated Levi into the secrets of heaven at the
time of his ascent.

But where did our sources get the idea that Levi actually ascended into heaven? No doubt the presence of this angel encouraged such an idea. On the other hand, Noah, Abraham, et al.
received their covenants on earth, and Levi's angel could equally
well have spoken to him down there. Significant, therefore, is the
phrase in Mal. 2:5 "he stood in awe before My name," which in

itself might suggest Levi's removal to some place of the divine presence. But it is further to be noted that the consonantal text here, ומפני שמי נחת הוא is somewhat problematic: the first two words, "from before [or: "from in front of"] My name," present a puzzling combination of a spatial preposition and the nonphysical "name." The next word, נחת, looks like the common root in Hebrew and Aramaic meaning "go down, descend." It seems plausible that an interpreter might therefore understand the text to be saying, "he went down from before [the place of] my name," that is, heaven, implying that Levi had earlier ascended to heaven, where he entered with dread and awe into a covenant with God, and then went back down to earth.[26] Indeed, it is even possible to vocalize the second word in this sequence not as "My name" at all but "My heavens," a reading that would even more strongly suggest that Levi had taken a heavenly voyage.

ECHOES OF MALACHI

I am aware of two other texts that may ultimately be based on a similar reading of this passage in Malachi. The first text is the first-century C.E. Greek romance *Joseph and Aseneth*, which at one point observes about Levi:

> And Aseneth loved Levi exceedingly beyond all of Joseph's brethren, because he was one who attached himself to the Lord and he was a prudent man and a prophet of the Most High and sharp-sighted with his eyes, and he used to see letters written in heaven by the finger of God and he knew the unspeakable [mysteries] of the Most High God. (*Jos. Asen.* 22:13)

That Levi "attached himself to the Lord" is patently an etymology of his name based on the verb לוה, "join, be joined" (the same etymology appears in *Jub.* 30:16; cf. Gen. 29:34). However, the idea that Levi was a "prophet" is nowhere adumbrated in Genesis. Instead, *Joseph and Aseneth* may here reflect an exegetical tradition that developed out of Malachi's mention of Levi's divine covenant with God, and perhaps in particular the words "True instruction (תורת אמת) was in his mouth, and no wrong was found on his lips" (Mal. 2:6). Especially given the understanding (common in Second Temple texts) of תורה as referring to *divine* teaching, this verse would seem to imply that Levi was indeed a true bearer of the divine word, that is, a prophet (a description that recurs in *Jos. Asen.* 23:8 and 26:6). Similarly, Levi's knowing the "unspeakable [mysteries] of the Most High" seems to reflect Mal. 2:7, "the priest's lips will *keep* knowledge"—that is, he will keep this knowledge to himself, keep it secret, because it is "unspeakable."[27] Thus, *Joseph and Aseneth* here seems to reflect a tradition, rooted in Malachi, that presented Levi as the bearer of esoteric knowledge, just as in the first vision, which I have labeled "Levi's Apocalypse." Indeed, *Joseph and Aseneth* may have inherited this notion not directly from Malachi but through the agency of some other text, the *ALD* or even (if I am right) an ancestor text that it incorporated, "Levi's Apocalypse."

The second text is from *Pirqei deR. Eli'ezer*, in the continuation of the passage cited earlier:

The angel Michael descended and took Levi and carried him up to God. [Michael] said to God: "Lord of the world, this one is Your allotted portion from among those that You have created." And He extended His right hand and blessed him, that the sons of Levi might serve Him on earth as the ministering angels in heaven. Said Michael to God: "Lord of the world, those who serve a king, does he not give them food to eat?" For that reason, He gave to the sons of Levi all the holy things that were His, as it says, "They shall eat the offerings by fire to the Lord as their portion" [Deut. 18:1]. (*Pirqei deR. Eli'ezer* 37)

Here, quite explicitly, an angel carries Levi to heaven, where he is granted a special role in the divine service—just as in the vision I have labeled "Levi's Apocalypse." It is likely that this text sounds like "Levi's Apocalypse" because it is in fact based upon it (either in its *ALD* incarnation or in some earlier form).[28]

Seven "Men" Anoint Levi

In contrast to "Levi's Apocalypse," the second vision—found in full in the *Testament of Levi* and in fragmentary form in the *ALD*—does not have any apparent interest in biblical exegesis per se. It shows no awareness of the Malachi passage and makes no further allusion to any of the things recounted there. Although Levi is once again to be informed of his special role by angelic beings, this text even fails to use the word "angel" (מלאך) found in Malachi; instead, it speaks of seven "men" in white robes. If the author of this text had had the slightest wish to anchor its words in the Bible, would there not be some allusion to this crucial passage in Malachi—the only passage in the Bible that even remotely suggests that Levi had indeed been granted some personal covenant with God, presumably, a covenant of the very priesthood that is such a central concern for the author of this second vision? But apparently this author has no need of such a biblical anchor. He seems simply to have inherited the idea that Levi had some sort of angelic encounter and then went about describing it in his own terms: Levi encountered the seven white-robed "men," each of whom then performed a different step in Levi's priestly initiation. By doing this, the author apparently sought to communicate to the reader in the most vivid way the idea that Levi himself had become a priest, having been duly invested and anointed by no less than seven divine emissaries.

HISTORICAL RELATIONS

My main concern until now has been biblical exegesis—tracing the biblical roots of such motifs as "Levi the Human Tithe," "A Chain of Priests," "Levi Enters Heaven," and so forth. But having also raised the possibility that Levi's two visions in the *ALD* derive from two originally separate *texts* that circulated independently for a time, texts that were first combined by the author of the *ALD*, I find myself obliged now to address the larger question of the historical relationship of the various texts and motifs discussed above.

As already mentioned, the *ALD* exists in several Qumran fragments. The science of paleography is quite well developed with regard to the Qumran scrolls, so that scholars can now establish with some confidence the period in which a given manuscript was written (if not necessarily when the text itself was composed) within a range of a few decades.[29] Of course, the Cairo Geniza fragments can be of little use in dating the *ALD*, since they are all medieval copies of this ancient text. Rather, it is the Qumran fragments that can help, since dating these manuscripts may give us some idea of the date by which the *ALD* must have already been composed.

In their survey of the Qumran manuscripts, scholars have observed a range of different hands characteristic of different periods. The earliest of these may be said to be a typical Hasmonean script, dated by F. M. Cross to ca. 125–100 B.C.E. (Other Qumran manuscripts of the *ALD* have been identified as late Hasmonean or early Herodian, that is, from about 50–1 B.C.E.) If the earliest of the Qumran manuscripts is not an autograph—that is, the original composition as penned by the author himself—then the actual composing of the *ALD* must go back to before 125–100 B.C.E. Oddly, however, estimates of the *ALD*'s actual date of composition tend to place it well before 125 B.C.E. Several scholars have even suggested that it goes back to the third century B.C.E.[30]

RELATIONSHIP TO *JUBILEES*

One crucial factor in dating the *ALD* is its relation to the book of *Jubilees*. The reason has already been seen: the two compositions share an account of how Levi, Jacob's third son, was elevated to the priesthood during his own lifetime. There is nothing in the book of Genesis itself to suggest such a turn of events. *Jubilees* and the *ALD* not only share this theme but also agree with each other on quite a few non-biblical details surrounding it, as we have seen: the visit to Isaac, Levi's vision at Bethel, and so forth. All this would seem to indicate either that one text borrowed from the other or that they shared a common source. If it can be established that the *ALD* borrowed from *Jubilees*, or if the opposite can be proven, and if the date of *Jubilees*' composition is more or less agreed upon, then dating the *ALD* may become significantly easier.

Most scholars date *Jubilees* to some point in the second century B.C.E. It would be difficult to date *Jubilees* any later than that, since part of one Qumran manuscript of *Jubilees*, 4Q216, columns 6–7 (and presumably the rest of this scroll, now lost), was written in a script dated palaeographically to the period 125–100 B.C.E.[31] (Indeed, James VanderKam, in his publication of this text, observed that his colleague Josef Milik—a gifted manuscript scholar— "prefers to date the script nearer to the mid-second century B.C.E.")[32] Thus, if this manuscript is not an autograph, the composition of *Jubilees* can scarcely be dated any later than 125 B.C.E.

It is certainly significant that the dating of this earliest *Jubilees* manuscript matches that of the earliest manuscript of the *ALD* (or is even earlier, according to Milik's dating). This means that, from the standpoint of palaeography, there is no reason to suppose that the composition of the *ALD* is any earlier than that of *Jubilees*—the opposite might just as easily be true. Yet many studies simply seem to assume that the *ALD* is the older of the two works.[33]

There are good reasons to doubt this assumption, starting with the very nature of the *ALD*. As we have seen, its central message concerns the exaltation of Levi and his descendants. According to the *ALD*, Levi is a pious and even prophetic figure, a person beloved by God and the recipient of two divine visions. "We have magnified you *over everyone*," an angelic speaker says to him at the conclusion of the second. In addition to being installed as a priest, Levi is also portrayed as a sage and champion of wisdom. Indeed, he says to his children that they will be "chiefs and judges and . . . [. . .] and servants [. . .] even priests and *kings* . . . your *kingdom* will be [. . .] and will have no end f[orever . . . and] will [not] depart from you until all . . ." (4Q213, frag. 2, 10–18).[34]

Presumably, a positive portrayal of Levi might have been composed at any time. But there is one element in the presentation of Levi that points to a particular moment in history. As just seen, this text claims that future kings will originate from among the descendants of Levi. Another fragment of the *ALD*, 1Q21, likewise says of Levi "and you will be king with . . ." (frag. 7, col. 1) and speaks of the "kingship of the priesthood" (frag. 1, col. 1). It seems most unlikely that such things could have been written about Levi before the rise of the Hasmonean dynasty in the second half of the second century B.C.E. Until then, kingship had always been considered the prerogative of the tribe of Judah, not only because the house of David, hereditary kings since the tenth century B.C.E, had come from that tribe, but because sacred Scripture itself had said that the staff of kingship "will not depart from Judah for all time" (Gen. 49:10).[35] How dare any other tribe usurp that right? However, after the revolt of the Maccabees and the solidification of Hasmonean power in the temporal as well as spiritual spheres, the Hasmoneans—descendants of Levi—sought to have themselves recognized as the legitimate kings as well as priests. As just mentioned, this went against what Scripture itself seemed to be saying. Therefore, an "ancient" document in which Levi is told explicitly that his descendants have been chosen to exercise just about every form of leadership in the future—to be both priests and kings, as well as judges and teachers and the bearers of wisdom—would be very convenient for these Hasmonean rulers to have. If so, it would appear that the *ALD*, at least as we know it from the present text, probably does not go back any earlier than the second half of the second century B.C.E.

The situation with *Jubilees* is somewhat different. One might begin with the relationship between this book and the Qumran community. As is well known, *Jubilees* was apparently quite popular at Qumran; the library found there included some fifteen separate copies of the book. At the same time, most scholars agree that *Jubilees* is not itself a product of the Qumran community. There is nothing in *Jubilees* to suggest its author was aware of this community's existence or even of any predecessor movement (if there was one) that might have led up to the community's creation. As far as *Jubilees* is concerned, there are no internal divisions within the Jewish world such as those reflected at Qumran, only the great divide that separates Jews from non-Jews. Moreover, there are doctrinal differences that separate *Jubilees* from the Qumran writings.[36] Of course, that does not mean that these differences stem from a *chronological* gap; the author of *Jubilees* may have been a contemporary of the Qumran community founders who simply disagreed with them on these fundamentals. This hypothesis seems unlikely, however, precisely because of the book's apparent popularity at Qumran; such respectful treatment is not likely to have been accorded to a captious rival or a rejected suitor of Qumran's founders, but rather to a revered predecessor with whom they agreed on many, if not all, major points.

Chronological precedence is suggested by yet other particulars, some of which argue for locating *Jubilees* even earlier in the second century B.C.E.[37] Thus, there is no hint in *Jubilees* that its author was aware of the revolt of the Maccabees or of the events in the reign of Antiochus IV that preceded it, starting around 175 B.C.E. The author intones against such Hellenistic practice as public nudity (3:31) but apparently knows nothing of the Seleucid infringement on traditional Jewish worship and other practices that preceded the Maccabean revolt. The author's battle against Hellenism and his ardent xenophobia might just as convincingly be dated to the third century as to the second. Diodorus Siculus cites Hecataeus of Abdera, ca. 300 B.C.E, as referring to the Jews' "antisocial and foreigner-hating way of life";[38] he could have been describing the grandfather or great-grandfather of *Jubilees*' author. In the light of all this, there really seems little reason *not* to date the composition of *Jubilees* to the years immediately preceding 175 B.C.E., if not still earlier.

Beyond such historical considerations, the literary relationship of the common material found in *Jubilees* and the *ALD* clearly suggests that the latter borrowed from the former, not vice versa. To mention but the most obvious case in the material already considered,[39] both *Jubilees* and the *ALD* refer to a certain journey undertaken by Jacob to visit his father Isaac. This journey is nowhere mentioned in the Bible. In the *ALD*, it is narrated in a single sentence: "And we went up to my father Isaac, and he too blessed me thus." In *Jubilees*, by contrast, this non-biblical journey is an important element, treated at length, since it fulfills a definite exegetical purpose. As we have seen, it explains why Jacob, when he first arrived at Bethel (Gen. 28:10–22), could not offer a sacrifice to God (he could not, according to *Jubilees*, because he was not a priest; his father Isaac, who was a priest, had not yet designated his successor), and why, by contrast, on his return to Bethel years later, Jacob *could* make such an offering (in the meantime he had made this non-biblical journey to Isaac, and there Isaac had designated Jacob's son Levi for the priesthood). All this is set forth in *Jubilees*, and the non-biblical journey is even given a clever biblical justification, the fact that Genesis mentions that Deborah, Rebekah's handmaiden, was buried at Bethel.

It seems most unlikely that the author of *Jubilees* could have read the one-sentence description of a non-biblical journey in the *ALD*, realized its exegetical possibilities, thought up the biblical proof that such a journey had in fact taken place, and then narrated the whole episode at length. It is far more probable that the author of the *ALD* was familiar with the longer account in *Jubilees*—complete with its biblical proof that such a journey happened—but, precisely because the whole matter had already been treated at length in *Jubilees* (indeed, perhaps because that book was already well known), he felt no need to provide the biblical proof and so simply summarized it in a single sentence. Of course, one might counter this argument by supposing that *Jubilees* and the *ALD* had both borrowed from a common source, now lost. Given the relentlessly exegetical character of the book of *Jubilees*, however, and the great attention this book devotes specifically to the subject of Jacob's doings at Bethel, it seems more likely that *Jubilees*' author himself is the proud originator of this clever bit of exegesis and the narrative that goes with it. To be sure, many ancient Jewish texts contain or allude to exegetical motifs;[40] *Jubilees* is almost unique, however, in its careful attention to interpretive problems in biblical narrative and, often, in its highly innovative solutions. This is precisely what one finds in the *Jubilees* account of Jacob at Bethel. It is difficult to believe that the author of *Jubilees* could have acquired this altogether characteristic bit of exegesis from some other source, especially since this motif of the non-biblical journey and its connection to Deborah's death is unattested outside of *Jubilees*.

This same common source, incidentally, would presumably have had the same interest in dating undated biblical events and supplying names to unnamed characters that is so characteristic of the book of *Jubilees,* since one finds evidence of these as well in the *ALD.*[41] It would also have used the same chronological system of dividing history into seven-year units ("weeks of years") that is used consistently throughout the book of *Jubilees,* since the *ALD* also evokes this system in one passage dealing with chronology (*ALD* 62). Finally, any common source of Levi traditions on which the *ALD* drew would seem to have been written in Hebrew[42] (see below)—coincidentally, just like the book of *Jubilees,* but unlike the other early apocalypses and retellings of biblical narrative known to us from Qumran. All this strains credulity. To put the matter squarely: the simplest explanation for each of the items mentioned is that the *ALD* did, in fact, borrow directly from *Jubilees.*

When these arguments are considered fairly, there appears to be no sound reason to date the *ALD* to the third century B.C.E, as some scholars have done. What, after all, is the most reasonable construal of the evidence? The palaeographic data do not suggest a date for the *ALD* any earlier than the last quarter of the second century B.C.E. The assertion that the Levites will be kings certainly seems to point to a Hasmonean dating for this text, that is, sometime after the middle of the second century B.C.E, whereas *Jubilees,* with its apparent chronological distance from the Qumran community and its apparent ignorance of the Maccabean revolt or the events that led up to it, seems to belong sometime earlier than midcentury (conservatively speaking). The literary evidence, as we have just seen, also points to *Jubilees* having preceded, and been used by, the *ALD,* not the other way around. There is nothing in the *ALD* itself to counter this evidence. In the face of these fairly straightforward considerations, it is difficult to understand how a reasonable person might end up reversing the order and claiming the *ALD* came first. If *Jubilees* was composed, in the common opinion, sometime in the second century, it would thus appear quite impossible to date the *ALD* to the third.

A Composite Work

However, our discussion thus far has also revealed a number of redundancies and inconsistencies in the *ALD*. Its author may have borrowed some things from *Jubilees*, but this fact alone will not account for all the overkill as well as the out-and-out contradictions that exist in the text. The *ALD* must have had others sources as well.

Some of the evidence for this has already been presented. The *ALD* reports two angelic visions, whereas Mal. 2:4–7—the biblical source that suggested such a vision in the first place—speaks of only one. Why, if it were starting from scratch, would the *ALD* have created two visions, thus undermining its own biblical legitimation? In this second vision, Levi is initiated into the priesthood by the seven "men" (*ALD* 4:11–12), but even this is apparently insufficient, since afterward Jacob "consecrated me and I became a priest of the God of eternity" (*ALD* 5:4). (If so, then what exactly had the seven men done?) In all, Levi is informed in four different ways that he has been chosen for the priesthood. While no single one of these redundancies rules out entirely the possibility that the *ALD*'s author was creating everything ex nihilo—authors do sometimes contradict themselves or repeat—when one considers all of them together, that possibility seems quite unlikely. The simplest explanation for them is that the *ALD*'s author was in fact reworking (and trying to reconcile) earlier source material—source material that included more than just the book of *Jubilees*.

Indeed, some of this same source material appears to have been known to *Jubilees*' author himself: we have seen that, at one point, *Jubilees* alludes to a dream-vision of Levi (32:1). The mention of

this dream does nothing to advance the action or explain anything in *Jubilees*; in fact, it too is redundant. It seems as if the author of *Jubilees* here was simply paying lip service to an existing
text or tradition—saying to his readers, "Yes, I know that you
have all heard of Levi having had some dream-vision about becoming a priest. This is when that dream-vision occurred."

   To this list one might add a few things not discussed above. For
example, many scholars have remarked on the fact that, toward
the end of the *ALD*, Levi finishes narrating the history of his own
life, even mentioning his own death at age 137 (*ALD* 12:9)—but
then he immediately turns to recounting how he summoned his
children at age 118 in order to give them what sounds very much
like his last words (*ALD* 13:1). Why should he begin passing on to
his children the lessons he had learned in life fully nineteen years
before his life is over—in the process, breaking ranks with every
other aged father in the Bible as well as in the biblical apocrypha
and pseudepigrapha? The biblical convention, it hardly needs saying, is that the time just before death is a privileged moment, a
time when a person attains to his greatest wisdom and even gains
a glimpse of what will happen in the future; see, for example, Gen.
49:1–2; Deut. 31:28–29, 33:1–25; 2 Sam. 23:1–7. Certainly *that* is
the appropriate time for passing on one's wisdom. The *ALD's*
awkward apposition of ages likewise appears to be the unhappy
result of its author trying to combine different sources that had
contained different dates.[43] In this same historical section, Levi
mentions that he was twenty-eight when he was married (*ALD*
12:7; Cambridge d, lines 19–20). But why should he bother to tell
us this when he already stated at the start of this historical section
that he married at the age of twenty-eight (*ALD* 11:1)?

   One scholar has pertinently observed another logical inconsistency in the *ALD*.[44] As we have seen, careful exegesis of Genesis
35 allowed the author of *Jubilees* to conclude that Jacob and
Levi had made a quick side-trip to visit Isaac before offering the

sacrifices at Bethel. This trip is summarized in a single sentence in
the *ALD*. But then the text goes on to describe a second visit to
Isaac, the occasion on which Isaac instructs Levi in the priesthood. The two trips are actually presented almost side by side:

> And we went to my father Isaac, and he too [blessed] me thus.
> Then, when **[my father] Jacob tithed** . . . everything which he pos-
> sessed in accordance with his vow (. . .) I was first at the head of the
> (. . .) **and to me of all his sons he gave** a sacrifice of (. . .) to God,
> and he invested me in the priestly garb and he consecrated me and I
> became a priest of the **God of eternity**. And I offered all of his sacri-
> fices and I blessed my father that he might live; and I blessed my
> brothers. Then all of them blessed me, and my father blessed me as
> well, and I finished offering his sacrifices at Bethel. Then we went
> from Bethel and stayed at the residence of Abraham our father,
> along with Isaac our father. And Isaac our father [saw] all of us and
> blessed us and rejoiced. When he learned that I was priest of the
> Most High God, the Lord of heaven, he began to instruct me and to
> teach me the law of the priesthood. (*ALD* 5:1–8 [4Q213b in bold-
> face, with surrounding text restored from Bodleian a and b:])

The trip mentioned in the first words cited is, as noted, the one-
line summary of the non-biblical visit narrated in *Jubilees*. The trip
four sentences later ("Then we went from Bethel . . ."), by contrast,
is a journey actually mentioned in Genesis. It takes place after the
events at Bethel: "And Jacob went to his father Isaac at Mamre,
Kiriath-arba (which is) Hebron, where Abraham and Isaac dwelt.
Isaac was one hundred and eighty years old when he breathed his
last and died, and he was gathered to his kin in a ripe old age and
was buried by his sons Esau and Jacob" (Gen. 35:27–28).

The puzzling thing is that in the *ALD*, it is only during this second visit that Isaac begins to instruct Levi in the ways of the
priesthood. This is counterintuitive: certainly Isaac should have

instructed Levi about the priesthood during the first visit, so that Levi could know what to do when he returned with Jacob to Bethel to offer Jacob's sacrifices there. Here too, it would seem, the *ALD* was not composing its text from scratch but was reworking earlier sources. One of these was *Jubilees*, which had cleverly created the first (non-biblical) visit to Isaac. But the source from which the *ALD* copied Isaac's priestly instructions was earlier than *Jubilees* and so knew nothing of such a visit; it knew only the biblical visit mentioned in Gen. 35:27–28, so that is where it—and, as a result, the *ALD*—located the priestly instructions.

Sometimes the *ALD* even shows an awareness of its own internal contradictions. We have seen, for example, that after his second vision Levi relates:

And those seven departed from me and **I awoke from my sleep. Then** I said: "This is a vision, and thus I am amazed that I should have any vision at all." And **I hid this too in my heart and** I revealed it **to no one.** (4Q213b in boldface, with surrounding text restored from Bodleian a, lines 9–13)

To put it in a more contemporary idiom, Levi wakes up and says, "Wow! *Two* visions! Why should I even have had one?" One could hardly ask for a clearer indication of the author's self-consciousness at including two visions when even one was not required for Levi to learn that he was to be a priest (all he needed was to be told by Isaac, which occurs in the very next sentence!).

To sum up so far: The *ALD* was written sometime in the latter half of the second century B.C.E. It was not, however, an ex nihilo creation; the many redundancies and internal contradictions indicate that its author was combining material from different sources. One of these sources was the book of *Jubilees*, which was probably composed in the first quarter of the second century B.C.E. It is obvious that the *ALD* borrowed from *Jubilees* the non-biblical visit to Isaac as well as a number of lesser details. Beyond this, however, there are indications of one or more earlier texts about Levi on which the *ALD* relied, and from which derives, in fact, most of the overkill observed thus far.

A number scholars, studying carefully the *ALD* fragments, have come to a similar conclusion, hypothesizing the existence of an earlier source, an ancient "Levi apocryphon" on which the *ALD* would have drawn.[45] The purpose and contents of this apocryphon remain cloudy, however; it has been invoked without any actual specification of its contents. Indeed, among those who wish to maintain that the *ALD preceded Jubilees*, this apocryphon has served as a convenient grab-bag of Levi traditions, so that whenever the *ALD* seems to be dependent on *Jubilees*, this hypothetical text can be alleged to have served as a common source for both.

In truth, however, this "apocryphon" is just a will-o'-the-wisp, the ad hoc creation of a few puzzled scholars. The *ALD*'s real sources need not be hypothesized. They are right there in the text for all to see, since the *ALD* is essentially a composite of two first-person Levi narratives, each of which had recounted a vision of Levi's. The first text was essentially a wisdom apocalypse derived from the exegetical elaboration of Mal. 2:4–7; the second— apparently taking from this same passage in Malachi (or from the wisdom apocalypse that was based on it) the idea that Levi had had some sort of interaction with an angel—described Levi's actual initiation by angels into the priesthood. The presence of these two contrasting visions side by side in the *ALD* is the very key to understanding the composite nature of this work and then to breaking it down into its original components.

How the *ALD* Came to Be

Sometime in the latter part of the second century, at the height of Hasmonean power, a writer was commissioned to assemble the extant Levi material and to combine it all into one great Book of

Levi, one that would not only sing the Levites' praises and fitness to rule but would also specifically "grandfather" the Levites' right to be kings back to the time of Levi himself. (Those who are skeptical about originally independent texts being stitched together by an editor on the basis of their common focus on a central figure might look no further than the example of Enoch in the biblical pseudepigrapha, or to the well known examples of such stitching found within the biblical canon itself.)

Accordingly, this writer turned first to an ancient text about Levi that had been around for some time. Its starting point was a biblical passage, Mal. 2:4–7, whose cryptic words this ancient text's anonymous author interpreted as referring to some heavenly journey undertaken by Levi. On this basis, he felt entitled to praise Levi as a visionary and sage, and to put in his mouth predictions of the brilliant future of his descendants, of the sort now found in the *ALD* (4Q213, fragments 1, 2, and 4 and the parallel Geniza fragments, as well as 4Q213a, fragments 1 and 2, completed by the parallel Greek text). This document had no particular interest in the priesthood, but it did apparently suggest that, during his heavenly journey, Levi himself was appointed a priest and the ancestor of all future priests in Israel, since the crucial Malachi passage did seem to refer to Levi himself as a priest (Mal. 2:7). (Moreover, if Levi had entered heaven and had been privileged to glimpse the future of his descendants, such an assertion virtually imposed itself. After all, the fact that Levi's descendants would end up inheriting the priesthood was the most obvious thing for Levi to "foresee" about them!) The main focus of this document, however, was Levi's status as an ancient heavenly traveler, so in keeping with the wisdom-imbued character of other Second Temple apocalypses, it is Levi the Sage, not Levi the Priest, who receives primary emphasis.[46]

Such an ancient text, with its praise of Levi's wisdom and prediction of the destined greatness of his descendants, might have been composed at almost any time in the postexilic period, when some temporal as well as religious authority (though not, to be sure, kingship) lay with the Temple priesthood, said to be composed of Levi's priestly offspring. The fact that these priests were priests hardly required affirmation; what this text had sought to assert was that they were also wise and ought to be listened to, deriving their mandate for leadership directly from God, as Mal. 2:4–7 attested. Whenever this text had originally been composed, it certainly must have found favor with the Hasmoneans after their rise to power. Its only fault was the absence of specific reference to kingship among the list of great things destined for Levi's descendants. But our Hasmonean-period writer could easily rectify that; several mentions of future Levite kings and the Levite claim to kingship were therefore simply written into its predictions.

This was not the only Levi material extant, however. A second text had presented a different first-person narrative of Levi's, one in which he relates how he was initiated into the priesthood by seven angelic figures (*ALD* 4:11–12). This second text had gone on to narrate Levi's receipt of detailed instructions from his grandfather Isaac about the offering of sacrifices (*ALD* 5:6–10:10)—chief among them the non-Pentateuchal provision of "covering the blood" of sacrificial animals (*ALD* 10:9).[47] Such a grandfatherly briefing was very important to the author of this second text, and altogether plausible; after all, Isaac was certainly still alive when Levi was an adult, and Genesis did report a certain journey of Jacob and his family to visit Isaac before his death (Gen. 35:27–28). Having Isaac transmit sacrificial procedures to Levi on that occasion—procedures that, Isaac repeatedly stresses, he learned from "my father Abraham" (*ALD* 7:4; 10:3, 10), who in turn learned some of them from the Book of Noah (*ALD* 10:10)—was to give these priestly details an unbeatable pedigree. They must be exactly what God had always wanted priests to do, and if they were not found in the Pentateuch, well, that was because such things had been transmitted orally from far earlier times—indeed, transmitted from the time of Levi onward via this very document. It goes without saying that the great theme of this second, ancient Levi text was the priesthood itself, the same element that is largely neglected in the Levi apocalypse just described.

These two ancient Levi texts were inherited by our Hasmonean writer and incorporated into the *ALD*. One could, of course, imagine that he had inherited only one of them, the ancient account of Levi's heavenly ascent based on Mal. 2:4–7, and that he was himself responsible for inventing the second vision, but that seems unlikely, as already explained. What would be the point of introducing a whole new angelic vision instead of simply interpolating new material into the already existing one? After all, Mal. 2:4–7 speaks of only one angelic vision. Since the author of the first vision seems to have tried hard to use this passage to provide his own words with some biblical legitimacy, why should the Hasmonean writer then go on to undermine this hard-won legitimacy by creating a second angelic vision with no biblical basis, instead of simply inserting everything he wanted to say into the first vision? Moreover, why should this same Hasmonean writer, whose text clearly refers to two visits to Isaac, not have stuck the priestly instructions (which, by this theory, he himself must have authored) into the first visit rather than the second? These, along with the other arguments adduced, make it clear that there was indeed such a second, separate text about Levi—a vision report that may have been intended (as Milik suggested) to be part 1 of a priestly trilogy, followed by the *Testament of Kohath* (4Q542) and the *Visions of Amram* (4Q543–548). Combining the ancient Levi apocalypse with this other first-person Levi text, the Hasmonean editor then fitted the two into a particular historical framework, the account of Jacob's doings at Bethel as found in the highly scholarly book of *Jubilees*.[48] In the process, however, he created the duplications and inconsistencies that have been pointed out by various scholars[49] as well as herein.

Once Again, Two Journeys

Since I have already remarked upon the two journeys to visit Isaac, I would like here to explain how I think they came about. As we have seen, one of the *ALD*'s sources (the one I have called "Levi's Priestly Initiation") sought to "grandfather" its particular rules of sacrifice back to Levi and through him back to Levi's grandfather Isaac—indeed, back to what Isaac had seen his father Abraham do as a priest. For this purpose Levi needed to be instructed personally by Isaac; the only possible encounter between the two, as far as this author knew, came about just before Isaac's death, when Jacob and his family had journeyed to be at his side (Gen. 35:27–28). That is why he located the priestly instruction there.[50]

At some later point, the author of *Jubilees* composed his book. He was not particularly interested in Levi, but he was troubled by the strange sequence of events at Bethel: Jacob has his vision of a ladder there in Genesis 28, then makes a vow to tithe his possessions to God, but offers no sacrifices at the time; instead, he simply sets up a stone pillar on the site. *Jubilees* accounts for this by means of the events he narrates after Jacob's return to Bethel some years later. If Jacob had not offered sacrifices the first time, *Jubilees* explains, it was because he had no right to: he had never been designated as a priest and did not have the faintest idea of what to do. For the same reason, after returning to Bethel, Jacob makes an immediate side-trip to visit Isaac in order to have Isaac accompany him back to Bethel; Isaac *is* a priest, so he ought to be the one to help Jacob now fulfill his vow. But Isaac says he is too old to travel; instead, he blesses Levi and in the process designates him as his priestly successor. Jacob then returns with Levi to Bethel, where Levi functions as a priest.

None of this was particularly connected to that other text, "Levi's Priestly Initiation"; *Jubilees* was concerned mainly with exegesis—in this case, with explaining Jacob's puzzling behavior at Bethel. But the author of *Jubilees* was certainly familiar with "Levi's Priestly Initiation" (he refers to it in passing in *Jub.* 32:1), and reading over this text, he asked himself a good question: what sense does it make to have Levi instructed about sacrificing *after* he has already offered the sacrifices at Bethel? The author of *Jubilees* could therefore have decided to transfer Isaac's instructions to the occasion of Levi's first visit to Isaac, which took place before the sacrifices. But in typically bold fashion, *Jubilees'* author went one step further: he transferred the priestly instructions back to Abraham's last words to Isaac (*Jubilees* 21). After all, if "Levi's Priestly Initiation" kept having Isaac refer to what he saw Abraham do as a priest, why not simply put the priestly instructions in the mouth of Abraham directly? And so he did.

We return, then, to the Hasmonean-period writer commissioned to put together the great Levi book. As mentioned, he started with his two ancient Levi texts. He incorporated the first, the "Levi Apocalypse," as a dream vision that Levi has in Abel Mayin. Levi prays a pious prayer, is ushered into heaven, sees the future (including the fact—not found in the original apocalypse—that Levi's descendants will be kings), and is told to take revenge on the Shechemites, which he does. This Hasmonean author then incorporated a second vision, the one narrated in "Levi's Priestly Initiation"; Levi is made a priest by seven angelic figures. But there was still more material about Levi in another, highly scholarly and authoritative book, *Jubilees*. The Hasmonean writer therefore included in his new text a brief, one-sentence reference to the *Jubilees* narration of a non-biblical journey to Isaac, followed by its account of Levi offering sacrifices at Bethel. The Hasmonean writer could not, however, follow *Jubilees* in placing the priestly instructions directly in the mouth of Abraham. After all, Abraham does not speak in this text; its first-person narrator is Levi—and how could Levi narrate Abraham's last words to Isaac (which were uttered long before Levi's birth)? The Hasmonean writer therefore left them as they were in "Levi's Priestly Initiation": Isaac instructs Levi after they meet in the biblical journey of Gen. 35:27–28. Thus was created the *ALD*, a great, but somewhat self-contradictory, Levi book assembled at the height of Hasmonean power in the last third of the second century B.C.E.

Chapter Six

JUDAH AND THE TRIAL OF TAMAR

udah is certainly a positive figure in the Bible, the one who offers himself in place of his younger brother Benjamin in the story of Joseph (Gen. 44:33) and the son to whom, as we have seen, Jacob in his dying words grants the hereditary kingship in Israel (Gen. 49:10). Yet, according to chapter 38 of Genesis, Judah's personal life was not exactly above reproach. He married a Canaanite woman, the daughter of Shua—clearly an unacceptable choice for a descendant of Abraham, Isaac, and Jacob (see Gen. 24:4, 27:46–28:1). Later, when their son Er was ready to marry, Judah arranged a bride for him, Tamar, but then Er died. Judah promised Tamar that she could be the bride of one of his other sons, but, after his second son died as well, Judah delayed and delayed while Tamar waited on the sidelines, unmarried. Finally, the daughter-in-law decided to take things into her own hands. She dressed up as a prostitute, her face heavily veiled, and sat at the entrance to Eynayim, where her father-in-law was to pass by. Sure enough, when Judah saw her, he availed himself of her services, leaving behind three personal items—his signet, cord, and staff—as security until he could bring her proper payment. As soon as he had gone, however, Tamar pocketed these personal items and disappeared. Three months later, Tamar began to show the first signs of pregnancy; her father-in-law, outraged at this evidence of indiscretion, said she ought to be killed. Tamar then produced the signet, cord, and staff and said: "The one to whom these belong is the man who made me pregnant." Judah shamefacedly recognized them as his, and her life was spared. She gave birth to twins, the immediate ancestors of the tribe of Judah.

It goes without saying that such a story cried out for interpretation.[1] How could Judah have married a Canaanite in the first place? And what was the point of recounting this whole, sordid incident of a man sleeping with his daughter-in-law? It was bad enough that such a thing had happened, but what was served by reporting it in scripture, indeed, by narrating the event in detail? Particularly ironic were Judah's words on discovering that he is the father; when Tamar produces the incriminating personal items, he says, "She is more righteous than me." But in fact neither of them seems particularly righteous—not Tamar, who tricked her father-in-law into sleeping with her, nor Judah, who married a Canaanite, prevented Tamar from remarrying, and had relations with a woman he believed to be a prostitute.

"She Wins: I'm the Father"

One interpretive motif seems to have had as its point of departure precisely the problematic sentence just mentioned. The assertion "She is more righteous than me" can be broken down in Hebrew into two separate components, literally: "She is righteous. From me." Doing so at least mitigated the obvious absence of righteousness in any of the main figures. For, when the sentence is divided in two, the first half of it can be understood in a judicial sense, "She is right" or "She wins," while the second might seem to answer the question just asked by Tamar, "To whom do these [personal items] belong?" (Gen. 38:25)—or perhaps another, related question, "By whom is Tamar pregnant?"

This motif is embodied, inter alia, in the Aramaic translation of Onqelos for the verse in question:

> And Judah recognized them and said, "She is right. She is pregnant *from me*, on account of the fact that I did not give her to my son Shelah." (*Targum Onqelos* Gen. 38:26)

Similarly:

> And Judah recognized [that is, admitted it] and said, "My daughter-
> in-law Tamar *is innocent*, inasmuch as I did not take her for my son
> Shelah" (*Targum Neophyti* Gen. 38:26)

A Court Proceeding

Underlying these translations is a prior assumption, namely, that
Judah spoke these words as part of some sort of judicial proceed-
ing, one that concluded in finding Tamar innocent. The assumption was natural enough: when Judah had learned that Tamar
was pregnant, he said, "Take her out and let her be burned"
(Gen. 38:24). Surely, ancient interpreters reasoned, these words
did not refer to some kind of vigilante justice: Judah must have
been referring to a sentence to be passed by a proper court of
law—indeed, he may have been one of the presiding judges:

> R. Jeremiah in the name of R. Samuel b. R. Isaac [said]: In three
> places God appeared [in court]: in the courtroom of Shem, in the
> courtroom of Samuel, and in the courtroom of Solomon. In the
> courtroom of Shem [as it says], "And Judah acknowledged and
> said, 'She is right. From me.'" R. Jeremiah in the name of
> R. Samuel b. R. Isaac [said]: God said to them, "You testify about
> what happened in public and I will testify about what happened in
> private." (*Genesis Rabba* 85:11 [Oxford MS 147])

> Shem, Isaac, Jacob, and Judah presided in the court. They said,
> "Take her out and burn her" (Gen. 38:24). (*Midrash Tanḥuma*, ed.
> Buber, 1:187)

THE *TESTAMENT OF JUDAH*

Long before the rabbinic sources cited above were committed to
writing, some of the same midrashic ideas found their way into
Jewish writings of the closing centuries B.C.E. and the first two

centuries of the common era. For example, there may be a hint of the judicial setting for Judah's words as early as the book of *Jubilees*:

> For in all sincerity he [Judah] had gone and demanded punishment; because Judah had wanted to burn her on the basis of the law which Abraham had commanded his children. (*Jub.* 41:28)

The phrase "had *gone* and demanded" implies that what Judah said, "Take her out and burn her," was not blurted out in the heat of the moment to the person who brought him the news. Instead, Judah *went* somewhere—presumably to some local authority— and presented this demand for punishment.

One particularly interesting source of exegetical motifs is the *Testament of Judah* section of the *Testaments of the Twelve Patriarchs*. As we have already seen, the author of the *Testaments* seems to have inherited a rich store of traditions about the biblical text. What is sometimes unique about this author, however, is that he has no hesitation in imputing character flaws and missteps to biblical heroes; on the contrary! The literary form he chose—a series of the patriarchs' last words to their children—actually favored his having these aging heroes admit to their faults and warn their children against repeating them. Thus, as we have seen (chapter 3), Reuben warns his children at length about falling into temptation in the way that he himself did with Bilhah. In the case of Judah's last words, the author of the *Testaments* decided to build his text around Judah's confession of two fundamental flaws, his weakness for liquor and his love of money. Neither of these has any connection with the real biblical portrayal of Judah, but both are nevertheless connected to specific biblical verses.

Judah the Drunkard

Judah's weakness for liquor comes principally from the description of Judah in Jacob's blessings in Genesis 49, which concludes:

Tying his donkey to a grapevine, his ass to a flourishing vine,

He washes his garment in wine, his robe in the blood of the grape.

His eyes are darker than wine, but his teeth are whiter than milk.

(Gen. 49:11)

Scholars have long seen in this passage an allusion to the vini-
culture that was an important part of the economy of the tribe of
Judah. But for ancient interpreters, these words were taken as a
reference not to the people of that tribe in general but to their
eponymous ancestor, Jacob's son Judah. If so, then it seemed that
Jacob here—having just praised his son's physical prowess and fitness to rule (Gen. 49:9–10)—was adding a slight note of criticism:
"Judah, you drink too much wine!" Indeed, the last line might be
translated: "His eyes are dark *from* wine" (חכלילי עינים מיין), that is,
bloodshot from overimbibing. The negative implications of this
phrase would not be lost on anyone who knew the Bible well. The
same expression occurs in Prov. 23:29–30, "Who has redness of
eyes (חכלילות עינים)? Those who linger late over wine, those who
keep trying mixed wines."

Money-Hungry Judah

As for Judah's love of money, this too is derived from the Bible,
specifically, from Judah's precise words to his brothers when they
propose to kill Joseph: "What will we gain if we kill our brother
and hide the crime?" (Gen. 37:26). He may have thereby saved
Joseph's life, but in Hebrew, Judah's formulation of this question
is nevertheless somewhat damning. He asks, more literally, "What
is the profit (מה בצע)?" The word בצע certainly has negative conno-
tations in biblical Hebrew: it is often the equivalent of "filthy
lucre" or "ill-gotten gains" in English (see Exod. 18:21; Judg.
5:19; Jer. 6:13; Hab. 2:9; Prov. 28:16; etc.). *Targum Onqelos* thus
puts Judah's question in somewhat blunter terms:

Then Judah said to his brothers, "What money do we stand to gain (מא ממון ניתהני לנא) if we kill our brother and cover over his blood?" (Gen. 37:26)

THE TESTAMENTS AND THE SEPTUAGINT

The *Testaments of the Twelve Patriarchs* is an odd text. While parts of it seem clearly to be derived from Hebrew and Aramaic sources (as we saw with the *Testament of Levi*, dependent on the *Aramaic Levi Document*) and sometimes seem to be written, therefore, in a stilted Greek full of Semitisms, other parts are quite the opposite and use Greek words and expressions that would not normally occur to someone translating from a Semitic text—at least not to someone who was seeking to render his source-text fairly literally. This has led more than one scholar to suppose that the *Testaments* as a whole were composed *ab initio* by someone writing in Greek.[2]

The debate about the original language of the *Testaments* is complicated, and if I have mentioned it here, in connection with the *Testament of Judah*, it is only because this text can tell us something about a related issue. Proponents of the Greek authorship of the *Testaments* have also suggested that there are, here and there, indications that the author of the *Testaments* read the Bible not in Hebrew but in the Old Greek translation, the Septuagint. If so, this might be a strong indication that the original author of the work was indeed writing in Greek.

Issachar the Farmer

The parade example for this line of argument comes in the *Testament of Issachar*, where Jacob's son Issachar is presented as a simple farmer. Now, Issachar is never quite called a "farmer" in the Bible—at least, not in the traditional Hebrew text. What Jacob says when he blesses this son is:

> Issachar is a strong-boned ass, crouching among the sheepfolds.
> But he found the place so nice, and the land so pleasant,
> That he bent his shoulder to the burden and became a worker
> for tribute.
>
> (Gen. 49:14–15)

The phrase translated as "worker for tribute" (מס עבד) is somewhat ambiguous; one recent translation renders it "a toiling serf" (JPS), another "a slave at forced labor" (NRSV). When this phrase was translated into Greek, however, it became far less ambiguous: the phrase was rendered simply as γεωργός, "farmer." To proponents of the *Testaments'* Greek authorship, the conclusion seemed obvious: the *Testament of Issachar*, since it speaks of Issachar as a farmer, must be directly dependent on the Septuagint. This was not a small detail since, in the estimation of some, Issachar's being a farmer was "the theme of the whole testament."[3] This idea could not have come from elsewhere, it was argued, since the Aramaic targums, Jerome, and rabbinic exegetical traditions all connect Issachar with studying, not farming. "The author of the Testaments must therefore have derived his theme for the *Testament of Issachar* from the Septuagint."

While it is an exaggeration to say that the entire testament is centered on agriculture, it is certainly true that the Septuagint calls Issachar a farmer (Gen. 49:15). However, this hardly proves that the author of the *Testament of Issachar* wrote what he wrote because his knowledge of the Bible came from the Septuagint. The fact that the phrase מס עבד is explained as *farm*-worker in the Septuagint hardly means that the Septuagint translators—Jews, let it be recalled, of the third century B.C.E.—were the only Jews in that century or subsequent ones to have come to this conclusion

(or to have received it from elsewhere). The idea that Issachar
was a farmer might simply reflect what was then a widespread
understanding of Gen. 49:15. After all, one fundamental meaning
of עבד is "to work the land, to plow." (In this sense it is a bit like
labourer in French; the equivalent Aramaic פלח means quite
specifically both "to till" and "to work.")[4] If one combines this
meaning with the immediately preceding phrases about Issachar's
finding the *land* pleasant and *bending his shoulder* to the burden,
one might easily come to the conclusion that the whole verse
refers to this patriarch's willingly taking on the heavy physical
labor of farming.[5] The description of Issachar in the previous
verse as a "strong-boned ass" doubtless also contributed to this
association with farm work.[6] Once established by ancient interpreters, this idea of Issachar-the-farmer might, like other bits of
ancient midrash, have circulated widely. Noteworthy in this connection is the *Samaritan Targum* of the Pentateuch, which is quite
independent of the Septuagint here; it renders מס עבד as אריס משמש,
"tenant farmer."[7] It is thus hardly surprising that the *Testament
of Issachar* depicts Issachar as a simple farmer, and it scarcely argues any dependence on the Septuagint. This presentation of Issachar seems to derive directly (like so much of the *Testaments*)
from the Hebrew description in Genesis 49 of the patriarch in
question; that it appears in the Septuagint or, for that matter, in
the *Samaritan Targum*, only suggests that this ancient interpretation of Gen. 49:15 as a reference to farming was widely disseminated, at least for a while. It was only long after both the
Septuagint and the *Testaments* were written that Jewish exegetes
came up with an entirely different way of interpreting מס עבד in
Gen. 49:15 and thus ended up depicting Issachar as a scholar in
the targums and rabbinic literature.[8]

On the other hand, the two main themes of the *Testament
of Judah* mentioned above, drunkenness and love of money,
would be lost on someone who knew the Bible only in Greek. The

Septuagint version of Gen. 49:12 says nothing of drunkenness but only of "making the eyes gracious (χαροποὶ) more than [or "from"] wine." Here there are no eyes bloodshot from overimbibing. As for Judah's love of money, this too would be lost on a reader of the Septuagint, which renders Judah's question about Joseph, "What will we gain . . ." as "What use will it be (τί χρήσιμον) if we kill our brother?" A Greek writer who knew the Bible via the Septuagint would hardly find in this verse the suggestion that Judah was motivated by an unseemly lust for money, so any imputation of greed to Judah would appear baseless to him.[9]

The Waters of Kozeba

The *Testament of Judah* does offer further biblical support for the idea that Judah overimbibed—but again, it is an argument that will only work if one knows the Bible in Hebrew. In the confessional part of his testament, Judah makes the odd claim that he ended up sleeping with his daughter-in-law because he had "become drunk at the waters of Kozeba" and consequently did not recognize her (*T. Jud.* 12:3). No such detail exists in the biblical narrative of Judah and Tamar; he is not said to be drunk at all, and there is no mention of a place called Kozeba. A biblical connection exists, however, between Judah and such a place. The traditional Hebrew (Masoretic) text of Genesis mentions that, when Judah's Canaanite wife gave birth to their son Shelah, "he [Judah] was in Khezib when she bore him" (Gen. 38:5). Khezib and Kozeba apparently refer to the same Judean site, the latter being the form of the name used in 1 Chron. 4:22.

It seems that an ancient midrashic tradition sought to connect the biblical place-name Khezib/Kozeba with what looked like its Hebrew root, כזב, "deception." In other words, if the Bible mentions such a place—apparently gratuitously—in Gen. 38:5, interpreters reasoned that it must have done so as a subtle hint to

Judah's condition when he married and had children with this Canaanite woman: he was not in his right mind; he was in "Deceptionville" at the time! The author of the *Testament of Judah* apparently knew this tradition; that is why he had Judah assert that "I knew that the race of Canaan is wicked, but . . . when I saw her [Shua] pouring out wine, I was *deceived* [that is, כזב] owing to the intoxication of the *wine*" (*T. Jud.* 11:1–2). In the same vein, Judah goes on to say that he had "become drunk at the waters of deception (מי כזב)" when he had relations with Tamar. Demon Alcohol was responsible for both sins! This is fine midrash—but again, quite pointless for whoever knows the Bible only in Greek.

The same sort of exegetical necessity underlies, by the way, that other excessive drinker in the *Testaments*, Bilhah. In chapter 4 we saw that many of the particulars in the *Testament of Reuben*'s retelling of the incident—that Reuben saw Bilhah bathing, that Jacob was away at the time, that Bilhah was an unwilling participant, that Jacob spurned Bilhah subsequently, and so forth—all derive from little details in the biblical text. But if Bilhah was indeed an unwilling participant—and the fact that she was not subsequently punished seemed to support this idea—why did she not cry out for help or resist? The author of the *Testaments* had an answer at the ready: Bilhah was dead drunk at the time. Someone unfamiliar with the midrashic basis of these two problem drinkers might conclude that the author of the *Testaments* was leading some sort of campaign against alcohol abuse.[10] But what he says about Bilhah seems designed, first and foremost, to solve an exegetical problem, just as Judah's alcoholism was.

"Before the Eyes of All"

According to the biblical account, when Tamar dressed up as a prostitute, she stationed herself "בפתח עינים which is on the road to Timnah" (Gen. 34:14). The indicated phrase seems to mean "at the gate [or: "opening"] of Eynayim," and this understanding is duly reflected in *T. Jud.* 12:1: Tamar "sat in the city Enam by the gate." Judah sees her there and, failing to recognize her, goes on to have relations with her. After the truth is revealed, however, he is said not to have approached her again—this in keeping with Gen. 38:26. The *Testament of Judah* does, however, add a further element. It suggests that Judah was not really sure afterward that he *had* committed a sin:

> I said, "Perhaps she did it in trickery, having received the pledges from another woman. . . . Moreover, those who were in the city had said that there was no harlot at the gate, because she had come from another place and sat for a while at the gate—so, I thought, no one knew if I had gone in to *her*." (*T. Jud.* 12:7–10)

In other words, at first Judah himself was not convinced that the woman in question had been Tamar, and there were no other witnesses to the event—as it says in Gen. 38:21, no one from the city had seen Tamar dressed as a prostitute. This is a fine, close reading of the biblical text. Later on in the *Testament of Judah*, however, Judah reflects again on this incident and says, "*Before the eyes of all* I turned aside to Tamar" (14:5). But I thought he just said that no one saw!

By this time, such inconsistency in a narrative text should easily be identified as another instance of **overkill**. Apparently, our author was in possession of two contrary traditions. The first sought to look deeply into Judah's state of mind: how *could* he be sure he was not being tricked, since there were no witnesses to Tamar sitting "at the gate of Eynayim"?[11] For this to work, the phrase בפתח עינים could only be taken to mean an actual city gate. However, a second midrashic tradition took this same phrase somewhat tendentiously as "at the opening of the eyes," that is, Judah sinned "before the eyes of all." Both these little bits of

exegesis were precious even if they did contradict each other, so
our midrash-minded author included them both.

Tamar Told Him the Secret Words

Let us return to the dramatic high point of the story of Judah and
Tamar, the moment when Judah is confronted with the evidence
that he is the father of Tamar's unborn child:

> Judah said, "Take her out and let her be burned." When she was
> taken out, she sent word to her father-in-law, "The man to whom
> these belong is the one by whom I am pregnant." And she said,
> "Recognize whose these are, the signet and the cord and the staff."
> Then Judah recognized them. (Gen. 38:24–26)

In the *Testament of Judah*, these events are related as follows:

> [Judah said:] Not knowing what she had done, I wished to kill her;
> but she privately sent me the pledges and put me to shame. And
> when I summoned her, I heard as well the secret words that I spoke
> in my drunkenness while sleeping with her. So I could not kill her,
> for it was from the Lord. (*T. Jud.* 12:5–6)

The sequence of events in this retelling is somewhat different
from that found in the Bible. Here, Tamar *first* sends the pledged
items, and then *afterward* Judah summons her and she speaks directly to him. Why did the author of the *Testaments* (or the exegetical tradition he was citing) create two different scenes when
the Bible speaks of only one? The reason is an apparent inconsistency in the biblical text: Tamar "sends word" to her father-in-
law (indeed, her message speaks in the third person of "the man
to whom these belong"), but later she seems to be addressing him
face to face, that is, she actually *says* (and *says* by addressing him

directly, in the second person), "Recognize whose these are."
Now, of course, we know that this is not really face-to-face
speech: it is simply part of the message that Tamar sends. But to
the midrashic way of thinking, if Tamar first "sends" and then
"says," and at the same time switches from third- to second-person
speech, there must be two different scenes here.

Why then should Judah have summoned her, and what could
Tamar have said at this face-to-face encounter? As we have seen,
Judah did have reason to suspect Tamar; she could conceivably
have received the pledged items from someone else. Therefore, according to the *Testament of Judah*, at their face-to-face meeting
Judah demanded additional proof—and she supplied it. "I heard
as well the secret words that I spoke in my drunkenness while
sleeping with her." To be sure, there is nothing in the biblical account about any "secret words." In fact, if Tamar first sent word
and then was summoned to meet Judah face to face, what the
Bible says she "said" in this putative second encounter really doesn't
make much sense: "Recognize to whom these belong, the signet
and the cord and the staff." After all, she had already sent the
pledged items with essentially the same message. But precisely
because the sentence "Recognize to whom these belong" adds
nothing new, our midrashist seems to have concluded that the
Bible was not telling everything about this face-to-face meeting—
something else must have been said. He therefore created the motif
"Tamar Told Him the Secret Words." He may even be suggesting
that we read Tamar's second statement somewhat elliptically,
"Recognize [who said these secret words. It is the same man] to
whom these belong, the signet and the cord and the staff."

This fine piece of midrash requires, however, two supplemen-
tary clarifications. The first is that, whatever its ultimate source,
the present text of the *Testaments* contains a glaring error here.
Judah says: "She privately sent me the pledges and put me to
shame." If she sent them *privately*, how was Judah put to shame?

On the contrary, sending them publicly, with a message that identified the personal items as Judah's own, is what would have put
him to shame; sending them privately, with a message that began
"The man to whom these belong," was apparently intended as a
way of sparing his dignity.

In fact this is a simple mistake. The original text doubtless said,
"She privately sent me pledges and *so did not* put me to shame."
This is altogether in keeping with the well-known rabbinic motif
connected with this same verse:

> It is proper for one to cast oneself into a fiery furnace rather than to
> put someone else to shame in public. Whence do we know this?
> From the case of Tamar, since she was even set on fire [a punning
> interpretation of מוצאת, "was taken out," in Gen. 38:25 as מוצת,
> "was set on fire"] yet still she did not put Judah to shame in public
> (b. *Berakhot* 43b and numerous parallels).

The point of this remark is that, even in imminent danger of
death, Tamar had sought to protect Judah's privacy by sending
the message that she sent. Our present Greek text—like that in
which Simeon and Levi tell their father that the Shechemites
ought *not* to be circumcised (above, chapter 3)—has apparently
been garbled in transmission and now says exactly the opposite of
what was originally intended.

A Divine Voice Called Out

The second matter requiring clarification is the idea that Judah
had spoken some "secret words" to Tamar at the time, and that
these words served as further proof that Judah was the father.
When one considers the matter, these "secret words" could have
proven very little. After all, Judah entertains the possibility that

Tamar had gotten the personal items from someone else—the real prostitute—and that Tamar was simply using them to get herself off the hook for being pregnant. But if so, what was there to prevent the same real prostitute from passing on to Tamar the "secret words" as well? What is more—and still more serious—is the logical flaw in this version of Tamar's trial, a flaw that is in fact present in the biblical story itself: just because Judah slept with Tamar did not mean that he was the father of her child. It might be that Tamar, eager for a child, had theretofore been quite promiscuous and was already pregnant before Judah came to Eynayim—that she had, again, devised the whole scheme as a way of exculpating herself. In the midrashic reading seen earlier in *Targum Onqelos*, Judah flatly declares, "She is right. [She is pregnant] from me"; the same motif appears frequently in rabbinic sources. But what made Judah so sure he was the father?

It is for this reason that an ancient midrashist came up with an idea glimpsed in passing above:

> R. Jeremiah in the name of R. Samuel son of R. Isaac [said]: In three places did God appear [in court]: . . . In the courtroom of Shem [as it says], "And Judah acknowledged and said, 'She is right. From me.'" R. Jeremiah in the name of R. Samuel son of R. Isaac [said]: God said to them, "You testify about what happened in public and I will testify about what happened in private." (*Genesis Rabba* 85:12 [Oxford MS 147])

The last remark is intended to address the obvious difficulty mentioned: how could Judah be so sure he was the father? God—or in other versions, "a heavenly voice" (בת קול or רוח הקודש)—tells Judah to limit his testimony to what he knows for sure, that he slept with her; God Himself will then testify as to who caused Tamar to be pregnant.[12]

Interestingly this same motif exists in a somewhat different form:

> "And Judah acknowledged and said, 'She is right. From me.'"
> R. Jeremiah in the name of R. Samuel son of R. Isaac [said]: A
> heavenly voice said to them, "From me came the secret matters
> (כבושים)." (*Genesis Rabba* 85:12 [Paris MS 149, Munich MS 97,
> Oxford MS 2355, etc.])

According to this narrative expansion, the only words Judah
spoke were, "She is right." Then a heavenly voice adds, "From
me"—meaning that the "secret matters," the true knowledge of
who had made Tamar pregnant, came from the heavenly voice
and not from Judah (who could not know for sure and therefore
could not testify in this matter).

The point of this version is basically the same as that of the
previous version of "A Divine Voice Called Out," but its wording
is striking. "Secret matters"—or, in another version, "the secret
things/words" (דברים—the Hebrew word means both)—is oddly
reminiscent of the motif of "Tamar Told Him the Secret Words"
found in the *Testament of Judah*. These are, technically, two **rival
motifs**, two quite different ways of explaining what went on at
Tamar's trial. Tamar revealed the secret words, or God (or a
heavenly voice) revealed the secret matters or "words." But they
are rival motifs that share a common **element**, something "secret"
that was revealed at the trial. The presence of this common element may be merely coincidental, but that strikes me as unlikely.
More probable is that one of these **rival motifs** is a development
of the other, that is, one source inherited the phrase "secret
things/words" in somewhat garbled form and then created a
whole new motif on the basis of this suggestion. But who borrowed from whom?

The *Testaments* are, in my opinion, an old text, going back to
the first century B.C.E. at the latest, whereas *Genesis Rabba* and

the other sources in which "secret things" appears are all considerably later. Nevertheless, it would seem likely that the version in the *Testament of Judah* is actually based on a misunderstanding of the words uttered at this putative trial, "From me came the secret things." Especially if the version of "A Divine Voice Called Out" that was consulted by the author of the *Testaments* (or by its source) had used both words seen in the manuscript variants of *Genesis Rabba*, דברים כבושים (secret *words*), it is easy to see how such a person might not understand what secret words were involved—and finding no easy referent at hand, made one up. The secret words, this reader reasoned, were actual words spoken by Judah in his drunkenness, words that only Tamar could know: "From me," Judah admits upon hearing her testimony, "came these secret words." As noted, the motif "Tamar Told Him the Secret Words" does not make much sense; those secret words could have been passed on to Tamar by someone else, and in any case, they would only prove that Judah had slept with Tamar, not that he was the father of her child. But it was the only explanation of דברים כבושים that this reader could come up with—and thus was created the odd sequence of events at Tamar's trial in the *Testament of Judah*.

Chapter Seven

A PRAYER ABOUT JACOB AND ISRAEL
FROM THE DEAD SEA SCROLLS

*T*he Dead Sea Scrolls may be, as is often said, the greatest manuscript discovery in history, but assembling the various fragments into readable texts, and then trying to make sense of them, is no easy task. The texts themselves usually come without titles, and in any case the opening column or more is often missing, so that any inquiry into the text must begin, quite literally, in medias res. What is more, even the surviving parts of the manuscripts have usually been eaten away to some extent, so that lines frequently break off in the middle or contain large gaps. (The case of the scattered Qumran fragments of the *Aramaic Levi Document*, examined in chapter 5, is altogether representative.) No wonder it is so easy to be misled about what one is reading or to overlook some crucial clue in a broken line somewhere.

Thus, when scholars first sought to make sense of the text designated 4Q369, they made an understandable mistake. The first column of this text is quite fragmentary, but fixing on the mention of the obscure antediluvian figure Mahalalel—known only from Gen. 5:12–17—and on the reference to Mahalalel's father as, apparently, someone else's *son* earlier in the same line, they concluded that the "someone else" in question was none other than Mahalalel's grandfather, the biblical Enosh (Gen. 5:6–11), and that this first column of broken text must therefore have been concerned principally with him. After all, Enosh was indeed an important figure to the Bible's ancient interpreters,[1] one on whom such a text might indeed focus. Since this text seemed to be a prayer of some sort, they styled it the "Prayer of Enosh." (Despite this title, they expressed the belief that the second, more readable column of the text was actually a prayer by a different figure—probably, they said, the biblical Enoch [Gen. 5:18–24].)[2]

This, as I hope to show, was an error, and it was compounded by another mistake. The second column, still apparently addressed to God, said, "You have made him a firstborn son for Yourself." Since the existence of a future king or messiah who might restore Israel's fortunes was certainly a subject of discourse during this period—and one that is clearly attested elsewhere in the Dead Sea Scrolls—it was not an unreasonable inference that the individual alluded to was none other than that promised king.[3] If so, then it was remarkable that he was being referred to as God's "firstborn son," especially in the light of later, Christian messianism.

Before considering these claims in greater detail, it might be well to present the four main fragments of 4Q369 as they were originally published:

4Q369 "PRAYER OF ENOSH" (PAM 41.518, 42.834, 43.357)

1, i: 1–10

1.]and to all
2.]to the mysteries[. . .][4] Your peace
3.]they will understand [. . .] that they will be made guilty
4.]all their [. . .][5] in their time periods
5. perio]d of Your miracles[6] for of old You decreed for them
6.]his judgment until the period of judgment determined
7.]in all the warnings[7] until
8. . . .] *vacat*
9.]his [son], and Mahalalel the fifth generation
10.]his son (בנו) Enoch a seven[th] generation

1, ii: 1–12

1. Your name. You apportioned his inheritance (נחלתו: that is, homeland) to cause Your name to dwell there[

2. It (i.e., this homeland) is the splendor (צבי) of Your earthly
   habitation and upon it You have deli[ghted [. . . שעת]שעה[8] [and You
   have set?]

3. Your eye upon it and Your glory is seen there f[orever . . . ?]

4. to his seed for generations as an eternal possession. And al[l

5. and Your goodly statutes You have made clear for him t[o

6. with an eternal and You have made him a firstborn son for
   Yourself [

7. like him as a prince and ruler over all Your earthly habitation[

8. heaven and the glory of the skies you have set
   ([סמכת]ה) [

9.]and Your angel of peace in his assembly, and[

10.]to him righteous laws, as a father to a so[n

11.   . . .] my love. May your soul cleave to[[9]

12.]for in them [. . .] Your glory[

2:1–5

1.] and the angel of the patriarchs is guarding[10][

2.]Your [T]orah, and to fight in all the la[nds

3.]to You by them peace[

4.]and Your [j]udgments against them[

5. a]ll Yo[ur] creatures[

3:1–5

1.] [

2.]for from You all that is and [

3.]from You [and] from Your hand is all the dominion[

4.]all Your dominions in their periods[

5. f]or(?)[

Reading through these fragments, it is apparent that 4Q369 is indeed a prayer, but the conclusion that it is a prayer of Enosh, or Enoch for that matter, seems unwarranted. The mysterious "he," "him," and "his" that appear throughout this prayer do not refer to either of these antediluvian figures, still less to the "eschatological messianic figure" that the editors wished to see in the reference to God's "firstborn son" in column 2, line 6. Instead, all of these refer to the people of Israel and their founding father, Jacob. There can be little doubt, for example, that it is within Israel's homeland—and not Enoch's, wherever it might be—that God, in the much used phrase of Deuteronomy, "caused His name to dwell" (line 1), and that it is that same homeland which is called the "splendor" (צבי, line 2) of the earth—certainly otherwise a rare word—twice by the prophet Ezekiel (Ezek. 20:6, 15). Moreover, the fact that God's "eye[s]" (line 3) are uniquely set upon the land of Israel is held to be, in fact, its distinguishing characteristic in Deut. 11:12, and God's "glory is seen" there prominently in Isa. 60:1–2 (*inter alia multa*). Thus, there can be little doubt that the place being referred to in these first three lines of column 2 is the national territory of the people of Israel. If so, then the missing antecedent of "his" in נחלתו, "his inheritance" (or more properly, "his territory") in line 1 would clearly seem to be Israel: God set off Israel's territory as the place in which to cause His name to dwell. So too with the "his" of line 4: God gave the land "to his seed for generations as an eternal possession": it was certainly to Jacob/Israel's seed that the land was given. Indeed, this line is virtually a word-for-word citation of God's promise to Jacob in Gen. 48:5, "And I shall give this land to your seed after you as an eternal possession."

Given all this, there appears to be little reason to look for a messianic figure in the word "him" of line 6, "You have made him a firstborn son for Yourself." As a matter of fact, the reference here is to Exod. 4:22, "Thus says the Lord, 'Israel is My firstborn son.'" So, for that matter, is Israel the antecedent of the other unidentified *him*s and *his*es in the rest of this same passage: "And your goodly statutes You have made clear for him" (line 5) refers to a well-known motif concerning the clarification of divine law to *Israel*; "like *him* as a prince and ruler over all Your earthly habitation" (line 7) means *like Israel*; the "angel of peace" is in *Israel's* assembly; and so forth.

In short, everything in this column seems to refer to Israel, and there is little justification in attaching the title of "firstborn son" to anyone else. Having noted this, however, I believe it important to explore further the exegetical intention behind these words in our Qumran text. For while this biblical assertion of Israel's first-born status was no doubt pleasing to Jewish sensibilities in Second Temple times, it nonetheless puzzled ancient biblical interpreters. In what sense could the people of Israel, the descendants of a single man, Jacob, himself descended from Isaac and Abraham, and all of them from the great family of Shem, Noah's son—in what sense could this little, late branch on the tree of humanity be called God's *firstborn*? To one who saw in sacred Scripture a great corpus of divinely revealed truth, this title of "firstborn" could hardly be explained away as a mere rhetorical flourish. But if it was not that, then what did it mean? Here, certainly, was a problem.

Heavenly "Sabbath Gentiles"

It is interesting that, among many other exegetical conundrums, this one was specifically addressed by the author of *Jubilees*. In order to understand the answer he provides, however, we must begin with another, albeit related, interpretive problem treated by *Jubilees*, this one concerning the Sabbath. The problem is this: the Bible says that God rested on the seventh day, but it says nothing about Him *ending* that Sabbath rest (nor, for that matter, does it mention God resting on any subsequent Sabbath). Interpreters no doubt found this problematic, since it could all too easily lead to the conclusion that God is still "resting"; this is the doctrine of an otiose creator, that is, He who had made the universe simply ceased all activity after the creation. Such a doctrine was certainly known to ancient interpreters:

> And it is plainly said by our legislation [that is, the Torah] that God rested on the seventh day. This does not mean, *as some interpret it*, that God no longer does anything. It means that after He had finished ordering all things, He so orders them for all time. (Aristobulus, cited in Eusebius, *Ecclesiastical History* 13.12.11)

Most interpreters, of course, maintained that God is indeed still active—but that only heightened the question: if God rested on that first Sabbath and then went back to work, why does the Bible fail to mention any subsequent divine Sabbaths?[11] Indeed, if the Sabbath was—as the creation account in the book of Genesis implies—a *universal* day of rest, why was Sabbath rest not imposed on all of humanity and observed in every subsequent week not only by the Almighty but by all his human minions? But clearly this was not the case. The Sabbath is mentioned again only much later, in the book of Exodus—and there it is being kept not by God, nor even by all of humanity, but by one small people on earth, the people of Israel. What is more, it sometimes rains or snows on the Sabbath, and the wind blows as usual. Does not this very fact further imply that God, to whom Scripture specifically attributes responsibility for such things (see, for example, Ps. 147:18), does not regularly rest on the Sabbath? Perhaps, indeed, God had observed only that first Sabbath after the creation and has been working ever since:

> Do not look askance if we [Christians] drink hot water on the Sabbath [in violation of the Jewish Sabbath laws], since God

does not cease directing the operation of the universe on that day, but He continues as on other days. (Justin Martyr, *Dialogue with Trypho* 29:3)

[A pagan said to R. Aqiba:] "If, as you say, God honors the Sabbath, then let him not cause the winds to blow on it or make the rain to fall [that is, things that He would not do if He were indeed resting]." (*Genesis Rabba* 11:5)

These same questions apparently troubled the author of the book of *Jubilees*, and that book presents its own, unique answer:

[An angel explains to Moses:] "He gave us a great sign, the Sabbath day, so that we might work six days and observe a Sabbath from all work on the seventh day. And He told us—all the angels of the presence and all the angels of the sanctification, these two kinds— that we should keep the Sabbath with Him in heaven. . . . Then He said to us: 'Behold, I shall separate off for Myself a people from among all the nations, and they also will keep the Sabbath. . . . They will become My people and I will be their God. I have chosen the descendants of Jacob among all of those whom I have seen [will be created]. And I have written them down as My firstborn son and have sanctified them for Myself. . . . I will tell them about the Sabbath days so that they may keep the Sabbath from all work on them.'" (*Jub.* 2:17–20)

Jubilees asserts that the Sabbath is fundamentally a heavenly institution, not meant for ordinary mortals—which is why there is no universal commandment to observe the Sabbath (even though it was the culminating part of the creation of the universe). Indeed, as the passage cited states clearly, the Sabbath is not even universally observed in heaven but is kept every week only by God and the two highest classes of angels: "And He told us—all the angels of the presence and all the angels of the sanctification, these two kinds—that *we* should keep the Sabbath *with Him* in heaven." Thus, if the world keeps operating on the Sabbath, it apparently only does so because the *lower* angels in charge of such mundane functions as the winds and rains are not allowed to rest; it is only God and the two highest classes of angels that rest. These lower angels are to God what the "Sabbath gentile" was to Jews in later times, performing activities which He could not because of the rest imposed by the Sabbath:

> For on the first day He created . . . the angels of the presence, and the angels of holiness, and the angels of the spirits of fire and the angels of the spirits of the winds, and the angels of the spirit of the clouds, and of darkness, and of snow and of hail and of frost, and the angels of the sounds, the thunders and the lightnings, and the angels of the spirits of cold and of heat, and of winter and of spring and of autumn and of summer, and of all the spirits of His creatures which are in the heavens and on the earth. (*Jub.* 2:2)

In short, it is these lower angels who continue to work on the Sabbath and keep the world going, while God and his two highest classes of angels rest.[12]

God Thought of Israel First

But it is precisely at this point in the creation that *Jubilees* adds a striking detail: God remarks to the angels in this context, "Behold, I shall separate off for Myself a people from among all the nations, and they also will keep the Sabbath. . . . They will become My people and I will be their God. I have chosen the descendants of Jacob among all of those whom I have seen [will be created]. *And I have written them down as My firstborn son and have sanctified them for Myself.* . . . I will tell them about the Sabbath days so that they may keep the Sabbath from all work on them." In other words, it was the very first Sabbath in history that caused God to think about the future of humanity. No peoples, no human beings but Adam himself (according to *Jubilees*), had been created at this moment—and yet, precisely now, God resolves to create a nation in the future which will observe the Sabbath with Him.[13] It is for this reason, God says, that "I have written them down as My firstborn son and have sanctified them for Myself." Israel was thought up—"conceived," one might say—way back at the time of the first Sabbath in history. And so, technically speaking, Israel *is* God's firstborn since Israel's existence as a separate people was set in motion way back in the very first week of creation.[14]

Firstborn by Dint of Discipline

There was, however, another way to approach the exegetical problem of Exod. 4:22, "Israel is my firstborn son." The phrase "firstborn son" could be understood not as a statement of fact—for how, indeed, could any people be deemed to be God's firstborn *son* in any literal sense?—but as an expression of the special relationship between God and Israel. Israel was *called* God's firstborn son in the sense that it was particularly dear to God, as a firstborn is to his father.

Something like this approach seems to underlie our text, 4Q369:

5. and Your goodly statutes You have made clear for him t[o

6. in the light of eternity and *You have made him for Yourself a firstborn son*[

The wording indicated above (ותשימהו לכה בן בכור) seems noteworthy for one particular reason. After all, in Exod. 4:22 God had flatly asserted that Israel "*is* My firstborn son," period. Here, by contrast, God at a certain point *made* Israel a firstborn son.

The difference may be subtle, but, when one thinks about it, significant nevertheless. Our Qumran text, 4Q369, seems to be saying that Israel was not *born* a firstborn, as it were, but only was "made" or declared to be God's firstborn as a kind of title or elevation to special status. Our text does not say when or why this status was conferred upon Israel, but the word ותשימהו certainly implies that Israel was already in existence when it became God's firstborn.

Indeed, if we take the sequence of items in this prayer seriously, the granting of this firstborn status may be connected to what immediately precedes it in the text, the fact that God "made clear" His "goodly statutes" to Israel "with an eternal light." That is, Israel became God's firstborn not only because it was particularly dear to Him but perhaps also because, like a father, He established certain rules for Israel—His "goodly statutes"—and so subjected this "son" to appropriate rewards and punishments for his obedience to them. Such a connection seems to be reinforced a few lines later on:

10.]to him righteous laws, as a father to a so[n

The lost beginning of line 10 probably said something like "*You [God] gave* to him righteous laws (חוקים צדיקים)." However, the next phrase, "as a father to a son," is rather curious, since fathers are not usually represented as exercising a specifically legislative function in the family. If the author of 4Q369 nonetheless says that God gave laws *as a father*, does he not again mean that these laws, given to Israel, were like the rules of behavior that a father establishes for his children? However, this is as much as to say that Israel is like God's son in precisely the same sense, namely, that *like a son* Israel had been subjected to God's fatherly discipline.

In short, while line 6 makes it clear that Israel was at some point *made* God's firstborn son, rather than born such, line 10 seems to be saying that Israel is like God's son in that God gave to him "righteous laws." Both, in other words, seem to agree that Israel's sonship is not a matter of birth but expressive of Israel's special relationship to God. Moreover, the mention of these "righteous laws," along with the "goodly statutes," in proximity to the "firstborn son" further implies that what entitles Israel to its status as God's "son" is the fact that God had given Israel its special set of rules—the Torah; in other words, Israel is God's son by dint of fatherly discipline.

Now, it is interesting that 4Q369 is not unique in maintaining this line of interpretation. Just such an understanding of things is found elsewhere in the Qumran corpus, in the set of prayers known as the "Words of the Luminaries":[15]

> Behold, all peoples are [as no]thing before You, [as] emptiness and nothingness are they accounted before You. But we have called upon Your name and for Your glory You have created us, and You have made us sons for Yourself in the eyes of all the nations, for You have called Israel "my firstborn son" and You have disciplined him as a man disciplines his son, and You have made us great. (4Q504 ["Words of the Luminaries"], col. 3, 2–7)

Here too, God "made us" (that is, Israel) his "sons"; the verb here, שמתנו, is the same one used in 4Q369.[16] The "Words of the Luminaries" is not, technically speaking, alluding to Exod. 4:22 here but to Deut. 14:1, "Children [or "sons"] are you to the Lord your God." But having evoked that verse, the author of this text goes on to mention Exod. 4:22—"for You have called [Israel] 'my firstborn son'—and then supplies his own interpretation of the meaning of both these potentially problematic biblical assertions with the aid of a third, Deut. 8:5, "For as a man disciplines his son, the Lord your God disciplines you." In other words, the people of Israel are not God's "sons" in any genealogical sense, and certainly not His "firstborn" among the table of nations. Nor

were they "first" in the *Jubilees* sense of having been planned
first. Instead, they were "made" His sons and "called" His firstborn at some later point in history,[17] and for one simple reason:
because it is God's way to discipline Israel in the same manner as
a human father disciplines his own beloved son, meting out obvious rewards and punishments "in the eyes of all the nations."
Presumably, none of the other nations could claim to be God's
"son," not only because they do not worship Him but because
their history hardly bears witness to the same divine manipula-
tions and interventions intended to teach them how to behave. (If
this author then adds that "You have made us great"—the text
breaks off after this word—it may well be that he is playing on
the sense of רב: it is not only that God has caused Israel to attain
to greatness, but He has also brought him up, raised him, through
fatherly discipline until he has achieved his present status.)[18] In
any case, this Qumran text, like 4Q369, sees Israel's title of "firstborn" as having been granted at a certain point in time in consideration of Israel's special standing with God, and it connects this
specifically with God's fatherly disciplining of Israel.

This same motif of "Firstborn by Dint of Discipline" is found
in another Second Temple text as well, namely, the version of Sir.
17:17–18 attested in some Greek manuscripts:[19]

> When he [God] apportioned out all the nations of the earth,
> for each nation He established a [heavenly] ruler, but Israel is the
> Lord's portion. Whom, being his firstborn, He brought up with dis-
> cipline, and allotting to him the light of His love, He did not aban-
> don him.

The sense of the second sentence is as follows: since Israel was
indeed God's firstborn, he had to be brought up "with discipline"
(παιδεία = מוסר), presumably, the discipline of the Torah; yet it
was not only the strictures of divine law but also "the light of His
love" that God granted Israel, so that, despite Israel's infractions

of the Torah, "He did not abandon him." Indeed, this text's juxtaposition of God's fatherly disciplining of Israel and God's gift of
the "light of His love" is reminiscent of the same juxtaposition of
these two items in 4Q369:

10. . . .]to him righteous laws, as a father to a son[
11. . . .] *My love.* May your soul cleave to[

There is yet another Second Temple period text that juxtaposes
Israel's firstborn status with the matter of divine discipline. The
Psalms of Solomon at one point state:

> Your judgments [are] upon the whole land in mercy, and Your *love* is
> upon the seed of Abraham, the sons of Israel. *Your discipline is upon
> us as upon a firstborn*, an only son. (*Psalms of Solomon* 18:3–4)

Here again are the same familiar elements: Israel is not genetically
God's son but is "as" (ὡς) a firstborn by dint of the discipline
(παιδεία = מוסר) imposed by God; however, the application of God's
"judgments" (κρίματα, presumably משפטים) to Israel is hardly to be
viewed as a punishment since it has been done "in mercy." Indeed,
along with these "judgments" God has given to Israel his "love."

Finally, notice should be taken of a passage in Pseudo-Philo's
Liber Antiquitatum Biblicarum which evokes this exegetical motif.
There, in the account of Korah's rebellion, Korah's sons assert:

> Our father [Korah] engendered us, but the Almighty created us.
> And now, if we walk in His ways, we will be His sons. (Pseudo-
> Philo, *LAB* 16:5)

These words reflect the same understanding of Israel's sonship:
while not "sons" in any biological sense (since "our father engendered us"), the people can nonetheless *become* sons "if we walk
in His ways," that is, sons by dint of divine discipline.

In short, the question posed by Exod. 4:22—in what sense could Israel be God's "firstborn son"?—engendered two **rival motifs**, "God Thought of Israel First" (found only in *Jubilees*) and "Firstborn by Dint of Discipline." According to the latter motif, Israel was not *born* God's firstborn at all; that is, God's assertion in Exod. 4:22 was not intended in any genetic or chronological sense. Instead, "firstborn" here was a title that Israel received after it was already in existence, in consideration of its special standing with God. God both loved Israel as a firstborn and likewise subjected him to fatherly discipline. This explanation of Exod. 4:22 was apparently well known, having been attested in the Qumran "Words of the Luminaries," one version of Ben Sira, the *Psalms of Solomon*, and Pseudo-Philo's *LAB*. It appears to underlie as well our column in 4Q369, with its assertions that God *"made* him [= Israel] a firstborn son" and gave him "righteous laws as a father to his son." Moreover, the mention of God's clarifying His "goodly statutes (משפטים) for him" in the line just preceding the mention of the "firstborn son" may partake of the same motif.

No Angel over Israel

The above-cited Sir. 17:17 alludes to a biblical passage that the author of 4Q369 must likewise have known well, namely, the description in Deuteronomy of God's "separating off" the people of Israel from all other nations:

> When the Most High was granting the nations their portions, at the
>   time that He separated humanity [into different peoples],
> He established the boundaries of peoples according to the number
>   of the sons of God.[20]
> But God's portion is His people, Jacob his allotted inheritance (נחלתו).
>
>   (Deut. 32:8–9)

The sense of this passage was clear enough to ancient interpreters: if God had established the "boundaries of peoples"—that is, the division of humanity into different nations—so as to have their number correspond to the number of the "sons of God," this was certainly done for a reason: each of those "sons of God"—an expression understood by interpreters in this and other contexts to refer to God's angels—was to be put in charge of a different people. However, Israel was to have no such guardian angel, since its fortunes are directly supervised by God: "But God's portion is His people, Jacob his allotted inheritance." So indeed was this passage interpreted in some Second Temple texts:

> He [God] chose Israel to be His people. He made them holy and gathered them apart from all mankind. For there are many nations and many peoples, and all belong to Him. But he made spirits [= angels] rule over all in order to lead them astray from following Him. But over Israel He made no angel or spirit rule because He alone is their ruler. (*Jub.* 15:30–32)

> For every nation he appointed an angel, but Israel is the Lord's own portion.
>
> (Sir. 17:17, all versions)

God Appointed a Guardian Angel

Yet here was a problem. For, the above notwithstanding, Second Temple writings elsewhere abound with evidence of the widespread belief among Jews that various angels did indeed involve themselves in human affairs, including those of Israel. In fact, there is scarcely anything more characteristic of Jewish writings of, especially, the latter part of the Second Temple period than their interest in angels. The people of Israel itself had, according to many sources, its own angelic supervisor or representative.

Thus, the biblical Daniel is told specifically about Michael, "the great angel who has charge of your people" (Dan. 12:l; see also Dan. 10:13 and 21), and this same angel appears as Israel's guardian at Qumran (1QM 9:15–16; and 17:6–7) and elsewhere.[21] In other texts Israel's heavenly representative is identified as Sariel, Phanuel, Israel, Melchizedek, and so forth. The Qumran Community Rule speaks of a "Prince (שר = angel) of Lights" who has dominion over all the righteous (presumably among the people of Israel):

> In the hand of the Prince of Lights is the rule over all the sons of righteousness, that they should walk in the paths of righteousness; and in the hand of the Angel of Darkness is the whole rule over the sons of wickedness. (lQS [*Community Rule*] 3:20–21)

The above passage has rightly been connected by scholars with a more generalized dualism attested in, for example, the "lots" of light and darkness or the "sons" of light and darkness mentioned elsewhere at Qumran. However, even outside of the dualistic worldview, the existence of a guardian angel for Israel must have struck many people in Second Temple times as an altogether logical inference. After all, if Israel's God is indeed the only true deity in the world, then it stands to reason that His particular people, Israel, ought to enjoy a privileged position in the world—or at least not be subject to the dominion of other nations, with their false gods and false beliefs. Yet since the return from the Babylonian exile, foreign domination had been the rule, not the exception. It was, to be sure, possible to attribute one or another political setback to divine punishment for past sins or to a divinely instituted test. However, as decades of outside rule stretched into centuries, no doubt other possibilities had to be considered. Certainly among these was the notion that God, while supremely powerful, had delegated His people's affairs to a guardian angel such as those named above. This angel was of course *not* supremely powerful; on the contrary, he was constantly in battle with the (angelic) forces of evil or, simply, the angelic representatives of other nations. So it is no accident that, in Qumran's *Community Rule* (1QS 3:20–21, cited above), the "Prince of Lights" stands in explicit opposition to the "Angel of Darkness," or that, in the book of Daniel, the angelic Michael stands against the angel of Persia and the angel of Greece (Dan. 10:13, 20).

Obviously this notion of an angelic guardian was difficult in one respect: the existence of such an angel taking care of the fortunes of Israel seemed contradicted by Deut. 32:8–9, which—as we have seen in the motif "No Angel over Israel"—was interpreted to mean that while all *other* nations had angelic intermediaries, Israel depended directly on God. One text from Qumran apparently sought to address this problem head-on:

> You [cr]eated [us] for Yourself, an eternal people, and You have granted us the lot of light, in keeping with Your faithfulness. [But] from of old You appointed the Prince of Light to help us, and in [. . .] and all the spirits [that is, the angels] of truth are under his rule. (1QM [War Scroll] 13:9–10)

In other words, God did indeed create Israel *for* Himself, but He nonetheless also created from the start ("from of old") an angelic "Prince of Light" to help them in their day-to-day affairs.

What remains of 4Q369 is certainly quite fragmentary, but it may be noteworthy that the beginning of column 2 of this text likewise does not speak of God setting off Israel for Himself, à la Deut. 32:8–9. Instead, it says:

1. Your name. You apportioned (פלגתה) his inheritance (נחלתו) to cause Your name to dwell there[

The rather unusual verb translated "apportioned" need not detain us here.[22] What is interesting is that this text does not evoke the motif "No Angel over Israel," but instead speaks simply of a divine designation of Israel's *territory*, a place where God will cause His name to dwell. Perhaps that is so because, in common with other Second Temple writers, the author of 4Q369 believed that Israel's fortunes were indeed under the direct control of one of God's angels. In fact, this author even seems to know that angel's name.

Israel's Guardian, the Angel of Peace

The "Prince of Light" (שר המאור) just mentioned is apparently a Qumran name for its guardian angel, a name that appears in nearly the same form, "Prince of Lights" (שר אורים), in 1QS (*Community Rule*).[23] However useful this name might have been at Qumran in suggesting a primal combat between light and darkness, good and evil, it had one salient disadvantage: it is not to be found in the Torah. Indeed, the Hebrew Bible altogether is notoriously short on angelic names. The only angels specifically named are to be found in the latter half of the book of Daniel, where, in addition to the references to Michael already mentioned, the angel Gabriel also appears briefly (Dan. 8:16 and 9:21). Other books that were doubtless also considered sacred—such as the various components of our present 1 *Enoch*—filled in a few more names, but the identity of Israel's angelic guardian, or even his very existence, had nonetheless been passed over in disturbing silence by most of sacred Scripture. This fact only compounded the difficulties of Deut. 32:8–9. One who wished to maintain that, despite the apparent meaning of this passage, Israel did nonetheless have a guardian angel had to be able to offer some scriptural support for this claim. It is thus hardly accidental that, from an early period, ancient sages scrutinized the Pentateuch and the prophetic corpus for the slightest hint of such an angel's existence and identity.[24]

One passage which proved to be crucial in this regard is found in the book of Isaiah:

> Behold, *Erellim* (אראלים) cry out outside, angels of peace (מלאכי שלום)
> weep bitterly; the roadways lie in waste, the traveler has ceased . . .
> the land is sorely grieving.
>
> (Isa. 33:7–9)

The Erellim mentioned at the beginning of this verse eventually became a class of angels in rabbinic writings, *Hekhalot* texts, and later literature.[25] But even before these emerged, the "angels of peace" mentioned here had enjoyed their own brief prominence for ancient angelologists. After all, if "angels of peace" were said by Isaiah to be grieving over Israel's fallen fortunes, then it stood to reason that these same angels were somehow allied with Israel's interests. From here, the leap to a specific "angel of peace" who intercedes on Israel's behalf is not far. Such an angel is indeed attested elsewhere in Second Temple writings:

> And now, fear the Lord, my children, and beware of Satan and of his spirits. Draw near to God and to the angel who intercedes for you, for he is the mediator between God and men for the peace of Israel, and he will stand up against the enemy's kingdom. Therefore the enemy is eager to trip up all those who call upon the Lord. For he knows that on the day when Israel believes, the enemy's kingdom will come to an end. The *angel of peace* himself will strengthen Israel, lest it succumb to an evil end. (*T. Dan* 6:5)

> For the way people end [their lives] indicates their righteousness [i.e., their degree of religious piety and observance], as they encounter [either] the angel of the Lord or of Satan. For if the soul departs in agitation, [this is because] it is being tormented by the wicked spirit

[= angel]. If, however, it departs in a state of peace, joyfully, it has encountered the *angel of peace*, who summons it in [to eternal] life. (*T. Asher* 6:4–6)

The disposition of the good man is not in the hands of the deceitful spirit, Beliar, for the *angel of peace* guides his soul. (*T. Benjamin* 6:1)

What is particularly noteworthy about the first two passages cited is that, on closer inspection, each is apparently seeking in its own way to explain the title "angel of peace." The first passage asserts that the angel of peace will serve as "the mediator between God and men for the *peace of* Israel." According to the second, on the contrary, the angel of peace is so called because he is the angel who greets the soul that "departs in a *state of peace*, joyfully." In other words, here are two rival motifs explaining the name of an angel whose existence was apparently well known at the time (that is, in my opinion, the first century B.C.E.) but whose precise function was, to put it mildly, still rather vague.[26]

It is interesting, in this light, to consider the appearance of this same "angel of peace" in the second column of our text:

8.]heaven and the glory of the skies You have set [
9.]and *Your angel of peace* in his assembly, and[
10.]to him right statutes, as a father to a so[n

The above hardly clarifies what it is that the angel of peace does, but at least one thing emerges on closer inspection: this angel's presence "in his [Israel's] assembly" comes in the midst of our text's catalogue of God's beneficent acts performed on Israel's behalf, a catalogue that occupies virtually the whole of this column. In other words, the putting of an "angel of peace" in Israel's assembly is yet another good thing that God has done for Israel, like giving him his territory or making him a "firstborn son." (There is scarcely any reason to doubt, even without considering the surrounding context, that it is in *Israel's* assembly that the angel has been put: the word "assembly" figures prominently in the Pentateuch and elsewhere in references to the whole of Israel's population.) If so, then it is a fair guess that our text understands the title "angel of peace" in a way somewhat similar to *T. Dan* 6:5, where this angel is also a national angel, one who intercedes with God for the sake of Israel. An apparent difference between the two texts, however, is that in 4Q369 there is no indication that this angel brings or maintains peace in the face of a continuous threat from the "enemy's kingdom." Instead, the peace mentioned here is in Israel's assembly, a source of well-being in Israel's midst—that is why God's assigning this angel to Israel was a beneficent act.

Israel Rules the World

Between the mention of God's granting Israel the status of firstborn son (line 6) and the mention of the "angel of peace" in Israel's midst (line 9) comes a curious description of Israel's exalted status:

6. with an eternal light and You have made him a firstborn son for Yourself[

7. like him as a prince and ruler over all Your earthly habitation[

8.]heaven and the glory of the skies You have set ([ה]תכמס)[

9.]and Your angel of peace in his assembly, and[

As mentioned, the editors initially saw these as references to the messianic figure otherwise alluded to as God's "firstborn." But since, as we have seen, it is Israel itself who is God's firstborn, then the "like him" in line 7 (if this is the proper reading) means "like Israel." There is little point in speculating on the precise wording of the missing part of line 6, but it seems at least probable that the line went on to refer here, as in line 4, to Israel's (i.e., Jacob's) progeny. Perhaps the missing words were ותשם זרעו ("You made his progeny") or הוא ודורותיו ("him and his offspring") or something similar. In any case, the meaning would have been that not only did God establish Israel/Jacob as his firstborn but that this status and Israel's role as "prince and ruler" over the whole earth applied as well to Israel's subsequent generations.

Prince and ruler over the whole earth? Throughout most of its recent history, as was just mentioned, Israel had been dominated by others. In what sense could the writer of our text maintain that God had appointed Israel to be "prince and ruler" over any- one? Perhaps such considerations are what helped lead the mod- ern editors of this text to their messianic interpretation. And yet, there was good reason to claim that Jacob/Israel and his progeny had indeed been appointed "prince and ruler" over the earth: after all, that is what Isaac had said of Jacob and his descendants in his famous blessing:

> May God give you of the dew of heaven, and of the fatness of the earth, and abundance of grain and wine. Let peoples serve you, and nations bow down to you. Be lord over your brothers, and may your mother's sons bow down to you. (Gen. 27:28–29)

If Isaac's blessing of Jacob had said, "Let peoples serve you, and nations bow down to you," then this is precisely what God must have wanted to grant Jacob and his descendants: dominion over all of God's "earthly habitation."[27]

The next line of 4Q369 should be examined in the same context:

8.]heaven and the glory of the skies You have set (סמכת[ה]) [

What can be speculated about the missing portion of this line? Finding the "characteristic base [should be: 'top']" of the letter *'ayin* at the beginning of this line, followed by a lacuna of three to four letter spaces, the editors restored the word עטרה, "crown" and translated: "the crown of the heavens and the glory of the skies You have set [on him]."[28] This seems to me most unlikely for the simple reason that a crown is never "set" on anyone in the Bible with the verb סמך. As a concordance will confirm, an עטרה (or כתר for that matter) can be "put"(שית or שים or נתן) onto the head, or it can "crown" or "surround" (עטר) the head, but no one in biblical Hebrew is ever said to have (סמך) a crown on someone's head. Indeed, the verb סמך's only direct inanimate object in the Bible are the hands themselves. (The verb סמך in the sense of "uphold" or "support" takes direct objects of persons [Isa. 63:5; Ps. 37:17, 145:14, etc.], but this would obviously not be appropriate for a crown; in any case, one does not "uphold" a crown on someone's head.) In other words, when used of things, the verb סמך does not mean "place" so much as "support" or "lean," specifically, to lean the hands on someone; in the same sense it means to "support" or "prop up" a person. In either sense, this verb could not be used for putting a crown on someone. For that reason I believe the restoration עטרת שמים , "the crown of the heavens" is wrong. But what could the text have said?

One particular occurrence of the verb סמך in the Bible may provide a clue. In this same chapter of Genesis, after Isaac blesses Jacob in the mistaken belief that he is blessing Esau, the real Esau walks in. Discovering the fraud, Esau pleads with his father:

> "Have you not reserved a blessing for me?" Isaac answered Esau, "Behold, I have made him your lord, and all his brothers I have given to him for servants, and with grain and wine I have sustained him (סמכתיו). What then can I do for you, my son?" (Gen. 27:36–37)

The above translation (that of the RSV) is certainly acceptable; it may be, however, that סמכתיו is being used here as a shorthand expression for סמכתי ידי, "I have laid my hand upon him" in the act of blessing,[29] in other words, "and with grain and wine I have blessed him." Whichever the case, it is clear that what Isaac is alluding to is the blessing that he had just accorded to Jacob (cited above):

> May God give you of the dew of heaven, and of the fatness of the earth, and abundance of grain and wine. Let peoples serve you, and nations bow down to you. Be lord over your brothers, and may your mother's sons bow down to you. (Gen. 27:28–29)

For this reason, I would restore the missing part of [. . . סמכת]ה in the next line not as the editors have, סמכתה עליו, but as סמכתו, to parallel Gen. 27:37. In other words, this line of 4Q369, no less than the preceding one, is an allusion to Isaac's blessing of Jacob, in which Isaac (or, rather, God via Isaac) granted Jacob dominion over other nations. As for the missing beginning of line 8, if it is not a heavenly *crown* that Isaac gave his son, what was it? In the biblical blessing, Isaac grants his son טל השמים, the "dew of heaven." I suspect that this "dew," or perhaps some restatement of its significance, is to be fitted into the block of text from the end of line 7 to the beginning of line 8.[30]

God Clarified His Statutes

I have saved until now what seems to me the most tantalizing line in this column of 4Q369, line 5:

> and Your goodly statutes You have made clear for him t[o

What is fascinating here is the word "made clear," בררתה. Although the editors of this text translated the word in keeping with its meaning in standard biblical Hebrew, to "purify," they wisely noted that it is "remotely possible that the word could be used in its mishnaic sense of 'clarify,' 'explain.'"[31] This does indeed seem

to be the intended meaning. God certainly did not "purify" his
goodly statutes nor even choose them (another Mishnaic Hebrew
meaning of ברר),[32] but clarified them, made them understandable,
"to him," that is, to Israel. This usage of ברר is widely attested in
Mishnaic Hebrew as well as Palestinian Aramaic, and it certainly
fits the overall context: another beneficent act performed by God
on Israel's behalf was the clarifying and explaining of divine law.

The reason why this is fascinating, however, is that it seems to
respond to a problem common to virtually all Jewish groups and
individuals in Second Temple times. On the one hand, Jews
wished to see in the Torah the great divine guidebook for daily
life; everything one needed was contained within it. On the other
hand, there were a great many things in ordinary Jewish practice
or belief—the just mentioned angelic guardian is but one example
among hundreds—which did not seem to be found in the Torah,
indeed, which seemed to be contradicted by the Torah's own
words.

Jews responded to this dilemma in basically two ways. One option was that of "outside information": God had indeed instructed Israel to follow this or that practice or to believe in this
or that thing, but that information had been given outside of the
Torah itself, through an appropriate human conduit of divine instruction. Such conduits included not only our canonical prophets
and sages but the various other biblical worthies who were alleged to have written apocalypses, last wills and testaments, or
the other books that constitute the apocrypha and pseudepigrapha
of the Hebrew Bible. Thus, for example, readers of the book of
Jubilees could find in it the precious information—inexplicably
omitted from the Torah itself—that the 364-day calendar was the
one chosen by God for determining all of Israel's festivals and
holy days. This information had been given to Moses on Mount
Sinai, but transmitted in an outside source, namely, *Jubilees* itself.
Another form that the "outside information" option took—though

obviously distinct from that of *Jubilees* and other books—is the Pharisaic contention that its "traditions of the fathers (or 'elders')" constituted an authoritative supplement to the Torah's instructions. Soon enough, this claim was likewise bolstered with the authority of Moses, who was said to have initiated a chain of orally transmitted material.[33]

However, there was another option entirely, interpretation. One could claim that, while a particular belief or practice was not openly espoused by the Torah, it had nonetheless been communicated therein, albeit in some hidden or nonobvious form: proper interpretation of the Torah's sometimes opaque wording would yield the missing information. The "interpretation" option and the "outside information" option were not mutually exclusive. The author of *Jubilees*, for example, believed that the 364-day calendar explicitly espoused by him was also implicit, *sous-entendu*, in the narratives of Genesis, if only they were properly understood. Similarly, the content of the Pharasaic oral traditions often concerned, or was attached to, proper interpretation of a particular biblical verse. In any case, the "interpretation" option could be, and was, applied to all manner of issues, Sabbath observance, Temple practice, and other aspects of daily life: if one looked deeply into the Torah's own words, a hidden message could often be extracted.

Our 4Q369 fragment says that God *clarified* His goodly statutes to or for "him," Israel, and this is a highly significant assertion since it seems to address precisely this problem. The meaning of the Torah laws, it says, was inherent in the laws themselves; all they required was "clarification." Moreover, it was God himself who clarified the goodly statutes: here was no outside figure who came with further information. True, our text says that God explained them to "to him" and not "to Israel," so one might still claim that there is some messianic figure or other interloper to whom the texts were clarified. But as I have been at pains to show, everything else in this column (indeed, in the whole text) refers to Israel. Let me be clear on this: there is not a single statement about the recurrent, unidentified "him" in column 2 which does not relate to something said about *Israel* in the Bible. Moreover, there is not a single statement about this unidentified "him" which is not paralleled by something said, in very similar terms, about Israel in the book of *Jubilees*, the *Testaments of the Twelve Patriarchs*, Ben Sira, and so forth. Thus, I think that there is little chance that the phrase "to him" in line 5 does not also refer to Israel.

In fact, I might point out that there is even a rather close parallel to this line elsewhere in the literature of the Second Temple period. It comes in Pseudo-Philo's *Liber Antiquitatum Biblicarum*—the passage has, for some reason, been largely neglected even by commentators on that book—in Aaron's words to the restive rabble at the time of the Golden Calf incident:

> And Aaron said to them: "Be calm. For Moses will come [i.e., down from Mount Sinai] and he will bring to us statutes, and he will make clear to us (*illuminabit*) the Torah and he will expound for us the law of God from his own mouth, establishing the rules for our people. (Pseudo-Philo, *LAB* 12:2)

The Latin *illuminabit* probably does not translate ברר in the hypothetical Hebrew original of Pseudo-Philo. More likely, the original word there was האיר. The semantic distance between the two is not great, however, and certainly the point is the same: God not only gave Israel the Torah but also explained it, interpreted it for Moses, at the same time.

I do not wish to overstate the similarity of these two texts. Pseudo-Philo is clearly more detailed and goes beyond what 4Q369 says. Indeed, his assertion that Moses "will expound (*exponet*) for us the law of God from his own mouth (*de ore suo*)" reflects a change mentioned earlier: at a certain point what the Pharisees had called the "traditions of the elders" began to be attributed to Moses himself. (Indeed, this is what is most striking in this passage, that the phrase *de ore suo* seems designed polemically to stress orality as the proper means for transmitting this additional information.) The text of 4Q369 by contrast says only that God clarified the statutes, and arguably this text could have in mind a clarification that was passed on either orally or in a separate book, like *Jubilees*.

Apart, however, from the fact that it was God who provided the clarification is the assertion that this clarification was given "to him," to Israel. It may be foolhardy to try to conclude anything more from our laconic text, but this strikes me as highly significant as well. For it was precisely on matters of *halakhah*, the correct way of carrying out divine statutes, that various groups in Second Temple times differed. To their mind, at least after a certain point, the Torah had *not* been made clear to all, or if it had, at least some Jews had forgotten or willfully turned away from such clarification. The correct meaning of the Torah was *the* sensitive issue. For this reason, had this text been composed in a world in which Israel was already divided into "the members of the covenant" and the "men of the Pit," it is difficult to believe that its author would have casually asserted that God clarified the Torah "to him," to collective Israel, without immediately adding that only one part of Israel has continued to understand it correctly.

What I am saying, in other words, is that this text seems to presuppose a world less polarized than that of the Community Rule, for example, a world more like that of the book of *Jubilees*, in which, while not all of Israel may know the true meaning of God's sacred laws, Israel is still a single polity; no one has been written off. In connection with this I would return again to the "angel of peace," whose establishment "in his assembly"—that is, Israel's—is one of God's beneficent acts. Once again, here is all of Israel. To put it another way, I suspect that the reason why the angel of peace, or for that matter Michael, Sariel, etc., were rejected by some Qumran texts in favor of the "Prince of Light[s]" is precisely that sectarianism had by then reached a point where an all-Israel guardian was no longer even desirable (since the Jewish people was now divided into good and bad, light and dark), and where putting an "angel of peace" in the midst of *all* of Israel's assembly ran counter to the dreams of some (including those at Qumran) of a "day of vengeance" in which the bad Jews would at last suffer violent retribution.

The Torah Is an Eternal Light

The line that immediately follows this mention of God's "clarifying" His "goodly statutes" is one that we have already examined for its reference to Israel's firstborn status:

5. and Your goodly statutes You have made clear for him t[o
6. with an eternal light, and You have made him a firstborn son for Yourself [

It is hardly possible to fill in the missing words between the end of line 5 and the beginning of line 6, but it certainly seems likely that the phrase "with [or "in"] an eternal light" (אור עולמים) was connected to the previous line, since after it a new clause starts: "and You have made him a firstborn son for Yourself." In other words, the phrase "with an eternal light" was the end of the clause or sentence dealing with God's clarification of of His laws. The letter ל, with which line 5 breaks off, might have been followed by a noun, but it is equally possible that this was the beginning of an infinitive phrase, something like, "and your goodly statutes You made clear for him *to guide him along Your paths*

with an eternal light." (I am not proposing this as an actual reading but simply as a way of showing how lines 5 and 6 might originally have been connected.)

If lines 5 and 6 were indeed connected—it does not matter precisely how—then it follows that this "eternal light" must somehow be related to God's giving Israel His laws. The relationship is
not hard to find: it is virtually a cliché of Second Temple writings
that the Torah itself was an eternal source of light.[34] As with
many ancient motifs, this one developed out of a number of separate biblical sites, each giving rise to a characteristic formulation,
but gradually these distinct formulations merged. Thus the idea
of Torah as light was stated outright in the Bible:

> For the commandment is a lamp, and Torah is light, and the re-
> proofs of discipline are the path of life. (Prov. 6:23)

But this mention alone hardly accounts for the popularity of the
motif. Another contributory factor was the presence of the "fiery
law" (so אשדת was understood from an early time)[35] in God's right
hand when He descended onto Mount Sinai, according to Deut.
33:2. Here was a clear statement that the Torah was like a great
fire—and in what sense save that it illuminated? Yet another contributing factor was that, immediately after it narrates the giving
of the Ten Commandments, the Bible says that all the people
"saw the thunderings and the לפידים" on Mount Sinai (Exod.
20:18). Modern translators rendered this word as "lightnings,"
but the Septuagint, perhaps encouraged by the sound similarity,
had rendered it as λάμπαδας; "torches" or "lamps," and the
same word was used by Jerome in the Vulgate. But what were
torches, normally a manmade device, doing on Mount Sinai
along with the divine presence? It seemed only reasonable that
this too was a figure of the illuminative power of Torah.

Given all, this, it is hardly surprising that, when proposing to give Israel the Torah at Mount Sinai, God should say, in one retelling:

> I shall give My light to the world, and I shall illuminate its habitations, and I shall place My covenant with the sons of men, and I shall glorify My people above all nations, upon whom I shall enjoin My eternal statutes, which will be to them as a light, but as a punishment to the wicked. (Pseudo-Philo, *LAB* 11:1)

Here, indeed, are both elements of our text's אור עולמים: the Torah is a light that illuminates the world, and its statutes are "eternal." In similar fashion, the Wisdom of Solomon speaks of the "imperishable [that is, undying, eternal] light of law" (18:4) while the *Testament of Levi* twice mentions the "light of the Torah" (14:4, 19:1).

I have suggested a few biblical sources for the Torah's being a light, a fiery law, and a torch or lamp. But what made its light in any of these cases "eternal"? The themes of the Torah's existence before the Creation and its eternal validity in the future had origins originally quite separate from the motif "The Torah is an Eternal Light."[36] Yet it seems that one reason why the word "eternal" was sometimes tacked on to references to the Torah as a "torch" or "lamp" (these stemming, as we have just seen, from Exod. 20:18) is that lamps in the course of things burn out, their supply of fuel finally used up. It was important, then, to assert that while the Torah illuminates like a torch or lamp, its light will never be extinguished:

> I will work through him [Moses] signs and wonders for My people, which I have not done for any other. And I will set My glory in their midst and proclaim to them My ways; and I, God, will light My *eternal lamp* for him, which will abide with him. (Pseudo-Philo, *LAB* 9:7, cf. 15:6)

Today I call to witness against you the heavens and the earth—for the heavens did hear, and the earth gave ear, when God revealed Himself from the end of the world so that He might set His majesty in your midst, and He kindled an eternal lamp (*sempiternam lucernam*) within you. Remember, wicked ones, when I spoke to you, you answered, saying, "All that God has said to us we will do and we will obey." (Pseudo-Philo, *LAB* 19:4)

Note also:

[Moses] brought the Torah to the descendants of Jacob and he *lit a lamp* for the *generations* of Israel. (*2 Bar.* 17:4; cf. 18:1–2)

For at that time [that is, the "time of the coming of Moses and of Aaron" mentioned in the previous verse] the *lamp of the eternal Torah,* which exists forever and ever, illuminated all those who sat in darkness. (*2 Bar.* 59:2)

In any event, the Torah as an "eternal light" or "eternal lamp" is well attested in the literature of this period, and given the sequence of items in lines 5 and 6 of our text, there is every reason to believe that the phrase אור עולמים here referred to the Torah as well. God "made clear" his "goodly statutes" to Israel in order that Israel might (walk about? the missing word could be להתהלך or something similar), "with an eternal light," namely, the Torah, and in consideration of this He further "made him a firstborn son."

CONCLUSION

To summarize: 4Q369 is a literary prayer or collection of prayers similar to those found in a great many Second Temple works (such as, for example, the prayer of acknowledgment in 1QM 13:7–16, or 4Q 504, *DibHam*, "Words of the Luminaries"), one which makes ample use of Scripture. (Particularly striking is the number of quotations from or allusions to the book of Deuteronomy.) The first column of fragment 1 is too poorly preserved to allow much speculation, but it may well have recounted God's deeds at the beginning of biblical history, before and just after the Flood. The second column of fragment 1, by far the largest readable unit, appears to be a catalogue of God's beneficent acts on Israel's behalf, suggesting a speaker who comes after, perhaps long after, the time of Israel's founder, Jacob. Among the beneficent acts of God mentioned are these: granting Jacob his national territory in order to "cause Your name to dwell there," a supremely beautiful land in which God delights (lines 1–2); keeping His eye on this territory and letting His glory appear there (line 3); granting this territory to Jacob's descendants in perpetuity (line 4); clarifying His laws to Israel and so granting it an "eternal light" (lines 5–6); making Israel His firstborn son (line 6); appointing Israel a "prince and ruler" throughout the land (line 7); blessing Israel with "heavenly glory" (line 8) establishing the "angel of peace" in Israel's midst (line 9); and giving Israel righteous laws "as a father to his son" (line 10).

As we have seen, many of these assertions were connected to perceived problems in this or that biblical verse, problems that were addressed elsewhere by ancient biblical interpreters. The biblical verses themselves, and the bits of interpretation adduced from such texts as *Jubilees*, Ben Sira, the *Testaments of the Twelve Patriarchs,* and so forth, demonstrate clearly that the unidentified recipient of God's beneficence in this column is indeed Israel, and the parallels between our text and the others mentioned anchor it firmly in the exegetical history of the Second Temple period.

* * * *

With this we conclude our survey of some of the most ancient exegetical traditions surrounding Jacob and his children. Our focus throughout has been on how the various motifs examined grew out of a sustained analysis of the biblical text—and how extraordinarily sophisticated some of them are: the *Jubilees* explanation of Jacob's doings at Bethel, for example, with its clever use of the Bible's casual mention of Deborah's death; or the motif "Rise and Fall of Empires," which so precisely accounts for all the details in Jacob's dream and turns them into a message of hope; or the way in which the *Testament of Judah* finds two different scenes implied in a single sentence of Tamar's. These and many of the other motifs examined highlight, I hope, the great creativity and scholarly care—two qualities often conceived to be opposites in our own day—that went into the formation of Israel's ancient exegetical traditions.

In an earlier study I tried to set out some general conclusions about the way exegetical motifs are created and how they interact with one another;[37] there would be little point in repeating those conclusions here. One matter, however, does deserve special mention in the light of the foregoing pages. What is particularly striking about the motifs examined here, beyond their creative reworking of the biblical material, is the extent to which they may be seen to have built on one another. "Rise and Fall of Empires," for example, might at first glance look as if it sprang directly from the biblical text; as we have seen, however, this motif was in all likelihood founded on an earlier exegetical idea, that Jacob's dream constituted a view of his descendants' future, and that the ladder was somehow a visual representation of what was in store for them. Technically, "Rise and Fall of Empires" is a rival of "Staircase of History," but as we have seen, the "Staircase" motif seems to have preceded "Rise and Fall of Empires" chronologically; despite their very different ways of construing the ladder, the earlier motif seems to have provided the basis on which the later motif was created. In other words, "Rise and Fall of Empires" did not derive exclusively from the contemplation of Genesis 28, but of Genesis 28 as it had been explained by

"Staircase of History." Similarly, with regard to Jacob's doings at
Bethel, I have stressed how different were the goals of *Jubilees* on
the one hand and the traditions about Levi collected in the *ALD*
on the other. *Jubilees'* main concern was to make sense of chapters 28 and 35 of Genesis; the Levi traditions were concerned very
little with Genesis but sought in various ways to exalt the figure
of Levi—Levi the ancestor of later priests and rulers, Levi the sage
and seer and transmitter of priestly lore. But what *Jubilees* has to
say about Genesis 28 and 35 depended not merely on the biblical
text but on an idea that *Jubilees* had inherited from these earlier
Levi traditions, namely, that the priesthood had not been
awarded to Levi's descendants alone, but that Levi himself had
been made a priest in his own lifetime. This idea (rooted, as we
have seen, in the exegesis of Mal. 2:4–7) provided *Jubilees'* author with the idea that Jacob himself had been skipped over in the
"Chain of Priests" and that this circumstance would explain perfectly why he did what he did in his two brief stays at Bethel.

This is, of course, not to say that all is unblemished artistry in
the world of ancient biblical interpretation. Sometimes ancient
exegetes, or ancient scribes, made a mess of things. We have seen
the sloppy interpolations in the Slavonic *Ladder of Jacob* text and
the great mass of contradictions and duplications in the *Aramaic
Levi Document*. Less obvious are the minor instances of **overkill**
in the *Testament of Levi*'s recounting of the revenge on Shechem,
or the two different ways of explaining "and Israel heard of it" in
the *Jubilees* version of the Reuben and Bilhah story, or the apparent misprision of the **element** "secret words" that led to Tamar's
peculiar testimony at her trial in the *Testament of Judah*. But even
these instances of exegetical bumbling could hardly be thought to
have spoiled the texts in which they are contained—for the fact is,
these texts were faithfully transmitted in their present form without anyone, apparently, being troubled by their flaws. Indeed,
sometimes a later misprision creates a version of a story far better

than the original—witness Cinderella's glass (*verre*) slipper, which originally had been, more logically but far less dramatically, made of fur (*vair*). (The reader will have to decide if Judah's drunken "secret words" in the *Testament of Judah* likewise qualify as an improvement over an earlier tradition.)

The title of this collection was intended in two rather different senses. In the narrow sense, of course, it refers to the incident recounted in Genesis 28 and the exegetical traditions assembled in chapter 2. But the image of a great ladder "set on the ground, whose top reached up to heaven" seems significant in a broader sense as well. The stories of Jacob and his children recounted in Genesis are what they are: etiological narratives and old-time historiography, things rooted in the soil of ancient Israel and its people in biblical times. Above that soil, however, there arose Jacob's ladder, a great chain of traditions about different biblical texts, one which was—for all its playing "fast and loose" with the biblical text, indeed, for all its occasional excesses—both "set in the ground" of those texts and, at the same time, directed to heaven and the glorification of sacred Scripture. What is more, considered together these traditions truly have the appearance of a ladder, with each rung connected to what had preceded and what followed it, in such a way as to make of this assemblage of biblical interpretations a single, ascendant structure—perhaps even one on which the angels of God may, at times, be glimpsed in their going up and down.

NOTES

CHAPTER ONE
JACOB AND THE BIBLE'S ANCIENT INTERPRETERS

[1]This is the famous first question raised by the medieval commentator Rashi in his Genesis commentary (Gen. 1:1): why does not the Torah start with the first commandment given to Israel, namely, at Exod. 12:2? In so doing, however, he is repeating an earlier, midrashic tradition cited in the name of R. Isaac: *Midrash Tanhuma* (Buber ed.) Gen. 11 etc, see the list of sources cited in D. Heiman and Y. Shiloni, *Yalqut Shim'oni* (Hebrew) (Jerusalem: Mosad Kook, 1977), 2: 187.

[2]I have discussed these four assumptions more fully elsewhere; see, in particular, *The Bible as It Was* (Cambridge, MA: Harvard University Press, 1997), 1–49 (= *Traditions of the Bible* [Cambridge, MA: Harvard University Press, 1998], 1–41). The connection of these four assumptions with, specifically, wisdom writings in ancient Israel was discussed in "Ancient Biblical Interpretation and the Biblical Sage," in J. L. Kugel, *Studies in Ancient Midrash* (Cambridge, MA: Harvard University Press, 1991), 1–26.

[3]In particular, in *Traditions of the Bible* (see note 2). Methodologically, the present volume is intended more as a sequel to my *In Potiphar's House* (San Francisco: HarperCollins, 1990), which also focused on the interrelationship of different sources.

[4]These titles also appear as subheads in the chapters of this book for easy reference; as subheads, names of motifs are always italicized to distinguish them from other, ordinary subheads. An index of motifs appears at the end of this volume.

[5]I discussed this motif in *Traditions of the Bible*, 299–301.

[6]Neither of these two phenomena is illustrated in the present study, but I have included them here for the sake of giving a complete account of how motifs interact; for further discussion of midrashic doublets and transfer of affects, see *In Potiphar's House*, 255–56.

[7]*Traditions of the Bible*, 351–401; 460–99; on Joseph, see *In Potiphar's House*, 28–154.

CHAPTER TWO

THE LADDER OF JACOB

[1]That is, the highest class of angels (corresponding to the "angels of holiness" and "angels of the presence" at Qumran and in the book of *Jubilees*). Presumably, it is their being called "angels *of God*" in Gen. 28:12 that led to this conclusion: their normal place was serving God in the heavenly sanctuary. (On this there is a vast literature: see especially M. J. Davidson, *Angels at Qumran: A Comparative Study of 1 Enoch 1–36, 72–108, and Sectarian Writings from Qumran* (Sheffield: Academic, 1992) and D. Dimant, "Men as Angels: The Self-Image of the Qumran Community," in A. Berlin, ed., *Religion and Politics in the Ancient Near East* (Bethesda: University of Maryland Press, 1996), 93–103. If so, what were these "angels of God" doing so far away from Him, on earth?

[2]The motif of forced exile might have suggested that, once the period decreed for the angels' punishment had reached an end, fairness dictated that they could no longer be kept a single day longer on earth. Perhaps for that reason, *Genesis Rabba* 50:9 specifies the exact length of time of their sentence (138 years). If Jacob's falling asleep and dreaming coincided with the very last minute of the 138th year, that might explain why the angels were allowed to reenter heaven before having escorted Jacob the whole way. But such an explanation is not given explicitly in any of the extant versions of this midrash.

[3]This idea may have been a development of another ad hoc rule, namely, that one angel cannot perform more than one task; this rule is evoked to explain why Abraham sees three angels, rather than a single one, at Mamre: one had been sent to heal Abraham from his recent circumcision, a second to destroy Sodom, and a third to save Lot from the destruction. On this, see Josephus, *Jewish Antiquities* 1:198; Justin Martyr, *Dialogue with Trypho* 56; *Targum Neophyti* Gen. 18:1 and parallels; b. *Baba Metzi'a* 86b and parallels: and my *Traditions of the Bible*, 341–42. It is well known that the three angels acquired a Trinitarian interpretation in Christian exegesis, and some scholars have alleged that the rule of "one angel per task" was created by the rabbis specifically to counter this Christian interpretation. But the presence of this explanation in

the writings of Josephus makes such a possibility most unlikely. Besides, the appearance of three angels when a single one would have been sufficient was certainly puzzling, especially since groups of angels are otherwise rare in biblical narrative.

[4]See below.

[5]In this case, the missing verb might be הסתכל (to gaze or contemplate) or הביט (look at, consider), both of which are regularly followed by the preposition "-ב". See in this sense *Midrash Tanhuma* (Buber ed.), ad loc.

[6]For a fuller discussion, see my *In Potiphar's House* (San Francisco: Harper-Collins, 1990), 115.

[7]The continuation of this passage actually presents a variant on the admiring angels motif; it finds in the phrase "descending upon him" a somewhat negative connotation and so, building on the ancient midrashic theme of the rivalry between angels and humans, suggests that the angels actually went down בו, in order to harm Jacob or curse him. See *Genesis Rabba* 68:12.

[8]That is, they associate the word בו, now understood as an elliptical way of saying "in order to gaze upon him," with both verbs: the angels went up to gaze upon him and they went down to gaze upon him.

[9]This motif developed out of the statement, "its top reached to heaven"; the same words might be understood as "his head reached to heaven" and thus to refer not to the ladder but to Jacob. I have discussed the origins of this tradition in *In Potiphar's House*, 112–20.

[10]Here, the word "glorified" in Isaiah is being interpreted rather more concretely as "beautified." In other words, God is saying that His throne (and, by extension, His own being) is beautified by Israel (another name for Jacob) since his portrait adorns it.

[11]The whole idea that the ascending angels actually *invite* the others to behold the faithful Jacob is unique here and may itself be connected to an entirely different motif, created for the story of the binding of Isaac, whereby the angels call out to one another in wonderment at Abraham and his son. This motif is attested in *Targum Neophyti* and *Pseudo-Jonathan* and in the *Fragment Targum*; see M. Bernstein, "The Angels at the Aqedah: A Study in the Development of a Midrashic Motif," *DSD* 7 (2000):277. As I seek to explain elsewhere

("Exegetical Notes on 4Q225," *DSD* [forthcoming, 2006]), the original purpose of these angels at the Aqedah came to be forgotten in later times and a new purpose had to be invented: the motif of their calling to one another in wonderment at the virtue of Abraham and Isaac came to replace the now-forgotten purpose, and that motif may have been subsequently transferred to this expression of angelic wonderment at the sleeping Jacob. After all, couldn't the angels have observed the faithful Jacob at any other point in his life, either by going down to earth (which they seem to be able to do elsewhere just fine without a ladder!) or simply by looking down from heaven?

[12]A Palestinian *amora* of the late third and early fourth centuries. This midrash is found in similar versions in *Genesis Rabba* (printed editions) 68 (end); *Exodus Rabba* 32:7, *Leviticus Rabba* 29:2, *Midrash Tanhuma, Vayyetse* 2; *Pesiqta deR. Kahana* 23 (Mandelbaum ed., 334); *Midrash ha-Gadol* Gen. 28:12; *Midrash Tehillim* 78:6; *Yalqut Shim'oni, Vayyetse* 121; *Yalqut Yirmiyah* 312; J. Mann, *The Bible as Read and Preached in the Old Synagogue* (Hebrew Section) (New York: KTAV, 1971), 171.

[13]Indeed, this midrash gives a new coloring to the words of the biblical text. "And your progeny will be like the dust of the earth, and you will extend westward and eastward, north and south" (Gen. 28:14)—these words are no longer a prediction of Israel's expansion and power but of its subjection and dispersion. What Jacob sees in the vision of the ladder is his own descendants' exile and subsequent domination by foreign peoples. Similarly, "I will be with you and guard you wherever you shall go" (Gen. 28:15) now sounds like a divine assurance that, despite the terrible times to come, Israel will never be completely abandoned. No wonder, then, that the biblical text says about Jacob when he awakens from this vision, "And he was afraid and said, 'How fearsome is this place!'" (Gen. 28:17).

[14]For these figures in rabbinic tradition, see *Seder 'Olam*, chaps. 29, 30 (Rattner ed., 133, 141); cf. b. *Megillah* 12a and parallels. Note also D. Flüsser, "The Four Empires in the Fourth Sibyl" in idem, *Judaism and the Origins of Christianity* (Jerusalem: Magnes, 1988), 317–44; and J. L. Kugel, "The Ladder of Jacob," *HTR* 88 (1995): 212. One late version of this midrash specifies that the Roman period of domination is to last five hundred years; see Mann, *The Bible as Read and Preached*, 171.

[15]See my *Traditions of the Bible*, 358, 366–67.

[16]See my discussion of this motif in *Traditions of the Bible*, 299–301.

[17]Margulies, *Vayyiqra Rabba*, 671–72. For other versions, see above, note 12.

[18]Indeed, this midrash apparently seeks to locate the two halves of Jer. 30:10 in two different time-frames: "Do not fear, my servant Jacob," was uttered by God when He first showed Jacob the ladder and asked him to climb it. But Jacob lost his nerve, and so the second half of the verse, "and do not be dismayed, Israel"—in the sense of "And do not *go down*, Israel"—was then uttered by God to Jacob's descendants.

[19]This work is found in an eclectic translation by Horace Lunt (based on published texts and several unpublished manuscripts) in J. H. Charlesworth, *OTP* 2:401–12; a translation by A. Pennington of two published recensions of the *Ladder of Jacob* is found in H. D. Sparks, *AOT*, 453–63. Previously, a translation of the text had appeared in M. R. James, *LAOT*, 96–103 based on G. N. Bonwetsch, "Die apokryphe 'Leiter Jakobs'," *Nachrichten von der Königlichen Gesellschaft der Wissenschäften zu Göttingen* (1900): 76–87. I am most grateful to Professor Lunt, my teacher in Slavonic, for having given me copies of the manuscripts used in the preparation of his translation. The work has been the subject of some recent articles; for bibliography see A. Orlov, "The Face as the Heavenly Counterpart of the Visionary in the Slavonic Ladder of Jacob," in *Studies in Scripture in Early Judaism and Christianity* 9, ed. C. A. Evans (Sheffield, U. K. Sheffield Academic Press, forthcoming).

[20]See R. Leicht, "*Qedushah* and Prayer to Helios," *JSQ* 6(1999): 140–76.

[21]The connection between this text and rabbinic exegetical traditions are, in my opinion, striking. These do not preclude an original Greek composition for the *Ladder of Jacob* but make it somewhat less likely. Moreover, the Hebrew words that survive in transcription in the text, along with other elements to be discussed below, likewise point in the direction of a Hebrew or Aramaic original. See also my brief discussion of this text in *In Potiphar's House*, 117–19.

[22]*bezakonbnъ* (= Greek ἄνομος). The Greek word was frequently used by Hellenistic Jewish and Christian writers to describe foreign nations or individuals.

In this respect, indeed, it was used in a way quite similar to "godless" ($\check{\alpha}\theta\varepsilon\text{o}\varsigma$) in the same literature; see W. Bauer, *A Greek-English Lexicon of the New Testament and Other Early Christian Literature,* translated and revised by W. F. Arndt and F. W. Gingrich (Chicago: University of Chicago Press, 1979), 72. Hence, Lunt's translation "ungodly" is the functional equivalent. In the Septuagint, $\check{\alpha}\nu\text{o}\mu\text{o}\varsigma$ often translates Hebrew רשע.

[23]In place of the word "interrogated" used by Lunt, we should probably read "tested" (Pennington translates "tried"). The Slavonic *istęzati* carries both meanings, and in context "tested" seems to make better sense. Tests in Second Temple writings were ordeals, indeed, long-term tribulations to be endured. See J. Licht, *Testing in the Hebrew Scriptures and Post-Biblical Judaism* (Hebrew) (Jerusalem: Magnes, 1973), 71–76. Alternately, this root might mean something like "afflict" or "torture" here (representing Greek $\tau\alpha\pi\varepsilon\iota\nu\acute{\text{o}}\omega$ = Heb. ענה), as does its modern Russian cognate.

[24]The word translated by Lunt as "against" here is indeed Slavonic *нa* (meaning, if followed by the accusative, "onto" or "against"), but the sense cannot be that these kings will rise up *against* Israel's iniquity but because of it. That is, God will allow these wicked kings to arise because of the sins of His people. (So similarly, two sentences later, the text explains that this site will become deserted "in the [divine] anger against your children"). Hebrew and Aramaic על can mean both "against" and "because of," and this is probably the source of the error.

[25]The manuscripts differ on whether these are four "ascents" or "descents" as well as on the "fourth ascent." On both see Lunt's translation and notes, (*OTP* 2:407, 409). My own readings are chosen for reasons that will be clear presently.

[26]Reading *pьrvo* for *pьrvoe* ("the first").

[27]The manuscripts read "struck" (*priraždjuštasę*), but this makes little sense; the verb here probably represents Hebrew פגע ("strike" but also "chance upon," "arrive at" cf. Gen. 28:10).

[28]A conjectural emendation; the MSS read *i,* "and."

[29]The verb used in the text is *priimati* ("receive," "accept") but the picture of the new ruler hosting a party for Israel's former tormentors makes little

sense. More likely it said something like "succeed" (*prĕimati*), or possibly, "surpass."

[30]The Slavonic *myslъ* here probably represents Hebrew, עצה which is both "thought" and "plan," "decree."

[31]The text reads, in various forms, *Falkonagargail*. Previous translators have sought here the name of a specific deity—without any notable success. The sense of the passage is clear enough, even if the word itself has proven elusive. On reflection, it seems to me more likely that the original text spoke of apostasy in general rather than a specific foreign god; that is, the original text referred to what is called in Aramaic *pulḥana nokhriyya* (the equivalent of Hebrew '*abodah zarah*, literally, "foreign worship," i.e., the worship of other gods) or more specifically *pulḥan gillulaya*, "the worship of idols." Such an expression would be a vivid way of referring to apostasy, turning away from the God of Israel to worship mere images, that is, foreign gods. The verb usually used with this noun phrase is "to serve, worship" ('*abad* in Hebrew, *pelaḥ* in Aramaic), which would accord with our text's "worship." Nor is it difficult to imagine a Greek translator leaving this expression in the original Aramaic (or, for that matter, a Hebrew author having used the Aramaic expression rather than the Hebrew) in order to, as it were, distance himself or the reader from this horrible prospect—much as Victorian translators of French or Italian novels sometimes left what appeared to them indelicate formulations in the original language. If left in the original Aramaic, *pulḥan gillulaya* might then be understood as a reference to a specific deity, that is, a proper noun; if so, its transformation into *Falkonagargail* can be easily accounted for. Incidentally, something similar happened with the biblical expression "a foreign god" ('*el zar*), which was transmuted into "the god Zar" in the *Paraleipomena Ieremiou* 7:29.

[32]In fact, the text goes on to evoke those ancient neighbors, Edom and Moab (6:15), but Edom here is simply the biblical Edom and not Edom-as-Rome, as it was in the insertion.

[33]See my *Traditions of the Bible*, 300–01, 312–18.

[34]Daniel speaks of 70 weeks of years, and this figure, 490 years, is the equivalent of 10 jubilees, as J. Milik has pointed out in *The Books of Enoch: Aramaic*

Fragments of Qumran Cave 4 (Oxford: Clarendon, 1976), 254; see also M. Black, *The Book of Enoch or 1 Enoch* (Leiden: Brill, 1985), 288. The *Sibylline Oracles* speaks of ten periods, as do *1 Enoch* 91:12–17; 11QMelch, and *Barnabas* 4:4. On these ten periods, see Flüsser, "Four Empires." The *Targum šeni* of the book of Esther (beginning) and *Pirqei deR. Eli'ezer* 11 both speak of ten kings whose reigns span all of human history (for the latter see the standard Warsaw edition [1852, reprinted many times], 28a and b). A number of Second Temple texts likewise speak of twelve periods or units, but there is no indication that they are based on a common tradition; twelve, like ten, was a conventional number, perhaps connected with the twelve months of the year and/or twelve hours of the day (cf. the specific mention of "hours" in *1 Enoch* 89:72, *Apoc. Abr.* 30:2). The twelve periods of *1 Enoch* 89:72 seem to extend from the end of the Babylonian exile until Alexander the Great (cf. Black, *1 Enoch*, 79, 273); our text's twelve periods in "this age" may have been fashioned in accordance with this. In *2 Baruch* 26:1–27:15 future time is likewise divided into twelve parts, but these are more precisely twelve stages of misfortune and not specific periods of time (contrast 28:1–2); nor are they connected with foreign rulers, as is made clear by 53:6 and chapters 56–70. Some versions of *4 Ezra* 14:11–12 speak of the "age" being divided into twelve "periods"; see Stone, *Fourth Ezra* (Hermeneia) (Minneapolis: Fortress, 1990), 414, 420–21. The *Apocalypse of Abraham* also speaks of twelve "times" of this age (29:2); see R. Rubinkiewicz, *L'apocalypse d'Abraham en vieux slave* (Lublin: Société des Lettres et des Sciences de l'Université de Lublin, 1987), 191–93.

[35]On this see J. L. Kugel and R. Greer, *Early Biblical Interpretation*, LEC (Philadelphia: Westminster, 1986), 40–51.

[36]The most common hypothesis is: Babylonians, Medes, Persians, and Greeks. See Dan. 2:39–41; also M. J. Gruenthaner, "The Four Empires of Daniel," *CBQ* 8 (1996), no. 1, 72–82 and no. 2, 201–12; C. Caragounis, "History and Supra-History: Daniel and the Four Empires," in A. S. van der Woude, ed., *The Book of Daniel in the Light of New Findings* (Leuven: Leuven University Press, 1993), 386f.; and J. J. Collins, *Daniel: A Commentary* (Minneapolis: Fortress, 1993), 166–70. Cf the four kingdoms of the fourth Sibylline Oracle, which are apparently present as well in 4Q243, 244 *Pseudo-Daniel*.

CHAPTER THREE

THE RAPE OF DINAH, AND SIMEON AND LEVI'S REVENGE

[1]Most commentators and translators have assumed that the text refers to forced, non-consensual intercourse, although the sequence of verbs in Hebrew, ויקח אתה וישכב אתה, is open to various interpretations. L. Bechtel, "What if Dinah Is Not Raped?" *JSOT* 62 (1994): 19–36, explores the interpretation suggested by her title; she is followed by T. Frymer-Kensky, "Virginity in the Bible," in V. H. Matthews et al., *Gender and Law in the Hebrew Bible and the Ancient Near East*, JSOT 242 (Sheffield, U.K.: Sheffield Academic, 1998), 79–96. This question, while intriguing, is not directly related to our study, which is concerned principally with the reaction of Dinah's brothers to what they clearly consider an "outrage" (Gen. 34:7).

[2]In so doing, of course, they inevitably gave expression to their own religious and cultural biases; to take up an earlier formulation, "the early exegete is an expositor with an axe to grind" (J. L. Kugel, *In Potiphar's House: The Interpretive Life of Biblical Texts* [San Francisco: HarperCollins, 1990], 248). Thus, finding the overall "pattern" in a particular exegetical work is never *opposed to* studying how that work addresses particular exegetical problems, as was suggested by a very recent study of some of the material in our chapter: L. Feldman, "Philo, Pseudo-Philo, Josephus, and Theodotus on the Rape of Dinah," *JQR* 94.2 (2004: 253–77). Indeed, the distinction between "pure exegesis" and "applied exegesis," which was made popular by Geza Vermes in *Scripture and Tradition in Judaism: Haggadic Studies* (Leiden: Brill, 1961)—and which, in truth, has its roots in various nineteenth- and early-twentieth-century attempts to present midrash as a kind of fantasy-filled folk literature, apart from a small quantity of actual "beth midrash" exegesis—is, I am afraid, doomed to fail. In my experience, at least, such a distinction in the long run comes to be quite arbitrary, an expression more of the prejudices of the scholar than anything native to the work being examined.

[3]A number of studies have examined (inter alia) the *Testament of Levi's* version of this biblical story from the standpoint of Jewish-Samaritan relations.

See in particular J. J. Collins, "The Epic of Theodotus and the Hellenism of the Hasmoneans," *HTR* 73 (1980): 91–104; also R. Pummer, "Genesis 34 in the Jewish Writings of the Hellenistic and Roman Periods," *HTR* 15 (1982): 177–88: and D. Mendels, *The Land of Israel as a Political Concept in Hasmonean Literature* (Tübingen: Mohr, 1981), 51–119. On the eventual schism between the Samaritans and the Jews, see F. Dexinger, "The Limits of Tolerance in Judaism: The Samaritans," in E. P. Sanders, ed., *Jewish and Christian Self-Definition*, 3 vols. (Philadelphia: Fortress, 1981), 2: 88–114; J. D. Purvis, "The Samaritans and Judaism," in R. A. Kraft and G.W.E. Nickelsburg, eds., *Early Judaism and its Modern Interpreters* (Philadelphia: Fortress, 1986), 81–91; R. J. Coggins, "The Samaritans in Josephus," in L. H. Feldman and G. Hata, eds., *Josephus, Judaism, and Christianity* (Leiden: Brill, 1987); and A. D. Crown, "Redating the Schism between the Judaeans and the Samaritans," *JQR* 82 (1991): 17–50. On other aspects of the texts discussed, see T. Baarda, "The Shechem Episode in the *Testament of Levi*: A Comparison with Other Traditions," in F. Garcia-Martinez et al., *Sacred History and Sacred Texts in Early Judaism: A Symposium in Honor of A. S. van der Woude*, CBET 5 (Louvain: Peeters, 1992), 11–73. (This article appeared at the same time as my own, "The Story of Dinah in the *Testament of Levi*," *HTR* 85 [1992]: 1–34, and, although different in approach, reached some of the same conclusions; see below.) More recent are the studies of M. Himmelfarb, "Levi, Phinehas, and the Problem of Intermarriage at the time of the Maccabean Revolt," *JSQ* 6 (1999): 1–24 and E. Puesch, "Le testament de Lévi en araméen de la Guéniza du Caire," *RevQ* 20 (2002): 511–56.

[4]It is difficult to justify this meaning in context—as we shall see—for how can two people attacking a whole city feel safe or secure? One possibility is that the word was intended to describe the inhabitants of Shechem and not the two attackers. Thus, one modern translation, the New Revised Standard Version, reads: "and they came against the city unawares." The last word refers to the Shechemites: *they* had the feeling of security.

[5]*Genesis Rabba* 80:10 and parallels explains בטח as בטוחים על כח הזקן, "relying on the power of the old man," that is, Jacob, whose power of influencing the outcome left them confident of victory. (This motif ultimately derives from Gen. 48:22, interpreted variously as a reference to Jacob's having joined

the fight or, possibly, as a metaphorical reference to Jacob's "prayer and supplication." See my *Traditions of the Bible*, 429–30.)

[6]This idea may be reflected as well in the version of the Dinah story preserved among the surviving fragments of the Hellenistic poet Theodotus (on whom see below). For in Theodotus's retelling, the biblical "And they came upon the city בטח" becomes "Levi and Simeon came *fully armed* into the city" (cited in Eusebius, *Praeparatio evangelica* 9.22.10). Here and throughout I have cited the translation of Theodotus made by F. Fallon in *OTP* 2: 785–93.

[7]Thus, *Midrash Tanhuma, Vayyehi* 9 (end): "מכרתיהם is Greek, for they call their swords מכירין." See also *Genesis Rabba* MS Vat. 99.5, in J. Theodor and Ch. Albeck, *Midrasch Bereschit Rabba*, 3 vols. (Jerusalem: Wahrmann, 1965), 1255 and notes.

[8]Intermarriage with the Canaanite tribes is proscribed in Deut. 7:3–6. It is clear that, in postexilic times, the issue was viewed in broader terms, and it remained a major concern: see, inter alia, Ezra 9:1, 10:2–5; Tob. 4:12; *Jub.* 20:4, 22:20, 25:4–9, 30:5; Philo, *On the Special Laws* 3:29; *T. Job* 45:3; *Jos. Asen.* 7:6; Pseudo-Philo, *LAB* 9:5, 44:7, 45:3.

[9]This is found in *Targums Ongelos, Neophyti, and pseudo-Jonathan* Gen. 34: 13. Note also that Isaac's words to Esau in Gen. 27:35, "Your brother came in *guile*," underwent a similar transformation to "wisdom" in the targums.

[10]If the correct reading nevertheless appears in Codex Graecus 731, this may be either a reflection of that particular manuscript's history of transmission, or, possibly, an emendation of the received text by a scribe who understood perfectly well the exegetical intentions of the *Testament of Levi* here. (My thanks to Michael Stone for this suggestion.)

[11]A later form of this text, represented by numerous Septuagint manuscripts, sought to solve this inconsistency by substituting the words "Simeon and Levi, Dinah's brothers, the sons of Leah," for the unspecified "they" of Gen. 34:14 in the Masoretic text. (That this is a later addition in the Septuagint text is apparent from Gen. 34:25, where, in the Septuagint as in the traditional [Masoretic] text, Simeon and Levi are presented as if for the first time: "Then two of the sons of Jacob, Simeon and Levi, Dinah's brothers, took their swords.") While the story in this form doubtless circulated widely, the exegesis underlying the

version of the Dinah story found in the *Testament of Levi* can, for reasons that will be apparent, only presume a text form like that of the Masoretic text.

[12]That is, he cursed instead of blessed (Gen. 49:7).

[13]The motif of Jacob's illness may be an attempt to account for the somewhat unusual wording of Gen: 34:30, "you have brought trouble upon me to make me odious (להבישני)." While the Hebrew word does mean "to make odious," a homonymous root in Aramaic means "to make bad" or "to make ill." See M. Sokoloff, *A Dictionary of Jewish Palestinian Aramaic of the Byzantine Period* (Ramat Gan: Bar Ilan, 1990), 83, 88. My thanks to Professor Gary Anderson for pointing this out to me.

[14]This reading thus follows the Masoretic text of Gen. 34:14; see chapter 2, note 9. But then why, according to such a reading, should the Bible say that they did so "with guile"? It seems possible that this line of interpretation could adopt the targumic strategy of understanding the phrase as meaning "with wisdom." That is, the brothers were quite right to say, "We cannot do this thing, to give our sister to one who is uncircumcised, for that would be a disgrace to us." This is precisely the interpretive line adopted by *Jub.* 30:11–14. In both, the Hebrew במרמה ("with guile") is apparently being associated with the similar-sounding בערמה, which can mean both "with craftiness" or "with wisdom."

[15]Here mention should be made of a tantalizing section of the ancient text known as the "Aramaic Levi document" (*ALD*), part of which is preserved in Cambridge Geniza Fragment col. a. This fragment was translated by R. H. Charles in idem, ed., *The Greek Versions of the Testaments of the Twelve Patriarchs* (Oxford: Clarendon, 1908), 245–56, and reexamined under ultraviolet light and republished by J. C. Greenfield and M. E. Stone, in "Remarks on the Aramaic *Testament of Levi* from the Geniza," *RB* 88 (1979): 214–30. The relevant section reads as follows: "[. . .] to do according to the law of *bk[. . .]* Jacob my father and Reu[ben my brother . . .] and we said to them [. . .] they desire our daughter and we will all be b[rothers . . .] and friends, circumcise the foreskin of your flesh, and you shall look l[ike us] and you will be sealed like us with the circumcision of [. . .]." It is impossible to be sure here who is telling what to whom. If the "we" of "we said to them" includes Levi, then Levi, Jacob, and Reuben together are apparently counseling the Shechemites to be

circumcised. On the other hand, our text of the *Testament of Levi* has no such threesome as a delegation, nor does Theodotus. On the contrary, Levi tells Jacob and Reuben to tell the Shechemites something, so the "we" here ought probably to be understood as referring to Jacob and Reuben alone. Perhaps what they are doing is reporting to Levi on their conversation with the Shechemites: "[Then said to me] Jacob my father and Reu[ben my brother, "We went to Shechem] and we said to them [since it had been made known to us that] they desire our daughter and that we all be b[rothers] and friends, 'Circumcise the foreskin of your flesh . . . [etc.].'" It would be after just such a report that Levi could introduce the sort of objection to this plan contained in the *Testament of Levi*.

[16]Indeed, there is one particular detail in *T. Levi* 6:3 that further ties these two versions together: "I advised my father and Reuben my brother that *he* should tell the sons of Hamor to be circumcised." It is not immediately clear who this "he" is, whether Jacob or Reuben, but it is most surprising that it is *he* at all. For, from the standpoint of both grammar and the biblical text, one would expect "they" (such a variant is in fact found in the Armenian text tradition; see de Jonge, *Edition*, 195). And why have "my father and Reuben" in any case? My hunch is that the *Testament of Levi*'s ultimate source simply said "my father," in keeping with the tradition preserved by Theodotus, but that, precisely because the biblical text says that the *sons of* Jacob had proposed the circumcision, this author also mentioned Reuben, who, as firstborn, would speak for the brothers. But in so doing, the author of the *Testament of Levi* inadvertently left the verb in the singular, "he would tell," as well as "our *daughter*" (she is Reuben's sister!).

[17]Barda arrived independently at the same conclusion, see "The Shechem Episode," esp. 36–40.

[18]Again this is apparently the view of Theodotus, frag. 4 (Eusebius, *Praep. Ev.* 9.22.56): "Jacob said that he would not give her until all the inhabitants of Shechem were circumcised and became as Jews."

[19]These may simply be the women, who were not slain according to the biblical account; see Jth. 9:4.

[20]Such discomfort is reflected as well in rabbinic exegesis: "For in their anger they killed a man: Did they kill only one man? And does it not say 'and they came

upon the city in certainty and killed all the males' [Gen 34:25]? But it means that they [the Shechemites] were accounted by God and by them [Simeon and Levi] as if they were only one man" (*Midrash. Tanhuma, Vayyehi* 10). See *Genesis Rabba* MS Vat, 99:5 (Theodor and Albeck, *Midrasch Bereshit Rabba*, 3: 1256).

[21]One might compare this exegetical maneuver to the well-known rabbinic interpretive rule that, when a general assertion is followed by a specification, "you must interpret in keeping with the specification." Note that Theodotus, on the contrary, apparently seeks to reconcile Gen. 34:25 with Gen. 34:26 by suggesting that Simeon and Levi slew all the males whom they encountered on their way to their only real objective, Shechem and Hamor. If so, it would still be the case that "in their wrath, they [each] killed a man," the rest being merely incidental victims sacrificed in the attainment of this goal. Note further that *T. Levi* 5:4 in most manuscripts seems to contradict the account of *T. Levi* 6:4–5, but this is doubtless because the text has been corrupted; the correct reading is perhaps preserved in the Armenian MSS: "in the midst of the sons of Hamor." See M. E. Stone, "The *Testament of Levi*; A First Study of the Armenian MSS of the *Testaments of the XII Patriarchs* in the Convent of St. James, Jerusalem" (Jerusalem: St. James, 1969), 73.

[22]If, of course, such a marriage is lawful and acceptable to the woman's family (as later interpreters make plain). For this point in the Temple Scroll and in rabbinic texts, see D. W. Halivni, *Midrash. Mishnah, and Gemara: The Jewish Predilection for Justified Law* (Cambridge, MA: Harvard University Press, 1986), 30–34. Note that, for later interpreters, this law of rape likewise applied to cases that we would describe as "statutory rape" and seduction.

[23]One might argue, of course, that the Torah had not yet been given to Israel, and that the law of leniency was thus not known to Jacob and his sons. But the notion that a preliminary revelation of scriptural law had been given to Israel's ancestors long before Sinai is well attested in many ancient texts, including the *Testaments* (see my *In Potiphar's House*, 99–101). Besides, why should God have allowed Simeon and Levi to act as they did if what they did was wrong? He ought to have punished them, or at the very least the biblical account ought to have condemned their act. That such was not the case—indeed,

that Levi's descendants later received the great gift of the hereditary priesthood—certainly implied that God approved of their action, and that, as a result, there was some crucial difference between Shechem and the rapist described in Deuteronomy.

[24]The three things mentioned here may be an attempt to elaborate on Shechem's actions as described in the biblical text: he "saw her . . . and seized her and lay with her and raped her" (Gen. 34:2). Why, an interpreter might ask, would Scripture have mentioned all these graphic details instead of just stating—indeed, in more modest language—that Dinah had been raped? The answer apparently being put forward in Judith is that each of the actions listed was in itself worthy of condemnation. Thus, this retelling expands Scripture's note that Shechem "saw her" into an indication that he *saw what he should not have seen*, that is, he "loosed the adornment of a virgin," perhaps an allusion to the hair-covering (on this see J. M. Grintz, *The Book of Judith* [Hebrew]) [Jerusalem: Mossad Bialik, 1986], 140–41). When the text says that Shechem next "uncovered her thigh," it may similarly be expanding upon the phrases "he seized her" and/or "he lay with her" in Genesis (the last especially would seem superfluous in view of the fact that it is followed by "he raped her"—superfluous unless "he lay with her" is understood to refer to something other than rape itself. All this would seem designed to build up the enormity of Shechem's offense and so justify the punishment meted out to him and his countrymen. At the same time, one ought to note a similarity between the sequence of three stages of sin detailed here and the three found in m. *Sotah* 1:7, as well as the "three things" (unspecified) by which Rahab is said to have sinned during her life as a prostitute (*Mekilta deR. Ishmael, Yitro* 1).

[25]See, for example, the rabbinic tradition represented by *Genesis Rabba* 40:5 (Theodor and Albeck, *Midrasch Bereshit Rabba*, 1: 392).

[26]In translating *T. Levi* 6:9, I have retained the common understanding of ὀγκούμενα as referring to the flocks being "big with young." Still, this is a strange notion. Did the Canaanites and Perizzites devise a method for causing Abraham's flocks to miscarry? I suspect that, in the Urtext, Abraham's flocks simply "become great," that is, numerous, and that "big with young" is a misunderstanding,

perhaps a confusion of *ntrbw* and *nt'brw* (or their Aramaic equivalents). Note also that the root מלא ("be full") was sometimes used of pregnancy; see E. Qimron, *The Hebrew of the Dead Sea Scrolls*, HSS 29 (Atlanta: Scholars 1986), 92.

[27]Note that Ebed itself is a proper name, Judg. 9:26, Ezra 5:6.

[28]See L. Ginzberg, *The Legends of the Jews*, 7 vols. (Philadelphia: Jewish Publication Society, 1909–1938), 5:314 n. 290. Note also the transformation of the biblical "Ebed Melek the Ethiopian" (Jer. 38:7) into "Abimelekh" (4 *Bar.* 3:12).

[29]These same crimes were also imputed to the Sodomites (in part on the basis of Ezek. 16:49–50) and were thought to have been the reason for their destruction; see, e.g., Wisd. 19:14; *Jub.* 16:5–7; *T. Naph.* 3, 4; *T. Benj.* 9:1; Josephus, *Jewish Antiquities* 1:194–95; *Targum Onqelos.* Gen. 13:13; 2 Pet. 2:6–7.

[30]For the historical background of this passage in Ben Sira, see J. D. Purvis, "Ben Sira and the Foolish People of Shechem," *JNES* 24 (1965): 89–94. The same thinking reflected in Ben Sira no doubt underlies two other early references to the same exegetical tradition, that found in 4Q372 as well as that reflected in *Midrash Tannaim*, both of which identify this foolish people with the Samaritans. See E. Schuller, "4Q372: A Text about Joseph," RevQ 14 (1989–90): 349–76; D. H. Hoffmann, *Midrash Tannaim Lesepher Debarim* (Jerusalem: Book Exports, 1977), 196. Note also the discussion of Samaritan origins in Josephus, *Jewish Antiquities* 12:257–64, and compare 9:288–91.

[31]Sovereignty (ἡγεμονία) here probably embraces both the priesthood and kingship; indeed, this combination is explicit elsewhere. Thus 1Q21 *Aramaic Levi Document*, frag. 1, line 2, speaks of the "kingship of the high priesthood" (cf. frag. 7, line 2), and the *Testament of Reuben* elsewhere says "For to Levi did the Lord give sovereignty" (*T. Reub.* 6:7). See further, chapter 5 below; also J. C. Greenfield and M. E. Stone, "Remarks on the Aramaic Testament of Levi from the Geniza," *RB* 86 (1979):218; and M. de Jonge, "The Testament of Levi and 'Aramaic Levi,'" *RevQ* 13 (1988):379–80.

[32]Perhaps he had in mind the Levites' slaughter of their (unidentified) fellow Israelites after the Golden Calf incident (Exod. 32:25–28).

[33]Above, note 2.

[34]See S.J.D. Cohen, *The Beginnings of Jewishness: Boundaries, Varieties, Uncertainties* (Berkeley: University of California press, 1999), especially chapter 8; citation from p. 261.

[35]C. Werman, *"Jubilees* 30: Building a Paradigm for the Ban on Intermarriage," *HTR* 90 (1997): 1–22.

[36]Werman, "Jubilees 30," does cite the article of mine on which the present chapter is based, "The Story of Dinah in the *Testament of Levi"* (*HTR* 85 [1992]: 1–34), but does not mention either Theodotus or the *Testament of Levi* in support of the early existence of this "second, permissive trend."

[37]M. Himmelfarb, "Levi, Phinehas, and the Problem of Intermarriage at the Time of the Maccabean Revolt," *JSQ* 6 (1999): 1–24.

[38]Ibid., 16. Note, however, that this article makes no mention of Theodotus, Judith, the *Testament of Levi,* or, from a somewhat later time, the *Psalms of Solomon,* and still later, Pseudo-Philo's *Book of Biblical Antiquities,* all of which may have some bearing on the question. I discussed the matter of Israel's "holy seed" and its treatment in some of these Second Temple documents in "The Holiness of Israel and the Land in Second Temple Times," in M. V. Fox et al., *Texts, Temples, and Traditions: A Tribute to Menahem Haran* (Winona Lake, IN: Eisenbrauns, 1996), 21–32. As for *Jubilees'* "characteristic idea of Israel as a kingdom of priests," I have difficulty locating this idea in that book. As will be shown below (chapter 5), Jacob, the embodiment of Israel and *Jubilees'* great hero, is pointedly *not* a priest, and the author of *Jubilees* shows some indifference throughout to issues of priestly ritual purity (chapter 5, note 36); his great issue is the impurity contracted by any Israelite (and not just priests) through contact with foreigners. Rather, I would say that *Jubilees'* "characteristic idea of Israel" is as an *angelic race* set off from the rest of humanity. See further Kugel, "The Holiness of Israel," esp. 25–27.

[39]Note also the study of C. Hayes, "Intermarriage and Impurity in Ancient Jewish Sources," *HTR* 92 (1999): 3–36, as well as the insightful treatment by G. Bohak of exogamy in Jewish communities outside of the land of Israel, "Ethnic Continuity in the Jewish Diaspora in Antiquity," in J. R. Bartlett, *Jews in Hellenistic and Roman Cities* (New York: Routledge, 2002), 175–92.

[1]Thus Ham's sin of merely seeing "his father's nakedness" (Gen. 9:20) results in the (apparently perpetual) enslavement of his son's descendants. Similarly, although the crime of raping an unmarried woman carries a relatively light penalty in Pentateuchal law (Deut. 22:28–29), Shechem is killed for having committed this crime, along with his father and countrymen (Genesis 34).

[2]Thus H. W. Hollander and M. de Jonge, *The Testaments of the Twelve Patriarchs: A Commentary* (Leiden: Brill, 1985): "The literary motif is universal, see David and Bathsheba, the elders and Susannah, Hermas and Rhode (Hermas, Vis. 1:1–2)" (99).

[3]Jonas Greenfield, "The Meaning of פחז," in Y. Avishur and J. Blau, *Studies in the Bible and the Ancient Near East Presented to Samuel E. Loewenstamm* (Jerusalem: E. Rubinstein, 1978), 35–40.

[4]That is, אל דאזלתא לקביל אפך הא כמיא. On this translation, see M. Aberbach and B. Grossfeld, *Targum Onkelos to Genesis* (New York: Ktav, 1982), 281.

[5]See the discussion in B. B. Levy, *Targum Neophyti 1: A Textual Study* (Lanham, MD.: University Press of America, 1986), 277–78.

[6]For the former see M. L. Klein, *The Fragment Targums of the Pentateuch according to Their Extant Sources*, 1 (Rome: Biblical Institute, 1980), 157.

[7]Cf. A. Shinan and Y. Zakovitch, *The Story of Reuben and Bilhah* (Jerusalem: Hebrew University, 1983), 33.

[8]A rabbinic term for the interpretation of a single (usually rare or difficult) term by breaking it down into two or more constituents.

[9]For others, see Ch. Albeck, *Genesis Rabba*, vol. 3 (Jerusalem: Wahrmann, 1965), 1205 n, 1253–54 n.

[10]It is noteworthy that *Jub.* 33:2 (cited above) specifies that Reuben had seen Bilhah "bathing *in water.*" The phrase "in water" may in itself be a reminiscence of the original exegetical connection between this motif and the phrase פחז במים.

[11]For a definition of **overkill**, see above, chapter 1.

[12]The phrase "Ephratah, house of Bethelehem" is modeled upon Gen. 35:16, 19 (cf. Mic. 5:1), but the word *house* seems strange here. Does it not represent a

double translation of the word בית in Bethlehem, as if a translator first read it as the common word for "house" and only then realized that it was the first syllable of a place name? If so, this would indicate that our text is indeed a translation. Cf. below, note 28.

[13]See H.F.D. Sparks, *The Apocryphal Old Testament* (Oxford: Claren, 1984), 102 n.

[14]It is apparently for precisely this reason that the Septuagint tradition adds the words "and it appeared evil to him" after "and Israel heard of it" (apparently on the model of Gen. 21:11, 38:10, etc.). Otherwise, why should Scripture have bothered to say "and Israel heard of it"? Cf. *Targum Pseudo-Jonathan*, "and Israel heard and it was evil to him." בראשית זוטא asks: "Why should the text say thus? So that you should not [later] wonder why the בכורה was taken from Reuben" (בראשית זוטא), ed. M. Cohen [Jerusalem: Mossad haR. Kook, 1962], 279).

[15]Hollander and de Jonge, *Commentary*, 99 n.

[16]The same basic exegetical idea is also to be found in rabbinic texts, where the assertion in Gen. 35:23 that Reuben is "the firstborn of Israel" is connected with the previous narrative and understood to mean that "even at the time of his going astray," Reuben was nonetheless declared to be Jacob's firstborn in genealogy, i.e., he was not utterly repudiated; see *Genesis Rabba* 82:11, b. *Shabbat* 55b and parallels. In other words, here too the juxtaposition of "and Israel heard" with the following list of descendants is interpreted as significant.

[17]P. Sandler, "Study of the פיסקא באמצע פסוק" (Hebrew), *PISBR* 7 (Jerusalem, 1959): 229–49, contains a review of scholarship; see, in English, S. Talmon, "Pisqah Be'emṣaʿ Pasuq and 11QS," *Textus* 5 (1966): 11–21.

[18]R. Kasher, "The Relationship between the *Pisqah Be'emṣaʿ Pasuq* and the Division into Verses . . ." *Textus* 12 (1985): 32–55. Talmon's theory (see note 17) is that the פיסקא באמצע פסוק is designed to direct the reader's attention to material found elsewhere, sometimes elsewhere in the Bible. In the case of Gen. 35:22, he thus suggests that the purpose is to direct readers "to the additional information which is recorded in 1 Chron. 5:1, to the effect that in punishment of this transgression, the [genealogical] rights of the firstborn were not divested from Reuben," but only the firstborn's double portion. But if so, then the Massoretes improperly divided the verses! Gen. 35:22 should have gone on to include

the next few words, "The sons of Leah: Reuben, Jacob's firstborn," since the fact of his still being (genealogically) the firstborn is, according to Talmon, the whole point. But it isn't. The whole point is that, as a result of Reuben's sin with Bilhah, Jacob had only twelve sons, which is why, having indicated the relationship of these two apparently separate matters, the Massoretes then broke the verse. (The same problem attaches to the arguments cited in Shinan and Zakovitch, *Reuben and Bilhah*, 23.)

[19]An ancient tradition understood that Reuben may have also lost the priesthood and kingship (alluded to, according to this interpretation, in Gen. 49:3 in the phrase יתר שאת ויתר עז) for the same sin; see below and *Targum Neophyti*, *Genesis Rabba*, ad loc. and chapter 5. A similar tradition about Simeon (who ought to have been next in line after Reuben for both offices) may underlie *T. Sim.* 5:6.

[20]Note the clear distinction here between revelation and application of the law. For, throughout *Jubilees*, the author alludes both to the existence of the "heavenly tablets"—which contain not only the Pentateuch-to-be but the true interpretation thereof, as well as, apparently, some other parts of the Bible—and the transmission of their revealed contents to Israel's ancestors. In the above-cited passage, however, our author makes it clear that while the *content* of (at least part of) the laws had been revealed to Israel's ancestors, the application of these laws to everyone had not, for this, in the view of *Jubilees*, was the reason (and apparently the only one) for the revelation at Sinai. Cf. G. Anderson, "Intentional and Unintentional Sin in the Dead Sea Scrolls," in D. P. Wright et al., *Pomegranates and Golden Bells: Studies in Honor of Jacob Milgrom* (Winona Lake, IN: Eisenbrauns, 1995), 49–64. Cf. L. Ravid, "The Specialized Concept of the 'Heavenly Tablets' in the Book of *Jubilees*" (Hebrew), *Tarbiz* 68 (1999): 463–71.

[21]See on this Kugel, *In Potiphar's House*, 82, 129–31.

[22]Hollander and de Jonge, *Commentary*, 90. The *Testament of Gad* thus holds that "the things by which a man transgresses, by these same things he is also punished" (*T. Gad* 5:10, cf. 5:9–11: *T. Sim.* 2:12). Note that this same principle is maintained in *Jubilees*: Cain kills his brother with a stone and is in turn killed when his (stone) house falls in upon him (*Jub.* 4:31–32). Cf. Wisd. 11:16

and the discussion in D. Winston, *The Wisdom of Solomon* (Anchor Bible) (Garden City, NY: Doubleday, 1979), 232–33.

[23]This is suggested by Shinan and Zakovitch, *Reuben and Bilhah*, 20–21.

[24]It is interesting that the medieval commentary *Ḥizquni* (*Ḥazzequni*) also explains this verse as if it was spoken of Reuben during his lifetime: "Let Reuben live and not die—since he sinned against his father's honor [with Bilhah] he was worthy of death, as it says, 'Honor your father and mother, so that your days may be lengthened . . . [Exod. 20:12], [implying] that if you do not honor them, your days will be shortened. That is why he said, . . . 'and not die.'"

[25]It is interesting that this problem of *when* this prayer was prayed bothered other rabbinic exegetes. Thus, *Sifrei Debarim* (347) reasons as follows: "*Let Reuben live and not die*: But was he not already dead? Then what is the meaning of *and not die*? [Let him not die] in the world to come. Another interpretation: *Let Reuben live* [because of his conduct] in the incident with Joseph [when he tried to save Joseph in Gen. 37:22], *and not die* [because of his conduct] in the incident with Bilhah." The first interpretation supplies the same explanation for "and not die" cited above from the targums, namely, "and not die in the world to come." But in so doing, the anonymous interpreter has failed to answer his own question ("But was he not already dead?"), for if "and not die" refers to the world to come, that still leaves "Let Reuben live" referring to this world, implying that these words could not have been said by Moses, unless he were quoting some earlier prayer. The second explanation in *Sifrei Debarim* offers a different way around the perceived redundancy of "live and not die": both these phrases presumably refer to life in the world to come, but the former is being urged on the basis of Reuben's meritorious behavior with Joseph, and the latter in spite of his sin with Bilhah. Cf. *Targum Onqelos* ad loc.

[26]Cf. Hollander and de Jonge, *Commentary*, 90 n.

[27]Kugel, *In Potiphar's House*, 68–69.

[28]The precise language here seems taken from Dan. 10:3, save for "wine and strong drink," a standard expression (Lev. 10:9, Num. 6:3, Deut. 29:5, etc.). The phrase "over my sin, for it was great" may reflect Ps. 25:11. If so, it is interesting to observe that this allusion does not match the language of the Septuagint,

which renders Hebrew רב ("great") as πολλὴ, whereas the *Testament of Reuben* uses μεγάλη. This may be another indication of the existence of an Aramaic or Hebrew original of the *Testament of Reuben* since a Greek original would presumably have alluded to the verse as it appeared in the Greek Bible. See also chapter 6.

[29]This motif is found as well in *Sifrei Debarim* 31 and *Midrash Tanna'im* 6:4; the connection between this motif and Reuben's repentance in the *Testament of Reuben* was pointed out by Shinan and Zakovitch (*Reuben and Bilhah*, 25).

[30]If this specific interpretation inspired Reuben's abstinence in the *Testament of Reuben*, then it is in conflict with *T. Sim.* 2:9, which on the contrary explains that Reuben was absent from the meal because he had gone to Dothan for supplies. But such an inconsistency would hardly be surprising, since double explanations (**overkill**), originating in two separate, competing motifs, often coexist in the same text. On the other hand, it may be that the author of the *Testament of Reuben* was just generally familiar with the idea of Reuben's penitence and fleshed in the details himself.

[31]Thus *Genesis Rabba* 98:4: "During the whole time that Rachel was alive, her bed was placed next to Jacob's. After Rachel died, Jacob took Bilhah's bed and placed it next to his own. Said [Reuben]: 'Is it not enough for my mother to have been made jealous while her sister was alive, but now even after her death?' He went up and upset the beds." This interpretation started from the fact that the whole incident in Gen. 35:22 is immediately preceded by Rachel's death. Seeking some causal connection between the two, this tradition then focused on the mention of *beds* in Gen. 49:4. The fact that the text seemed to speak literally of "your father's *beds*" (in the plural) might have led interpreters to conclude that Jacob was not reproaching Reuben for having slept with Bilhah, since that would presumably only involve one bed. Instead, if Reuben's sin involved *beds*, perhaps he literally did something to some beds. In keeping with this, the word חללת ("defiled, rendered impure") in Gen. 49:4—which, to an exegete well acquainted with the laws of purity and impurity, might seem particularly strange—was then explained as if it referred to some damage inflicted on the beds themselves, ill-treating them in some fashion; in the version cited, this comes out, via the similar-sounding קלקלת, as "upset" or "disarranged."

CHAPTER FIVE

HOW LEVI CAME TO BE A PRIEST

[1]Currently numbered as 1Q21; and 4Q213, 213a, 213b; 4Q214, 214a, and 214b. Emile Puesch has suggested that 4Q540, 541, and 548 were also part of the *ALD*, but this proposal has not gained much support to date; beyond an interest in the priesthood, there is not much to connect it to the *ALD* specifically.

[2]Cambridge University Geniza Fragment T-S 16 fol. 94; Bodleian Library Geniza Fragment, MS Heb c 27, fol. 56. See further J. Greenfield and M. E. Stone, "Remarks on the Aramaic Testament of Levi from the Geniza," *RB* 86 (1979): 214–30. To complicate matters somewhat, someone appears at some point to have translated this Aramaic document, or parts of it, into Greek; sections of this Greek translation were then inserted into one manuscript of the *Testaments of the Twelve-Patriarchs*, the tenth-century manuscript from Mount. Athos, Koutloumousiou 39. A translation of the Cairo Geniza fragments was printed in Charles, *APOT*, 2: 364–67; a later translation is that of M. E. Stone and J. C. Greenfield, which appears in H. W. Hollander and M. de Jonge, *The Testaments of the Twelve Patriarchs: A Commentary* (Leiden: Brill, 1985), 457–69. This has since been supplemented by official publication of the Qumran fragments, coordinated with the overlapping Geniza fragments, by Stone and Greenfield which appears in G. Brook et al., *Discoveries in the Judaean Desert*, Part XXII: *Qumran Care* 4 XVII, *Parabiblical Texts,* Part 3 (Oxford: Clarendon, 1996), 1–214. A number of recent studies have focused on the *ALD*—too numerous to mention here. For an excellent bibliography and survey of scholarship, see R. Kugler, *From Patriarch to Priest: the Levi-Priestly Tradition from* Aramaic Levi *to* Testament of Levi: SBL-EJL 9 (Atlanta: Scholars, 1996); also H. Rapp, *Jakob in Bet-El: Gen 35, 1–15 und die Jüdische Literatur des 3. und 2. Jahrhunderts* (Freiburg: Herder, 2001). While the present volume was at the press, a new, comprehensive edition of all the *ALD* material appeared: J. C. Greenfield, M. E. Stone, and E. Eshel, *The Aramaic Levi Document* (Leiden: Brill, 2004 [2005]). For the convenience of future students of the *ALD*, I have adopted this edition's new division of the text into chapters and verses.

[3]It is implied elsewhere in the *Testaments* as well, in such passages as *T. Reub.* 6:7–12, *T. Jud.* 21:1–5, *T. Iss.* 5:7, etc.

[4]The identification of this "man" as an angel is found in Hos. 12:4–5 and throughout later retellings and commentaries.

[5]As with many exegetical motifs in *Pirqei deR. Eli'ezer*, this one is found as well in *Targum Pseudo-Jonathan ad loc*. See C.T.R. Hayward, "Pirqei deRabbi Eliezer and Targum Pseudo-Jonathan," *JJS* 42 (1991): 215–46. On this passage and the continuation of this section of *Pirqei deR. Eli'ezer*, see below.

[6]This motif also appears in some manuscripts of *Midrash Tanḥuma*, whence it apparently found its way into Rashi's commentary.

[7]See Theodor and Albeck, *Bereschit Rabba*, (Jerusalem: Wahrmann, 1965), 2: 968, 972 and notes for parallels; also, S. Buber, *Midrash Aggadah* (Vienna: A. Fanto, 1894), 86 (Gen. 35:1).

[8]Technically, the verse each of them is out to explain is Gen. 35:7, which implies, without quite saying so, that Jacob paid off his vowed tithe when he returned to Bethel. But both in fact depend on the same underlying idea—that it was not Jacob himself who did the sacrificing, but that his son Levi had at some point been made a priest and was thus the obvious candidate to offer the sacrifices. In other words, both "Levi Dreamt He Was Ordained" and "Levi the Human Tithe" provide somewhat different scenarios for the same **basic motif**, "Levi Was Appointed a Priest." The question to be addressed is, Where did anyone get the idea that Levi himself was made a priest?

[9]The narrator of the book of *Jubilees* is an angel, the "angel of the presence."

[10]One could, of course, claim that Isaac's blessing of Levi as a future priest was simply the expression of a pious wish, a wish that was only subsequently put into action. The trouble with this is that, in biblical narrative, blessings (and curses) are not merely an expression of wishes but a kind of enactment—such is the case, for example, with Isaac's blessing of Jacob and Esau in Genesis 27. As I hope to make clear, however, Isaac's blessing of Levi, here as in *Jubilees*, in fact represents still more: from the standpoint of the "Chain of Priests" scheme dear to the heart of *Jubilees'* author, what Isaac is doing is officially transferring the priesthood from himself to the next incumbent.

[11]With regard to the issue of the timing of Levi's elevation to the priesthood, it is to be noted that Cambridge fragment d contains the same chronological note

found in *T. Levi* 12:5, to the effect that Levi was eighteen at the time of the revenge against Shechem and nineteen when he became a priest (this is the same sequence of events presented in *T. Levi* 2:2–3, but not in *T. Levi* 5:2–3).

[12]The normal biblical understanding is that it is the firstborn male who belongs to God (Exod. 13:13–15, Num. 18:15), but that would obviously not work here, since Levi was *not* a firstborn and yet ended up with the priesthood. Perhaps, a champion of the "human tithe" argument might claim, Reuben, the firstborn, had had to be eliminated because of his sin with Bilhah (see below), and as a result the principle of tithing was substituted in this case.

[13]Rabbinic expositors too were bothered by the fact that Simeon was passed over in favor of Levi; see *Sifrei Debarim* 349, *Midrash Tanna'im* 214–15.

[14]Other rabbinic texts presuppose the same system of counting backward: see thus *Sifrei Debarim* 355 (cf. *Midrash Tanna'im* 220), where Asher is said to have pointed out that the levitical office could either belong to him, if the counting started from Reuben, or to Levi, if the counting started from Benjamin.

[15]See the note of R. David Luria in פרקי דרבי אליעזר עם באור ר' דוד לוריה (Jerusalem: [n.p.l.], 1970), 86a and b.

[16]See L. Ginzberg, *Legends of the Jews*, 1: 332: 5: 199 n. 79, 283 n. 89. For a possible reflection of such a list of priests in *Jubilees*, see *Jub.* 19:24, 27.

[17]See on this J. C. Endres, *Biblical Interpretation in the Book of Jubilees*, CBQMS 18 (Washington, D.C.: Catholic Bible Association, 1987), 18–19.

[18]One might describe this more accurately as a "high-priesthood," for it appears that there could not be two such priests simultaneously. Thus, after Abraham appoints Isaac to be a priest, he (Abraham) is no longer eligible to offer the firstfruit sacrifices; in the next chapter, they are offered by Isaac.

[19]The reference to the altar that Jacob "established" (ויצב) in Gen. 33:20 was apparently less of a problem, since no sacrifices are mentioned and the unusual verb used here (instead of בנה, "build") might allow an interpreter to conclude that what Jacob did was something less than what was done by the priests Abraham and Isaac, both of whom are said to have *built* an altar and "called on the name of the Lord" (Gen. 12:8 and 26:25). Whatever the case, *Jubilees* makes no mention at all of this incident; Jacob is thus a nonpriest throughout the book.

[20]It is certainly significant that the *ALD* passes over this blessing in a single sentence: "And we went to my father Isaac, and he likewise blessed me thus"

(*ALD* 5:1). Here, Isaac's blessing is specifically subordinated to Levi's previously reported visions: *they* are what usher Levi into the priesthood and Isaac's blessing only confirms their message. If the "Chain of Priests" motif was important for *Jubilees*, it apparently was not so crucial for the *ALD*.

[21]The text says Rebekah's "nurse," but I have discovered this is somewhat confusing for readers of English, since nowadays it might seem to imply that the woman in question had nursed Rebekah herself, whereas clearly the text intends to say that she was a wet-nurse who had helped Rebekah with her infant children and, apparently, stayed on as a household servant. For that reason I have used the word "servant" rather than "nurse," here and throughout.

[22]The connection of this passage with the *Jubilees* material was already pointed out by J. C. VanderKam, "Jubilees and the Priestly Messiah of Qumran," RevQ 13 (1988): 353–65.

[23]So, incidentally, is the verse rendered in the Septuagint.

[24]Note that the blessing of Moses (Deut. 33:9) likewise alludes to a divine covenant between God and the Levites: "for they kept what You had said, and will hold fast to Your covenant." Here, however, the plural verb leaves room for the notion that this covenant is in fact with the Levites as a tribe rather than with the individual named Levi.

[25]Of course, מלאך can refer to a human as well as divine emissary in biblical Hebrew, but that is quite irrelevant here, for "emissary of the Lord of hosts" certainly implied a divine emissary, an angel, and so this phrase was interpreted from the Septuagint on.

[26]Just such an understanding of נחת as "go down" in this verse is reflected in b. *Berakhot* 12 b; the verse is adduced to support the idea that one should "go down" (= bow down or remain bowed) at the mention of the divine name.

[27]As for Levi's reading what was "written in heaven by the finger of God," this may be a reference to Jacob's reading the seven tablets from heaven in *Jub.* 32:20–26, which he then wrote down (v. 26) and apparently passed on to Levi before his death (*Jub.* 45:16).

[28]It seems unlikely, in any case, that *Pirqei deR. Eliʿezer* was dependent on the later, Greek *Testament of Levi* for this section. (Many scholars theorize that elsewhere *Pirqei deR. Eliʿezer* is indeed dependent on Greek sources.) The expression

translated as "food to eat" in the above passage, טרף מזונם, is a somewhat strange turn of phrase; it seems as if מזונם ("their food")—the common word for food in Mishnaic Hebrew—is actually a kind of gloss here for the rarer, biblical word טרף ("food"). But what could there have been in a Greek text that might have led the author of *Pirqei deR. Eli'ezer* to dredge up this biblical word and then give it a gloss in Mishnaic Hebrew? (Note that the meaning of טרף, problematic in rabbinic times, is explicitly the subject of the discussion in b. *Sanhedrin* 108b.) As R. David Luria observed in his commentary on *Pirqei de R. Eli'ezer* (86a and b), its use here seems to be a deliberate allusion to Malachi's use of the word טרף in Mal. 3:10. But no such allusion to טרף could carry through in a text preserved in Greek. It thus seems that *Pirqei deR. Eli'ezer* was relying here on some ancient text in Hebrew or Hebraizing Aramaic.

[29]In this respect, palaeography has thus proven itself to be somewhat more accurate than another procedure for establishing a manuscript's age, carbon dating, which usually allows the chemical content of a given manuscript or other object to be dated within a range of half a century or more. On its use with Qumran material, see G. Bonani, M. Broshi, et al., "Radiocarbon Dating of the Dead Sea Scrolls," *'Atiqot* 20 (1991): 27–32; M. Broshi, "The Dating of the Judean Desert Scrolls through Examination of Carbon 14 and Its Significance," *Qadmoniyot* 30 (1997): 71–73; and particularly G. Doudna, "Dating the Scrolls on the Basis of Radiocarbon Analysis," in P. W. Flint and J. C. VanderKam, *The Dead Sea Scrolls after Fifty Years: A Comprehensive Assessment* (Leiden: Brill, 1998), 1: 430–71, which explains the significance of the chronological range of 197–105 B.C.E established for 4Q213. On the technique in general: R. E. Taylor, *Radiocarbon Dating: An Archaeological Perspective* (Orlando, FL: Academic Press, 1987); S. Bowman, *Radiocarbon Dating* (Berkeley: University of California Press, 1990); R. E. Taylor and M. Aitken, *Chronometric Dating in Archaeology* (New York: Plenum, 1997), 65–96. As for dating the texts on linguistic grounds, the Aramaic dialect of the *ALD* was identified by Greenfield as Standard Literary Aramaic, similar, for example, to the *Onqelos* and *Jonathan* targums; if so, it can offer no real help in pinpointing the date of the text's composition. See Greenfield and Stone, "Remarks on the Aramaic Testament of Levi," 227–29. Note also J. Fitzmyer, "The Aramaic Levi Document," in *The*

Provo International Conference on the Dead Sea Scrolls (Leiden: Brill, 1999), 453–64, which seeks to distinguish the Aramaic of the Qumran fragments of the *ALD* from that of the Geniza fragments, arguing that both the latter and the Greek *Testament of Levi* represent "revisions of, if not completely new compositions based on, the ancient Jewish Levi text now known to us from Qumran" (426).

[30]This is true, for example, of M. E. Stone, "Aramaic Levi in Its Contexts," *JSQ* 9 (2002): 307–26, and R. A. Kugler, *From Patriarch to Priest: The Levi-Priestly Tradition from* Aramaic Levi *to* Testament of Levi, *SBLEJL* 9 (Atlanta: Scholars, 1996). A second century B.C.E date has been urged by P. Grelot, K. Beyer, and A. Hultgård.

[31]The same approximate dating has been suggested for another *Jubilees* manuscript, 4Q222.

[32]In H. Attridge et al., *Discoveries in the Judaean Desert Part XIII: Qumran Cave 4 viii, Parabiblical Texts, Part 1* (Oxford: Clarendon, 1994), 2.

[33]Kugler, *From Patriarch to Priest* notes (p. 4) that this tradition goes back to an article published by R. H. Charles and Crowley in 1907, though, to be accurate, they had hypothesized the existence of an original Hebrew Levi text, used both by *Jubilees* and the *ALD*. Kugler himself begins by asserting the precedence of *Jubilees* to *ALD* as an established fact (p. 3), although, to be fair, he does go on to consider other possibilities.

[34]For this passage see Stone and Greenfield, "The First Manuscript of *ALD* from Qumran," *Le Muséon* 107 (1994): 274; idem in Brooke et al., *Parabiblical Texts, Part 3,* 20.

[35]See my *Traditions of the Bible* (Cambridge, MA: Harvard University Press, 1998), 468–74, 491–96. Note in particular 4Q252, which explains Gen. 49:10 in the straightforward sense of "a ruler from the tribe of Judah will not depart so long as Israel has dominion"; see M. Bernstein, "4Q252: From Rewritten Bible to Biblical Commentary," *JSJ* 45 (1994): 1–27. In other words, this "plain sense" reading understood the verse to say that kingship in Israel will always belong to the tribe of Judah.

[36]Thus, there is no hint in *Jubilees* of the belief in a future messiah, but this belief is well documented at Qumran. Recent research has also shown that

Jubilees has a different set of Sabbath laws from that of Qumran (L. Ravid, "Sabbath Halakhot in the Book of *Jubilees*," *Tarbiz* 69 (2000): 161–66); and a somewhat different calendrical system (See L. Ravid, "The Book of *Jubilees* and Its Calendar—a Reexamination," *DSD* 10 [2003]: 371–94); some further differences are summarized in Kugler, *From Patriarch to Priest*, 142. Moreover, as VanderKam notes, *Jubilees* rejected any use of the moon for calendrical calculations, whereas the lunar calendar "is now well attested for Qumran"; see his *The Dead Sea Scrolls Today* (Grand Rapids: Eerdmans, 1994), 115. No one disputes that the Qumran documents display a great concern for the priesthood and ritual purity; at the same time, these texts make clear the community's alienation from the Jerusalem temple under its then-current leadership. In *Jubilees*, the situation is quite the reverse. Its author has nothing bad to say about the Jerusalem priests themselves (although he does believe that they are using the wrong cultic calendar); on the other hand, he shows a marked lack of interest in the priesthood and in matters of ritual purity. At one point *Jubilees* even arranges things so as to have Jacob, Israel's founder, come into contact with the dead body of his grandfather, although there is no scriptural warrant for such a scene and no exegetical purpose in it. It almost seems as if the author of *Jubilees* were saying, "The priesthood, with all its concern for ritual purity, is not the be-all and end-all of Israel's religion. Look at how things were back in the days of the patriarchs!" (On this: L. Ravid, "Purity and Impurity in the Book of *Jubilees*," *JSP* 13 [2002]: 61–86; cf. J. VanderKam, "Viewed from Another Angle: Purity and Impurity in the Book of *Jubilees*," *JSP* 13 [2002]: 209–15.) Neither Jacob nor anyone else in *Jubilees* is ever said to undergo ritual purification. Indeed, although Abraham, Isaac, and other early figures are presented as offering sacrifices and functioning as priests, Jacob, the great hero of *Jubilees*, is pointedly *not* a priest. Surely there is a message here. By contrast, the author of *Jubilees* shows an overriding interest in what has been called "moral impurity," particularly that deriving from contact with non-Jews; of such impurity the Qumran community documents have a rather different view (see J. Klawans, *Impurity and Sin in Ancient Judaism* [New York: Oxford, 2000], 74). All this makes it clear that a significant gap separates the world of *Jubilees* from that of Qumran.

[37]R. Doran, "The Non-Dating of Jubilees: Jub. 34–38; 23:14–32 in Narrative Context," *JJS* 20 (1989): 1–12. Note that VanderKam, while sticking to his original dating of *Jubilees* to between 161 and 152 B.C.E, has taken cognizance of the arguments of Nickelsburg and Goldstein for a *terminus post quem* of 170 B.C.E (for a summary of the arguments, see G.W.E. Nickelsburg, *Jewish Literature between the Bible and the Mishnah* [Philadelphia: Fortress, 1981], 78–79). VanderKam thus concludes, "It seems safe to claim that the Book of Jubilees was written between the years 170 and 150 B.C." (J. C. VanderKam, *The Book of Jubilees*, CSCO 511 [Scriptores Aethiopici Tom. 88], vi). For my part, I do not believe that there is any firm reason to establish even 170 B.C.E as a *terminus post quem*; about *Jubilees* 23, which forms much of the basis for this dating, see my "The Jubilees Apocalypse," *DSD* 1 (1994): 322–37. (My position on this is thus somewhat misrepresented in Rapp, *Jakob in Bet-El*, 92 n.) See also note 38, below. I do not find the broad resemblances adduced between the *Jubilees* version of the events leading up to the Flood and those in the "Book of Dreams" section of 1 *Enoch* to require *Jubilees*' dependence on the "Book of Dreams." What both texts seem to share is the book of Genesis and the exegetical traditions that arose to explain its cryptic words in 6:1–4. This body of ancient exegesis is one of the earliest and most exhaustive in our possession; see my *Traditions of the Bible*, 191–221. For this reason, it seems altogether likely that some of these traditions go back long before the "Book of Dreams" and circulated independently; cf. J. VanderKam, "Enoch Traditions in *Jubilees* and Other Second Century Sources," *SBLSP* 13 (1978): 1:229–51.

[38]*Bibliotheca Historica* 40:3; the passage is reprinted in M. Stern, *Greek and Latin Authors on Jews and Judaism* (Jerusalem: Israel Academy of Sciences, 1976), 1: 26.

[39]For others see below, as well as my article, "Levi's Elevation to the Priesthood in Second Temple Writings," *HTR* 86 (1993): 1–64.

[40]I have chronicled quite a few of these in *Traditions of the Bible*.

[41]See below, note 48, on the chronology of *ALD* 11:1–12:9 and the common mention of Milcah, Levi's wife, in *Jub.* 34:20 and *ALD* 11:1. Note that here, as evidenced elsewhere in *Jubilees* (e.g., 4:15, 20, 27; 8:1, 5, 6; 11:14; etc.), an unnamed character has been assigned a proper name known from elsewhere in the

Bible; this would also support the proposition that the *ALD* here depends on *Jubilees.*

[42]One instance of this is Isaac's blessing of Levi (*ALD* 5:1) in *Jub.* 31:12–17. Among other things, Isaac here informs Levi that his descendents will be ראשין ושפטין. As the editors of the *ALD* themselves point out, the second word "is extremely rare in Aramaic, and is in all likelihood a Hebraism. . . . The phrase has an antique flavor and is surely based on a Hebrew Vorlage." That "Hebrew Vorlage" is in fact none other than the book of *Jubilees,* where Levi is told that his descendants "will become judges and rulers" (*Jub.* 31:15). A word that was indeed extremely rare in Aramaic had been altogether natural in the Hebrew of *Jubilees;* thus, in this case as well, there can be little doubt who borrowed from whom. For other Hebraisms in the *ALD,* see Fitzmyer, "Aramaic Levi," 464; cf. S. E. Fassberg, "Hebraisms in the Aramaic Documents from Qumran," in T. Muraoka, *Studies in Qumran Aramaic,* AbrNS 3 (Louvain: Peeters, 1992), 48–69.

[43]I believe that in one of the *ALD*'s sources, the vision I have called "Levi's Apocalypse," there had been no mention of Levi's exact age at the time of his death. All that mattered to the creator of this vision was Joseph's death at the age of 110, which appeared prominently in the last verse of Genesis (Gen. 50:26); this, as far as he was concerned, set the scene for Levi to assemble his children and instruct them. However, the *Jubilees*-influenced author of the *ALD* felt obliged to give his own historical summary of Levi's life, right down to the exact year of his death, which is mentioned in passing in the book of Exodus in a list of Levi's descendants (Exod. 6:16)—and so the dissonance was created.

[44]C. Werman, "Levi and Levites in the Second Temple Period," *DSD* 4 (2003): 211–25.

[45]See Kugler, *From Patriarch to Priest,* 130–31 and passim.

[46]The *Damascus Document* refers to "the three nets of Belial, about which Levi the son of Jacob spoke" (4:15). These words seem indeed to refer to some text attributed to Levi, and the "three nets" might well have come in one of the wisdom speeches (now lost) of this ancestor of the *ALD.* The Damascus Document's reference to these three nets hardly proves, as Stone seems to assume (most recently in "Aramaic Levi in Its Contexts," 319) that the *ALD* itself

preceded the Damascus Document; that would be so only if it could be proven that the *ALD* had no ancestor but was created ex nihilo. (This indeed appears to be Stone's position, but it runs into difficulty with those passages in which the *ALD* contradicts itself.) J. C. Greenfield, in "The Words of Levi son of Jacob in Damascus Document 4.15–19," *RQ* 13 (1988): 319–22, sought to find a reference to Belial's "three nets" in the present *ALD* text, but his case rests on the improbable emendation of ההין to פם. More likely, the "three nets" passage was in part of the *ALD* now lost—and in an ancestor document.

[47]On this: C. Werman, "The Rules of Consuming and Covering the Blood in Priestly and Rabbinic Law," *RQ* 16 (1995): 621–36. It seems to me plausible that this second text, "Levi's Priestly Initiation," did not contain *all* the priestly instructions now found in *ALD* 6:2–10:10. Some may have been added by the *ALD*'s own author; note that the rules in *ALD* 8:1–9:18 have no correspondent in *Jubilees* 21.

[48]In a recent article, "Isaac's Blessing of Levi and His Descendents in *Jubilees* 31," (in D. W. Parry and E. Ulrich, *The Provo International Conference on the Dead Sea Scrolls*, STDJ 30 [Leiden: Brill, 1999], 497–519), J. VanderKam, has resisted my contention that the *ALD* is dependent on *Jubilees*, suggesting instead that they shared a common source, since "[t]he dates in *Aramaic Levi* and *Jubilees* do not tally at all where they can be compared." I find this observation a little less devastating to the case of the *ALD*'s direct dependence on *Jubilees* than VanderKam does. What this comparison shows, in fact, is precisely the opposite: the striking similarity of *Jubilees* and the *ALD* in the passages to which VanderKam refers (*ALD* 11:1–12:9; *Jub.* 28:15, 30:1, 32:2, 44:8). Thus, the *ALD* and *Jubilees* turn out to be the only two texts that seem to know that Levi's wife was named Milcah; moreover, the two texts here agree exactly on the sequence of events in Levi's life and even on the intervals of years separating those events. The only difference between them is that the ages specified for Levi in the *ALD* come out to be consistently three years more than the age that Levi would have had if his birth year were 2127 *anno mundi*, as *Jubilees* maintains (28:15). This would suggest that the author of the *ALD* either deliberately changed or miscalculated the year of Levi's birth, putting it in 2124 rather than 2127 (Unfortunately, he did not have R. H. Charles's edition in front him, with

its convenient noting of all dates *anno mundi* in the margin!) Then the years would match up perfectly, if not quite down to the month. It is, of course, troubling to depend on sloppy mathematics to explain the texts as we have them; however, any *other* accounting for the sequence of dates in these two texts must similarly presume an error or deliberate change on someone's part. That is, if *Jubilees'* author copied from the *ALD*, he too must have slipped up (and how likely is it that this careful chronologist made such an elementary mistake?). If the two of them copied from a common source, one or both must have miscopied. Alternately, as mentioned, one author may have deliberately changed what the other had written—but again, this gives no reason for preferring one theory of precedence to the other.

[49] Above, note 44.

[50] The matter of *when* Isaac instructed Levi had no particular urgency for this author. He knew nothing of the pressing need to have Levi become a priest in time to offer Jacob's sacrifices at Bethel or any of the exegetical issues that were to animate the author of *Jubilees*. In fact, it would even be a bit inaccurate to say that he subscribed fully to the "Chain of Priests" theme so beloved to *Jubilees'* author; if he did, there would have been no reason to have with the seven angels initiate Levi—Isaac would have simply given Levi the nod and the priesthood would have been his. But for this author what was important was that Levi and the Levites had been *divinely* selected for the priesthood and, in fact, initiated into it; that is why this selection had to be enacted by angels. That Isaac and Abraham and others had functioned earlier as priests may have been true, but this was, for our author, an interim measure: the true hereditary priesthood began with Levi. Consequently, Isaac's instructions to Levi about sacrificing are not really one priest's preparation of his successor for the job; Isaac was, for this author, only a stopgap priest. Rather, these instructions of Isaac's represent the transmission of divinely revealed knowledge, passed down from the time of Noah onward. Noah himself had instructed his sons about not eating blood (Gen. 9:4, understood as "But flesh with its soul—[that is,] its blood—you shall not eat"). He must at the same time have instructed them about covering the blood. These things, for our author, concerned all Israelites, not just priests. See Werman, "Rules of Consuming and Covering."

Chapter Six

Judah and the Trial of Tamar

[1]The interpretive history of the story of Judah and Tamar has been treated in detail in two studies, A. Shinan and Y. Zakovitch, *The Story of Judah and Tamar: Genesis 38 in the Bible, the Old Versions, and the Ancient Jewish Literature* (Jerusalem: Hebrew University, 1992); and E. Menn, *Judah and Tamar (Genesis 38) in Ancient Jewish Exegesis: Studies in Literary Form and Hermeneutics* (Leiden: Brill, 1997). The present chapter is intended to supplement these excellent studies.

[2]This is the long-held view of M. De Jonge; see, for example, H. W. Hollander and M. De Jonge, *The Testaments of the Twelve Patriarchs: A Commentary* (Leiden: Brill, 1985), 27–29. The same view is espoused by R. Kugler, in *The Testaments of the Twelve Patriarchs* (Sheffield: Sheffield Academic, 2001). The stilted Semitisms would thus, according to this view, represent a Greek author's attempt to "sound biblical," adopting unusual or awkward phrasing found in the Septuagint. This is indeed a recognized phenomenon in Greek pseudepigrapha of the Bible. Note, however, the cautionary study of G. Alon, "Mishnaic Hebrew in the *Testaments of the Twelve Patriarchs*," *Tarbiz* 12 (1941): 268–74. (While most of his examples are altogether convincing, his claim that the use of ἐπισκέπτομαι as a calque of בקר in connection with caring for the sick appears, however, to be in error: actually, the opposite is true.)

[3]M. De Jonge, *Testaments of the Twelve Patriarchs: A Study of Their Text, Composition and Origin* (Assen: van Gorcum, 1975), 78.

[4]M. Jastrow, *A Dictionary of the Targumim, the Talmud Babli and Yerushalmi, and the Midrashic Literature* (New York: Jastrow, 1967), 1178.

[5]Combined with this, the word מס then suggests the payment of part of the farmer's gain as tax or tribute. That is, Issachar is being described as a *tenant* farmer; see below.

[6]Note, however, that this connection is lost in the Septuagint's τὸ καλὸν ἐπεθύμησεν (apparently reading חמד for חמר).

[7]See A. Tal, *The Samaritan Targum of the Pentateuch*, vol. 1 (Tel Aviv: Tel Aviv University, 1980), 212. For אריס as "tenant farmer," see M. Sokoloff, *A*

Dictionary of Jewish Palestinian Aramaic of the Byzantine Period (Ramat Gan: Bar Ilan, 1990), 74. Note that same phrase, מס עבד , appears in Josh. 16:10, where the *Jonathan* targum renders it מסקי מסין פלחין, "payers of tribute, [farm-]workers."

[8]On the development of this tradition, see M. Beer, "Issachar and Zebulon," *BIA* 6 (1978): 167–80.

[9]It is noteworthy that de Jonge did not grasp the exegetical basis of all this: he says "These passages show that the author dealt very freely with the contents of his sources and altered the stories to make them illustrate his exhortations" (*Testaments: A Study*, 67).

[10]"The author of the *Testament of Reuben* may have changed the original story in order to draw attention once more to the evil effects of drunkenness" (de Jonge, *Testaments: A Study*, 73).

[11]The matter of Judah's actual guilt was related to another question, namely, the meaning of the phrase לא יסף in Gen. 38:26. The sense was far from clear in ancient times (see b. *Soṭah* 10b and parallels): Did it mean that Judah did not know her again, or, perhaps, just the opposite, that he *did not cease* to know her? If the latter, then certainly he must have been guilty of nothing.

[12]So the passage seems to imply. In all probability, however, it is to be understood in keeping with other versions (see below), which hold that the words "From me" were not spoken by Judah at all, but by God (or a heavenly voice) testifying in Judah's name.

CHAPTER SEVEN

A PRAYER ABOUT JACOB AND ISRAEL FROM THE DEAD SEA SCROLLS

[1]S. Fraade, *Enosh and His Generation* (Chico, CA: Scholars, 1984).

[2]H. Attridge and J. Strugnell, "The Prayer of Enosh," in *Qumran Cave 4.VIII Parabiblical Texts*, part 1, H. Attridge et al., *Discoveries in the Judaean Desert* 13 (Oxford: Clarendon, 1994). An earlier version of it appeared in B. Z. Wacholder and M. Abegg, *A Preliminary Edition of the Unpublished Dead Sea Scrolls: The Hebrew and Aramaic Texts from Cave 4* (Washington: Biblical Archaeology Society, 1991–92), 2: 233–36. The translations of Qumran texts cited here are my own.

[3]This suggestion by the editors was then taken up by C. A. Evans, in "A Note on the 'First-Born Son' of 4Q369," *DSD* 2 (1995).

[4]Here the editors proposed to read the word מלאך, "angel."

[5]The editors proposed to read מועדיהם, "their festivals."

[6]Cf. Dan. 12:6.

[7]On this sense of תעודה see my article, "Biblical Apocrypha and Pseudepigrapha and the Hebrew of the Second Temple Period," in T. Muraoka and J. F. Elwolde, eds. *Diggers at the Well: Proceedings of a Third International Symposium on the Hebrew of the Dead Sea Scrolls and Ben Sira* (Leiden: Brill, 2000), 166–77.

[8]The verb שעשע could be construed intransitively, as in Isa. 11:8, or it could have Israel as its direct object. The possibility of a substantive, שעשועה, should also be considered. All of these seem a bit more probable than the שעה proposed by Evans ("A Note," 196 n. 37).

[9]The editors proposed reading here: "his love your soul cleaves to." My only hesitation at this reading is that the "your," apparently referring to God, would turn this line into a reference to the divine "soul." While such references do exist in the Hebrew Bible (2 Sam. 22:16, Isa. 30:33; Job 4:9, 32:8, 33:4, 37:10—all with נשמה, none with נפש), they are relatively rare. Perhaps, then, it would be better to see this as an internal quotation, that is, God speaks of "My love" and urges Israel that "Your soul cleave to Me" (or "My service" or something similar). These words would apparently have been uttered by God when He delivered His "righteous laws" to Israel. See further below.

[10]It has been suggested, on the basis of Syriac אבוהא, that Hebrew אבות means "intercessors": see P. Wernberg Møller, *The Manual of Discipline* (Leiden: Brill, 1957), 53–54. The editors therefore translate the term as "angel of intercessions," certainly a possibility; still "fathers" seems far likelier. Instead of their "prison" for משמר, it might be better to read this as a verb, "is guarding."

[11]See, in this connection, John 5:17, "My Father is working still, and I am working," a statement apparently implying that God rested *only* on the first Sabbath and has kept no others since. Philo maintains that God continues to create on the Sabbath (*Allegories of the Law* 1:18).

[12]See further: J. Kugel, "The Holiness of Israel and the Land in Second Temple Times," in M. V. Fox et al., *Texts, Temples and Traditions: A Tribute to*

Menahem Haran (Winona Lake, IN: Eisenbrauns, 1996), 25–26; L. Doering, "The Concept of the Sabbath in the Book of Jubilees," in M. Albani et al., eds., *Studies in the Book of Jubilees* (Tübingen: Mohr-Siebeck, 1998), 179–205; J. Kugel, *Traditions of the Bible* (Cambridge, MA: Harvard University Press 1998), 88–90.

[13]For this very reason, according to *Jubilees*, Israel's observance of the Sabbath bears witness to the special status of that people. Israel is, in this book's view, a quasi-angelic nation (and corresponding to the highest angels at that!), its observance of the Sabbath constituting but one way in which it is connected directly to God and unlike any other nation on earth. Again, Kugel, "The Holiness of Israel," 25.

[14]This theme is comparable to another one, which held that the Torah (= divine wisdom) was created before the world itself, and that Israel was even at that early date designated as the Torah's future recipient. See Bar. 3:32–4:1, *T. Moses* 1:12. *4 Ezra* 6:55–56 (also: 6:59, 7:11), Pseudo-Philo, *LAB* 28.4, and the discussion of these and other texts in my *Traditions of the Bible*, 86–87.

[15]On this passage, see E. G. Chazon, "A Liturgical Document from Qumran and Its Implications: 'Words of the Luminaries' (4QDibHam)" Ph.D. dissertation, (Hebrew University, Jerusalem, 1991), 248–49; note also 4Q504, frag. 26, 4-6, " . . .]nations[. . .]firstborn[. . .]your land[. . . and her comments on p. 176. Overall, the resemblance between the "Prayer of Enosh" and the "Words of the Luminaries" is striking.

[16]The wisdom text 4Q418, frag. 81, 5 similarly reads, "He [God] made your glory exceedingly great, and He made you (וישימכה) a firstborn to Himself." Unfortunately, it is impossible to know from the fragmentary context if this assertion was connected to the theme of divine discipline. (My thanks to Torleif Elgvin for pointing this out.)

[17]Similarly: "Have mercy on the people called by Your name, Israel whom You *named* Your firstborn" (Sir. 36:17). Note also the marginal version of Hebrew MS B of Sir. 44:23, "And He *called him* by the firstborn's portion"; also, "But we are Your people, whom You *have called* Your firstborn" (4 *Ezra* 6:58); "And to Jacob his [Isaac's] son, the third [generation], whom You *called* 'firstborn.'" (Pseudo-Philo, *LAB* 18.6). Even *Jubilees*, with its quite distinct

explanation of Israel's firstborn status (seen above), says that God had *written them down* as My firstborn." (This tradition may have also been influenced by the wording בכור אתנהו in Ps. 89:28.)

[18]Note also in this connection Isa. 1:2, "Sons have I raised and lifted up" (גדלתי ורוממתי).

[19]Those belonging to the so-called GII edition of Ben Sira; see on this J. Ziegler, *Sapientia Iesu Filii Sirach* (Göttingen: Vandenhoeck & Ruprecht, 1965), 203.

[20]MT: "sons of Israel." The reading "angels of God" is found in the Septuagint version, cf. 4QDeut[g] ". . .] בני אל"; and P. W. Skehan, "A Fragment of the 'Song of Moses' (Deut. 32) from Qumran," *BASOR* 136 (1954): 12–15; and E. Tov, *The Text-Critical Use of the Septuagint in Biblical Research* (Jerusalem: Simor, 1981), 290.

[21]M. J. Davidson, *Angels at Qumran*, JSPs 11 (Sheffield: JSOT, 1992), 263.

[22]The editors of the "Prayer of Enosh" translated this word as "divided," but Evans correctly rendered it as "allotted his portion," pointing out that פלג is used elsewhere at Qumran in this sense ("A Note on the Firstborn," 196; to his example might be added 1QH 1:18; 13:13, and instances in 4Q509, 4Q511, etc.). Interestingly, the verb is used in the same sense and in the same context in the new readings of the *Genesis Apocryphon*: ". . . apportioned the whole earth[. . .]" (*GA* 3:17); "the portion that his father Noah apportioned (פלג) to him and gave to him . . . Japhet also apportioned (פלג) among his sons" (*GA* 17: 15–16). See M. Morgenstern et al., "The Hitherto Unpublished Columns of the Genesis Apocryphon," *AbrN* 33 (1995): 30–54. It is not beyond the realm of possibility that פלג was used in this context because of its biblical associations with Peleg, who was so named because "in his days the earth was divided (נפלגה)" (Gen. 10:25). If so, then it was at that time that Israel as well received its territorial inheritance; the land was, as it were, *peleged* off to Israel after the great flood.

[23]On these see Davidson, *Angels*, 144–58, 224–27.

[24]This whole subject has been adeptly surveyed in S. Olyan, *A Thousand Thousand Served Him* (Tübingen: J.C.B. Mohr, 1993).

[25]See Olyan, *Thousand*, 52–53, 73 n.

[26]This same angel of peace is attested at Qumran, in 4Q228 ("Text with Citation from Jubilees," frag. 1, col. 1, line 8); 4Q428 (*Thanksgiving Hymns* 17:3); and 3Q8 (Unclassified Documents). The latter have been published by M. Baillet in *Les "petites grottes" de Qumran, DJD* 3, (p. 100). Unfortunately, little can be deduced about the nature of this angel from these fragments. An "angel of peace" also accompanies Enoch in the "Book of Parables (or 'Similitudes')" (1 *Enoch* 40:8, 52:5, 53:4, 54:4, 56:2, and 60:24); he serves as Enoch's personal guide and is clearly different from Michael et al. (see 1 *Enoch* 40:9), though again, details of his function or powers are lacking.

[27]The fact that these words were Isaac's and not God's—indeed, the fact that Jacob obtained them by fraud—was hardly an impediment to ancient interpreters who wished to see in them a true, divinely granted blessing. As *Jubilees* states explicitly and later interpreters repeat, Isaac "did not recognize him [Jacob] because it was a distraction from heaven to turn aside his mind . . . so that he should bless him" [*Jub.* 26:18]. In other words, the blessing was indeed intended by God. Similarly, an angel tells Isaac after he has blessed Jacob, "My beloved Isaac, all the peoples which are in the world, if they were gathered together in one place, would not be able to undo your blessing upon Jacob; because, at the time that you blessed him, he was blessed by the supreme God . . ." [*T. Isaac* 2:20]. A similar understanding may have attached to "Israel is My firstborn," namely, that God endorsed Esau's sale of his firstborn's rights to Jacob for a bowl of lentils and that it is in this sense that Jacob/Israel was God's firstborn. This may be the sense of Ben Sira's statement—probably somewhat garbled in all textual witnesses—about Jacob,

> And to Isaac as well He gave a son, for the sake of his father Abraham.
> The covenant of all the former ones He gave him, and a *blessing rested* upon the head of Israel.
> And He recognized him as the firstborn [or: "called him by the firstborn's portion"] and He gave him his inheritance.
>
> (Sir. 44:22–23)

In other words, Jacob's purchase of the firstborn status was "recognized" (the same word used in regard to the firstborn of Deut. 21:17) by God and made official when He declared, "Israel is My firstborn son" in Exod. 4:22. The same understanding appears later, in rabbinic writings:

> What is the meaning of "Israel is My firstborn son"? [Exod. 4:22]. This is spoken about our father Jacob, who bought the birthright so that he might serve [as a priest] before God. (*Exodus Rabba* 5:7)

It is, of course, possible that a similar exegesis underlies 4Q369, but, alas, in its present state the text cannot warrant such a conclusion.

[28]Attridge and Strugnell, "The Prayer of Enosh," 357.

[29]That the act of blessing required the laying of the hands upon the head of the one to be blessed is evident from, for example, Gen. 48:14.

[30]Hanan Eshel has suggested to me the possibility of ערפלי טל השמים here. The root ער"פ is used of dew in Deut. 33:28, and the form ערפלי appears with "rain" in 4Q286, frag. 3, line 4; cf. Deut. 32:2.

[31]Attridge and Strugnell, "The Prayer of Enosh," 358.

[32]See E. Qimron, *The Hebrew of the Dead Sea Scrolls*, HSS 29 (Atlanta: Scholars, 1986), 89.

[33]On this subject in general, see H. Najman, *Seconding Sinai: The Development of Mosaic Discourse in Second Temple Judaism*, SJSJ 77 (Leiden: Brill, 2003).

[34]See, for example, Sir. 24:27, 32, etc., as well as G. Vermes, "The Torah Is Light," *VT* 8 (1958): 436–38.

[35]See Kugel, *Traditions of the Bible*, 670–71.

[36]The former derives from the identification of Torah with divine wisdom (Sir. 24:9, Bar. 3:36–4:1, and so forth; these are all exegetical developments of Prov. 8:22–27); again, see my *Traditions of the Bible*, 44–47, 54, 60.

[37]*In Potiphar's House*, 247–70.

SUBJECT INDEX

Aaron, 115, 212

Abel Mayin, 124, 167

Abraham, 135, 164, 167; acted as a
priest, 131–32; God's covenant with,
22, 30, 145, 147; was persecuted by
Shechemites, 56, 59–61

ALD (*Aramaic Levi Document*),
115–16, 123, 151, 152, 157–58,
234n15; cannot have been
composed in third century B.C.E.,
157–58; compiled from two
first-person Levi narratives, 162–65;
contradictions in, 159, 161, 220;
Levi's two visions in, 124–26,
142–44; palaeographic dating of,
151–52, 157; relationship to
Jubilees, 152–58, 161–62; side-trip
to Hebron in, 124–26, 141

Alexander Polyhistor, 45

ancient interpreters: not authors of
commentaries, 37; four assumptions
of, 3–4; interpreted verses, not
chapters, 4

angel(s), 13, 20, 202; accompanied
Jacob to Bethel, 12; anointed Levi,
124, 142, 150; capable of only one
task, 224n3; descended and
ascended to see Jacob, 16–17,
18–19, 225n8; lower order of, do
not keep Sabbath, 199; opened gates
of heaven, 124, 147; of the presence
and of sanctification, 192–93,
224n1; told Jacob about Reuben
and Bilhah, 93–96; provided
weapons to Simeon and Levi, 38, 39,
41; punished for revealing secrets or
for arrogance, 13–14; rule over
different nations, 20–21; do not rule
over Israel, 200. *See also* Angel of
Peace; Erellim; Michael; Phanuel;
Prince of Lights; Raphael; Sariel

Angel of Peace, 190, 204; greets
departing souls, 205; guards Israel,
204–5; 213–14; in 4Q228, 261n26

Aqiba, Rabbi, 192

Aramaic Levi Document. See ALD

Aramaic targums, 18, 42. See also
Fragment Targum; *Samaritan
Targum*; *Targum Neophyti*; *Targum
Onqelos*; *Targum Pseudo-Jonathan*

Aseneth, 148

Baal Peor, sin of, 70

Babylon. *See* Four Empires

HEBREW BIBLE INDEX

INDEX OF MOTIFS STUDIED